Praise for
Organizing & Preserving Your Heirloom Documents

"Family documents are among the most valuable heirlooms passed from one generation to the next. Katherine Scott Sturdevant has provided a valuable guide that demystifies the handling of historical family documents while offering practical tips on their care, preservation, and publication."

—Michael E. Stevens, author of
Editing Historical Documents: A Handbook of Practice

"At last a do-it-yourself guide that makes sense out of "documentary editing." *Organizing and Preserving Your Heirloom Documents* is an excellent book. After twenty-five years in the field, I still learned a great deal from reading it."

—Larry Bland, editor of *The Papers of George Catlett Marshall*

In an engaging style, Sturdevant examines all the components of this genre, from acquisition and authentication of documents, through transcription and proofreading texts, continuing with selection, arrangement and annotation, and ending with indexing and publishing the volume. Everyone interested in family history should have this instructive and easily accessible guide on their bookshelf as an important reference work.

—John P. Kaminski, Director of
The Center for the Study of the American Constitution
Past President, Association for Documentary Editing

Praise for
Bringing Your Family History to Life Through Social History

Required reading for every American genealogist. If [Sturdevant's] advice is followed, we can look forward to much more interesting and informative family histories.

—Harry Macy Jr., FASG,
The New York Genealogical and Biographical Record

Sturdevant has produced an engaging guide that demystifies social history, explains how and where to find it, and shows how to combine disparate finds into an interesting and meaningful family saga. *Bringing Your Family History to Life Through Social History* is a book to read for enjoyment as well as instruction.

—Kay Ingalls, CGRS, *National Genealogical Society Quarterly*

Ms. Sturdevant shows us all how to [make our ancestors come alive] by placing the people within their own social context. Use this book, and you will end up with a history that others will want to read.

—Paul Milner, Federation of Genealogical Societies *Forum*

Bringing Your Family History to Life Through Social History is *stupendous*! A splendid achievement, a major contribution to the field of genealogy. It has expanded my own knowledge, giving me new insights and ideas, and it will find its way into many of my classes and bibliographies.

—John Philip Colletta, Ph.D., author of
Only a Few Bones and *They Came in Ships*

Organizing & Preserving Your

Heirloom Documents

Katherine Scott Sturdevant

BETTERWAY BOOKS
CINCINNATI, OHIO

www.familytreemagazine.com

About the Author

Katherine Scott Sturdevant, M.A. and Ph.D. candidate, is a social historian. She has taught college-level American history for nearly twenty years, including an innovative, team-taught course combining history and genealogy. Her first Betterway book, the highly regarded *Bringing Your Family History to Life Through Social History*, reveals new methods of doing family history in a social history context. Trained as a documentary editor at the Institute for the Editing of Historical Documents, Kathy has been a historical editor for twenty years. She lives in Colorado Springs, Colorado, with her husband, Rick, who is deputy director of the Air Force Space Command History Office.

Other fine Betterway books are available from your local bookstore or on our Web site at www.familytreemagazine.com. To subscribe to Family Tree Magazine Update, a free e-mail newsletter with helpful tips and resources for genealogists, go to http://newsletters.fwpublicat ions.com.

06   05   04   03   5   4   3   2

Library of Congress Cataloging-in-Publication Data

Sturdevant, Katherine Scott
  Organizing & preserving your heirloom documents / Katherine Scott Sturdevant.
    p.   cm.
  Includes bibliographical references and index.
  ISBN 1-55870-597-X (alk. paper)
    1. Genealogy. 2. Manuscripts—Conservation and restoration. 3. Archival materials—Conservation and restoration. 4. History—Sources—Conservation and restoration. I. Title.
CS14 .S78   2002
929'.1—dc21   2002066524
                                                                      CIP

Editor: Sharon DeBartolo Carmack, CG
Production editor: Brad Crawford
Production coordinator: Sara Dumford
Cover designer: Clare Finney
Interior designer: Sandy Conopeotis Kent
Icon designer: Cindy Beckmeyer

Main cover photo by Pam Monfort, Bronze Photography. Other cover photos by Al Parrish.

DEDICATION

*This book is dedicated to the two professors
at San Francisco State University
who first asked me to be an editor
and who helped determine my future in so many ways,
Kay S. House, Ph.D. (English)
(now editor in chief of the writings of James Fenimore Cooper)
and
Jerald A. Combs, Ph.D. (history),
and to all of the editors, documentary or otherwise,
who contribute so much with so little credit.*

Acknowledgments

Organizing & Preserving Your Heirloom Documents is a natural extension of my first book, *Bringing Your Family History to Life Through Social History*. Documentary editing for family historians might have been a chapter of the first book were there not so much more than a chapter's worth to say about it. To acknowledge the people who helped me realize what is in this book, I have to thank a series of folks over my lifetime. I apologize if it sounds like an Oscar speech. Now you know it has to begin with my mother.

My mother raised me to know her mother, Kate Dickey Harper, even though Kate died a decade before I was born. My mother and her brother had asked Kate to write her memoirs when they feared she was dying of grief after losing her first son, Leonard. My mother asked me to care for and someday publish Kate's memoirs. My father, James A. Scott, on the other hand, always wanted to be a writer—or perhaps a painter, a sculptor, a pianist, a leather worker, a copper engraver, a potter, or a master gardener—to pursue an art to a high enough standard that he would win approval from some wider audience. He didn't, and yet he did. His friendliness, storytelling, and high standards of service made him a local public hero in his job. As a sales manager and clerk in San Francisco, "Scotty" was famous. Like a young boy with relics of half-finished hobbies under his bed, he struggled with the writing he wanted to do. I believe the furthest he got was to submit some tidbit, unsuccessfully, to *Reader's Digest*. Finally, for me, he started to record his stories before he lost his senses, and he left enough material for a book-length memoir. He knew it needed an editor, and he would smile somewhat wickedly at me and say, "That's what I have a daughter for."

In about 1978 or 1980, two of my favorite professors at San Francisco State University asked me to do some editing for them based on what they had seen of my writing. This was an unexpected honor. Kay House, my favorite English professor, asked me to be a "vetter" (an expert reader) on her authoritative edition of James Fenimore Cooper's *The Pilot*. After she explained what a vetter did, I knew I would enjoy it. We read and counterread versions of that novel until we could read no more, precisely pinning down Cooper's original intentions. Jerry Combs, my model history professor, asked me to edit and proofread his next book. That was when I was the department TA, or teaching assistant, for nine professors at once, at fifty dollars per professor. Although editing is always plenty of work, I was glad to do it for my fifty dollars in contrast to grading exams and papers. Thanks to my best teachers, I was starting to think of myself as an editor.

At Combs's instigation, I went to the University of California at Santa Barbara for my Ph.D. program. There, I got the position as book review editor for my program's periodical, *The Public Historian*, and thus began years of editorial experience. In 1983 I applied to the NHPRC (National Historical Publications and Records Commission) Institute for the Editing of Historical Documents in Madison, Wisconsin. It is a credit to that program that it accepted me, even though my proposed project for the course was editing my grandmother's memoirs. I had feared that documentary editors who worked on the papers of "great men" would sneer at me and my grandmother. I was wrong. Larry Bland, editor of *The Papers of George Catlett Marshall*, was assigned to be my instructor. He taught me that I could experiment with whatever way seemed best with the memoir, as long as I applied the standards I was learning.

Christie Dailey hired me for my first full-time job in history: historical editor for the State Historical Society of Iowa. Later, I continued to edit for periodicals, such as *Journal of the Southwest* for Joe Wilder, as well as for authors, publishers, and acquaintances. Joe Gordon of the Center for Southwest Studies at Colorado College had me edit an anthology of papers from a symposium dedicated to the late great writer Frank Waters. No editing experience will ever beat watching Frank Waters edit my biographical essay about Frank Waters. Each editing experience trained me for what I write here. Shifting my emphasis to teaching led me into teaching others to do family history. Speaking to genealogical audiences about family history methods led me to introduce the idea of documentary editing for family historians. So, thanks to all of the teachers, employers, students, and audiences who led me to apply historical editing toward family documents.

Once again genealogical author, editor, and friend Sharon DeBartolo Carmack championed and shepherded my project. Numerous friends and colleagues who provided examples or information that I use in this book include Rick W. Sturdevant, Wendell F. Sturdevant, the American Institute for Conservation of Historic and Artistic Works, Robert Fineberg, James Harper, Heritage Preservation, Birdie Holsclaw, Roger Joslyn, Janet Lecompte, Michael McColgin, Marcia Mensing, Sean Merrill, the New England Historic Genealogical Society, the anonymous "Parker" family, Marion C. Parker (no relation), Brenton Simons, Sherry L. Smith, the Society of American Archivists, and *Writer's Digest*'s Writers Online Workshops.

Three leading documentary editors generously read some or all of the manuscript at one stage or another. So in addition to my primary readers—Rick W. Sturdevant, Sharon DeBartolo Carmack, and Brad Crawford—I am proud to acknowledge the following editors, in alphabetical order. Any inadequacies or errors remaining in this book exist in spite of their help.

Larry I. Bland, editor of *The Papers of George Catlett Marshall*

John P. Kaminski, director of the Center for the Study of the American Constitution, University of Wisconsin; editor of the Documentary History of the Ratification of the Constitution; and past president of the Association for Documentary Editing

Michael E. Stevens, state historian, Wisconsin Historical Society and coauthor of *Editing Historical Documents: A Handbook of Practice*

Rick, thank you for all of your love and encouragement and for trying so hard to be patient, even though it doesn't come naturally. You have sat across the room in your rocking chair and watched me write two books now, and only interrupted me every fifteen to thirty minutes. Thank you for giving me such a nurturing mother-in-law, whose spirit, along with my parents', oversaw this project. Carol, this is your book, too. To my Daddy and Mommy, now I can work on getting your documents into print. I've written the book on how to do it.

Table of Contents At a Glance

Table of Contents

You have valuable family heirloom documents such as diaries, letters, and scrapbooks. You want to take care of them properly, make them known to others, perhaps even publish them, but are unsure how to do so. Documentary editing might have the answers you seek. Learn this new way to view your papers, the basic steps to working with them, and how to declare your own collection: the (Your Surname) Family Papers.

View your ancestor-authors the way a biographer, an aficionado, a literary critic, or a documentary editor would. Your family papers are a type of literature. You can be the keeper and teller of your ancestors' and relatives' life stories. Your ancestors might have even wanted an audience of readers that you can give them. Bring their writings to light.

The professional approaches will make your documents available to larger audiences, but your personal knowledge will add an element that no unrelated professional could. Learn what guidebooks and organizations exist to help you work with your family heirloom documents.

How do you find documents you didn't even know existed? How do you locate missing documents and obtain them from relatives and others? Serendipity can play an exciting role. Be sure to investigate who holds copyrights to your documents. By writing and interviewing, you can also create new family history documents worth preserving.

Why do documents deteriorate so easily? How should you handle them? What environmental hazards threaten them, and how can you protect or repair them? Learn how conservators preserve documents, how to adapt their methods to your own circumstances, and how to hire a professional if needed. You can copy your originals in special ways, display them, and even save your documents from natural disasters, such as floods.

6   Your Selection Process, 62

Begin your documentary project. Learn about the main types of family documents—diaries, journals, memoirs, letters, baby books, scrapbooks, account books, cookbooks, etc.—and how to select the right ones for your project. A case study of autograph albums shows how entertaining yet revealing their seemingly silly messages can be.

7   Organizing Your Documents, 80

Stop! Don't reorganize your documents from their original order until you read this chapter. The original scheme might be important. In addition to organizing them, learn why it is crucial to organize your time for large documentary projects. Journaling can help. Learn means of physically organizing the amounts of paper, even if you just have a big mess. Archival methods help put your family papers in proper order. You can have control!

8   Organizing Your Project, 94

Here's how to internally organize the documents you choose for your project. Chronological order makes historical sense. As you organize, check documents for authorship and authenticity so you know where to put them. Learn how to determine dates that are missing on your documents and how to put papers in order even after someone else has shuffled them.

9   Transcribing Your Documents, 108

Transcribing is a tough job, but you are the best one to do it. You have the qualifications, and there are guidelines, professionals, and even machines to help. Transcribing involves analyzing handwriting and old type, revisions, and previous transcriptions. Transcribing oral history might be even more technical. Practice here.

10   How to Edit and Proofread, 124

Follow professional standards for emendation (changing the original). Here is how to solve mysteries and add your own "corrections" to clarify the originals. Also here are tips for proofreading. Make the chore historically intriguing by breaking your ancestors' secret codes about private life. Make it amusing and more accurate by proofreading aloud with a partner and a sense of humor.

11 Annotating Your Documents, *135*

Decide how to annotate, with footnotes, endnotes, integrated text, or whatever method suits the documents and the audience. Is that mysterious reference in the text really common knowledge, or do you need to explain it? Consider the age and experience of the audience to determine whether Gen-Xers or Millennials may need you to identify that older item. Learn a variety of annotation methods. A scrapbook provides an excellent case study of how a string of documents— obituaries—can tell a family history with minimal annotation, but how annotation might add to the documents.

12 Illustrating Your Documents, *151*

Discover how much richer your papers will be, too, with illustrations. Guidelines help you decide when you need a picture to help your ancestors say the words. Your papers will mandate certain photographs—"musts" to include. Then, you can creatively illustrate with the help of some research. Examples here and throughout this book will help you see the possibilities.

13 Researching Annotation and Illustrations, *161*

Learn methods and tips for historical research, whether you need specific tidbits of information, general historical background, or illustrations. Remember that delicate matters such as ancestors' no-longer-acceptable bigotry may require research to understand and writing skills to explain their prejudices in context.

14 To Keep or to Donate?, *171*

Envision your documentary editing projects and how to complete them. One completion might be to donate the originals, sooner or later, to repositories for research. Here's how to ask the right questions, prepare for donation, and find the best home for your family heirloom papers.

15 Publishing Your Documentary Book, *178*

Learn ways to locate an appropriate publisher for your documentary volume. If you wish to publish, your collection will need an introduction, epilogue, and index. The introduction is your place to explain your decisions as an editor. To compose an epilogue, think of how folks love sequels and further adventures of favorite "characters." Make the index a social history index, based on the Elements of Social History, and you will offer researchers a wonderful tool.

Icons Used in This Book

Case Study
Examples of this book's advice at work

Printed Source
Directories, books, pamphlets, and other paper archives

Citing Sources
Reminders and methods for documenting information

Quotes
Useful words direct from the experts

\di'fin *vb*
Definitions
Terminology and jargon explained

Reminder
"Don't-Forget" items to keep in mind

For More Info
Where to turn for more in-depth coverage

Research Tip
Ways to make research more efficient

Hidden Treasures
Family papers and home sources

See Also
Where in this book to find related information

Idea Generator
Techniques and prods for further thinking

Sources
Where to go for information, supplies, etc.

Important
Information and tips you can't overlook

Step By Step
Walkthroughs of important procedures

Internet Source
Where on the Web to find what you need

Supplies
Advice on day-to-day office tools

Library/Archive Source
Repositories that might have the information you need

Technique
How to conduct research, solve problems, and get answers

Money Saver
Getting the most out of research dollars

Timesaver
Shaving minutes and hours off the clock

Notes
Thoughts, ideas, and related insights

Tip
Ways to make research more efficient

Oral History
Techniques for getting family stories

Warning
Stop before you make a mistake

ONE

Your Family Heirloom Papers

Y ou open it slowly. It is the box your cousin sent you after your great-aunt died. In it you find assorted trinkets that Great-Aunt had saved from the family: locks of hair, pieces of jewelry, photographs, and papers. Because you are a family historian, each is important to you. **Then you find the greatest treasure: a bundle of letters tied with a disintegrating ribbon.** You look at the postal cancellations: 1918. You look at the return addresses: home, and France. It dawns on you that you have your great-grandparents' World War I love letters. You not only have a family history treasure, you also have historical documents that tell a story. It is your ancestors' experiences through their eyes and words. Even strangers would enjoy reading this story. You have primary sources that historians could use as resources. Now what?

Perhaps you are like my friend Sean. After he introduced me to his delightful, eighty-something-year-old father, I said, "Is he a World War II veteran?" Sean said, "Yes, he and his brother were in the Navy." Sean reached into his wallet and showed me a small black-and-white snapshot of two young sailors. "I have his diary," he continued. "Well, I don't actually have it. He still has it, and that's how it should be. It will be mine someday, though, and I hope to write a book from it." I asked, "How? Do you mean fiction, base a story on it?" Sean looked bewildered. "Well, no, I'm not sure, but somehow I want to get it out there, have it published, so people can read it. It would be a tribute to him. People should know about it, and know him."

Maybe one of your family members wrote a memoir. My grandmother Kate Dickey Harper did, and she was a good storyteller. But her memoir is somewhat short and incomplete, as was her life. She wrote when she was ill, at her children's request. She wrote on brown paper, folded like a book, in pencil, making the pages difficult to sort in order and the handwriting faint and hard to read. Yet she described a girl's life on the Kansas, Colorado, and Arizona frontiers— again, material of general and historical interest. It cannot stand alone, though, because it is not book length and because it is full of references to people, places, and events that would be mysterious to outsiders. Like Sean for his father, I

Hidden Treasures

Figures 1-1 and 1-2 Ephemera such as souvenir booklets from World War II can reveal the service experiences of the veteran who owned them. Scott Family Papers circa 1942–1945, in author's possession.

want to do her justice, to get her life out there for others to read. My mother always wanted me to do this for her mother. "Mama was a good writer, story-teller, and a real ham," my mother said. "Mama would have liked a larger audience."

My father, James Scott, set about his memoir also, especially once he got a home computer. He was a fine storyteller, too, from years of practice. I begged him to record his stories for me. He wrote at length about American childhood in the 1920s and 1930s and about his World War II experiences. Yet his memoir consists of scattered stories kept in no chronological order, with some on out-dated, unreadable floppy disks and some on disheveled tractor-fed paper in dot matrix type. As senility set in, he lost track of the titles and numbers. Then, he began to rewrite the same two or three stories over, repeatedly, moving no further than the first line, in multiple notebooks and computer files. Neverthe-less, he always proudly remembered two legacies of his life: me, and the stories that he wrote down. Thus, I have a lingering responsibility to "do something" with his memoir. He had always dreamed of being a published writer. (See Figures 1-1 and 1-2 above for some of his souvenirs.)

Then there's Ron's story. Ron's ancestor was a Dutch adventurer who wrote an autobiographical account of his years in Tasmania and New Zealand when it was a gold rush frontier in the early to mid 1850s. The account was published more than a century ago and waited in obscurity for Ron to discover it. The precious book was all in Dutch, archaic Dutch at that. Ron needed to unlock its secrets for himself, and those secrets would interest many of us. He wanted to get the account out there with his ancestor's colorful words translated into English and also share, in print, the background and excitement of finding this treasure during his family history search. He wasn't sure how to prepare the original book for publication and include with it his own story of discovering it.

In addition to such singular documents, you may have your entire collection of original family papers: a hodgepodge of old letters, certificates, diplomas, clippings, scrapbooks, and receipts. If only these all belonged to someone famous, or if someone had already expertly organized them and discovered their significance in social history, then, you think, an archive would be more likely to take and keep them. Will your children, siblings, cousins, or strangers care about them as you have, or will the boxes and files of memorabilia be only so much trash when you're gone?

A prominent Pennsylvania family donated a room full of documents centering on their father to the New England Historic Genealogical Society with the understanding that the society's publishing arm, Newbury Street Press, would produce their family history. Father had kept everything, it seemed: receipts, yearbooks, school-event programs, and letters. The society hired genealogist-authors Patricia Law Hatcher and Sharon DeBartolo Carmack to develop a volume of genealogy and family history. Hatcher would do the genealogy, and Carmack would do a narrative account based on the documents.

I will not forget the day Sharon Carmack, my friend and longtime teaching partner, telephoned me unexpectedly at my work from a crowded storage room in the society. "Help! I only have three days here. I'm surrounded by boxes of every kind of paper. I don't know what to do!" If you are a Keeper of Everything, or inherit the boxes from one, you know how Sharon felt. Buried in those boxes, however, were love letters from the World War I era, between Father and Mother, before they married. The letters drew Sharon like a magnet, and she couldn't stop reading them. Ultimately, then, that family's narrative became a documentary editing project in which Sharon transcribed the best of the letters and used the other documents for annotation and additional narrative. The result will be a lovely book of both historical significance and general human interest.

Perhaps you are aware of some original records that you think should be available to more people than they currently are. Genealogists often volunteer their time to transcribe and publish, both in print and online, records of local institutions such as cemeteries. There is the case of Birdie Holsclaw, a professional genealogist, and the Colorado School for the Deaf and the Blind. She had special familiarity with its records because her genealogical research took her there. The school's records, however, were accessible only to the public who could walk in and sort through them. Birdie had firsthand experience with researching in those records and saw patterns in them. What could she do to make those records more available to others?

WHAT CAN YOU DO?

Did your ancestors leave you diaries, memoirs, travel journals, letters, baby books, autograph albums, or a collection of papers and memorabilia that almost tell a family story by themselves? Perhaps you don't know yet whether such treasures exist in your family, but you want to find them and find out what to do with them. You may know that your ancestors' written materials exist but some other relative or agency has them. **Whatever the situation, you are likely the person who will make the most of your family's papers.**

Important

Genealogically speaking, you can extract names, dates, places, and events from these documents to help you with your research. Your traditional genealogical goal would be to compile that detail on charts and ultimately self-publish a genealogy book as a record of all of the names and dates in your family lines. You may even dream that the genealogy of your family is so exceptional that a commercial press might publish it. Unfortunately, it is rare for any of us to produce a purely genealogical book with that much commercial potential.

Historically speaking, you could extract from your documents stories, quotes, and information that you might use in a family history narrative. In *Bringing Your Family History to Life Through Social History*, I recommend ways to weave such information together with social history about your family's times to make an interesting and important narrative. Only the best of such narratives will capture the investment of publishers, however. In addition, scholarly historians, who could use the information from your documents for examples in their works, will have no access to your documents unless you make them available.

Worst-case scenario: The precious family documents become lost forever. After all, you thought it was a miracle to find them. Other family historians have expressed envy: I wish I had my great-grandfather's diary! This frequent reaction indicates how rare our treasures are. The documents are already crumbling, the ink fading, and they have had several brushes with loss or destruction. Even if we cherish them, enclosing the diaries or letters in safe archival containers, in our favorite hiding spots, or in safe-deposit boxes, some day they may be lost. **Once these originals are gone, they are lost forever unless someone has reproduced the contents.**

Warning

You could copy the documents by photocopying, scanning, or transcribing, but if you do not reproduce them using the highest standards, your copies will never be as reliable as the originals. Inevitably you will later find that something about the original is missing from the copy: hard-to-read writing that you skipped over, hidden features you did not see, and mysteries you could not solve until later. Then there's the intangible, almost indescribable thrill some of us get when we see and touch the original, knowing that the author wrote on those pages. Don't lose that. You'll want to share that thrill with others.

Reading a diary, memoir, or letters is like reading a good book, but they are not really book length, or they have gaps that don't make sense. They refer to many names and events without explanation; even you are not always sure what they meant. Sometimes the writers just hinted at events that must have been fascinating, dramatic, and important enough to make the history books,

PARAGON OF FAMILY PAPERS: THE SNEDEN COLLECTION

To see a good example of what a historical society might do with an unusually valuable family collection, go to <www.sneden.com/about/discovering.html>. The Sneden Collection is the diaries and drawings of a mapmaker, Robert Knox Sneden, who served in the Army of the Potomac in the Civil War. The collection came to the Virginia Historical Society from a grandson of Sneden's nephew and from dealers. The society even paid an undisclosed amount for the materials, which is unusual, but was funded by two benefactors. The society later edited the documents into a published volume, *Eye of the Storm: A Civil War Odyssey*, built a major exhibit from the originals, and even developed a small line of related merchandise for its gift shop. There are indications that a film project may result as well. Although most of us wouldn't have a collection comparable to the Sneden, Charles Bryan of the Virginia Historical Society commented, "It never ceases to amaze me what's still out there in private hands" (*Richmond Times-Dispatch*, 9 December 1998).

but didn't elucidate. Other times the ancestor mentioned a social custom that is long forgotten without explaining it. A publisher would not want these diaries, memoirs, or letters as they are, nor can you assume that the publisher would pay an editor to "fix" them for you.

What should you do?

GO TO THE PROFESSIONALS

We, who call ourselves experts, scholars, or professionals, say: Bring the documents to us! This should be your first consideration for the sake of your rare documents. I recommend your state historical society as a place to start. This is safer than trusting any local individual or group with limited resources, and it is more practical than casting the average family net toward the Smithsonian Institution or other national repositories (although do not rule them out entirely). Understand that taking your documents to your state historical society probably means donating them to the society as a whole and negotiating your rights to them. The organization may publish them, archive them, or not be interested in them. You can somewhat dictate the role you and your family will play. Be prepared for rejection if your materials appear ordinary or if, for whatever reason, the society cannot help you with them. Hundreds of people bring their family "stuff" to historical societies, and some staffers may respond as though they have seen it all before.

You can find your state historical society or similar agencies in the American Association for State and Local History's (AASLH) *Directory of Historical Organizations in the United States and Canada.* This book is similar to *Ancestry's Red Book, The Handy Book for Genealogists,* or *The Genealogist's Address Book.* The AASLH directory, however, is more comprehensive than any other directory about *his-*

Printed Source

torical agencies. It lists agencies that have special collections, museums, and archives, and it indicates whether the agency in question has a publications program, although you will need to research the nature and extent of each program further. Many public libraries will have copies of an old edition of the directory, but the long-awaited fifteenth edition is available. For more information contact AltaMira Press, 1630 N. Main St., Suite 367, Walnut Creek, CA 94596 or (800) 462-6420 or <www.altamirapress.com>. The AASLH Web site is <www.aaslh.org> and its e-mail is history@aaslh.org.

Tip

Another institution that might place your papers in its archive is a college or university, especially if your ancestors or family members were alumni of the college or if that college collects local history where your family was integral to the community. A substantial college might be well funded enough to preserve your materials and would most likely employ professional staff and standards. Investigate whether there is such an option for some of your papers. If you aren't sure what colleges your family attended or how to reach them, try *The College Blue Book, HEP Higher Education Directory,* or *Baird's Manual of American College Fraternities.*

You need to determine what institution might be most interested in your family papers and be best able to care for them. It might be your local or state public library, perhaps in its genealogical collection. Some libraries have special collections departments that house papers from local families, especially diaries, memoirs, and letters. It might be a college with an archive or a museum that preserves papers as well as artifacts. It might be your state historical society, state archives, or state museum. Look for an agency that uses modern archival methods and equipment to protect your papers and that may even have a qualified staff or faculty member to prepare them for publication.

"DO IT YOURSELF"

With care and the proper guidelines, you can "do it yourself." More and more family historians are becoming sophisticated enough to organize, preserve, edit, and publish their own family papers. Perhaps, too, you need to organize your own archive before a society will take it seriously. You can use the ideas and ethics, methods and skills, resources and materials, and standards and models of a professional field called *documentary editing.* It is the purpose of this book to introduce the basics of this field to people who want to do the right thing with their ancestors' treasured writings. It is work, time, and effort, but it is rewarding. By this means you may find a publisher for the best parts of your family history, and you may bring your ancestors' lives into the light.

\di'fin\ *vb*

Definitions

Documentary or historical editing is collecting, organizing, and preparing for publication or other dissemination historically significant primary sources such as diaries, journals, memoirs, letters, and papers of an individual, family, organization, or theme. It is a field of expertise usually directed at the papers of famous individuals such as presidents, military or political leaders, prominent families, and the most significant scientists, inventors, and leaders. By necessity, documentary editing projects are often married to archival projects because someone has to

WHAT IS SOCIAL HISTORY?

Social history is the study of ordinary people's everyday lives. It is history from the bottom up instead of the top down, not focusing exclusively or primarily on the elite and famous. Social historians tend to identify something's importance by how many people it affected more than by how singular it was. We even organize history differently: by trends rather than by just the actions of "great men." Having a social history perspective means that one sees historical events as they affected groups collectively, not just how they affected exceptional people individually. We study "the common people" and the frameworks within which they lived. Social history is much more inclusive of ethnic minorities, women, and age groups than is traditional political history. But social history is not "history with the politics left out," as some have accused. Instead, social historians will tend to look at the people side of politics: grass roots campaigns, local politics, the formation of parties, and reform movements. Again, this is a help to the family historian. Your ancestors were more liable to participate in politics at these levels than as presidents of the United States.

—*Bringing Your Family History to Life Through Social History*, 6

collect, organize, and preserve the primary sources in order to publish them or make them available to the public. The documentary editor

- locates and acquires documents
- arranges them in chronological or topical order
- painstakingly transcribes them
- researches information with which to annotate the documents

Annotation may be in the form of explanatory footnotes, headnotes, integrated text, introductions, epilogues, and indexes. Every decision the documentary editor makes must follow careful consideration and professional standards. A goal of documentary editing is to reproduce the original documents in a printed form that scholars and researchers can rely upon when they do not have access to the original documents.

Although it is still true that famous people's papers form the best-known documentary editing projects, many organizations today build projects around the papers of lesser known or unknown families like yours and mine. Coinciding with the popularity of social history, documentary editing has become less elitist in recent years. Social history relies upon the stories of families like ours to construct collective pictures of whole societies. As historians have recognized the value of ordinary folks' life stories, we have searched for records of their lives. The more difficult it was to find famous examples of lifestyles, the more valuable the ordinary person's recollections became.

The diary or letters of a simple woman without any fame may have once been a minor novelty of interest only to her family. Now, however, her descriptions of her life and activities—say, as a housewife, midwife, homesteader, or nurse—

Figures 1-3 and 1-4 Scraps of ephemera can reveal and illustrate women's wartime activities. In 1889 Sarah Sturdevant paid dues to the Women's Relief Corps (WRC), the auxiliary to the Grand Army of the Republic (GAR), the Union veterans' organization. Her husband was a veteran. Meanwhile, a later female family member, probably Maybelle Sturdevant, worked with the Women's Christian Temperance Union (WCTU) to make tokens for World War I soldiers. Maybelle's husband was one such soldier. Sturdevant Family Papers, with permission of Rick W. and Wendell F. Sturdevant, in author's possession.

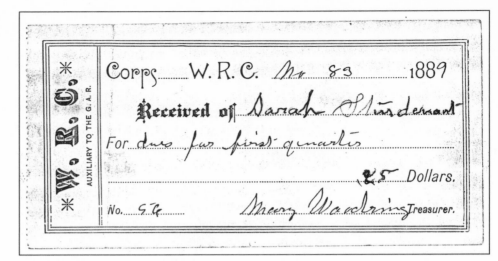

might offer historians valuable insights into that aspect of all women's lives. (See Figures 1-3 and 1-4 above for some women's artifacts.) Other previously unsung historical groups, such as African Americans, Native Americans (Indians), or immigrants, were even less liable to leave their own recollections than

MORE THAN JUST GEORGE WASHINGTON:
ONE DOCUMENT, MANY INTERESTS

In a letter dated "June [c. 1] 1777" (note the editor's brackets to show a speculation), George Washington wrote to his brother John Augustine Washington from his Revolutionary War headquarters in Middlebrook, New Jersey. Here is the end of one paragraph and the beginning of another:

> The different States must fall upon some decisive measures to compleat their regiments or no one can say what the consequences will be.

> I hope I may congratulate you & my Sister on her happy recovery from the Small Pox, together with your Children. the loss my brother Sam has sustaind will I fear, be very sensibly felt by him *[footnote number removed by KSS]* some mismanagement must surely have been in the way for the Small Pox by Inoculation appears to me to be nothing;

How many different historical subtopics can you see in this single passage? Someone might be pleased to find this passage because of researching George Washington, the Revolutionary War, state militia, family life, women's history, disease and medical care, child raising, and more. A genealogist might be researching the Washington family and its in-laws. A family historian writing narrative might use the Washington experiences and comments to help explain what went on in his own family. A history teacher like me will use the information to further describe what a time George had building an army and how Americans were dangerously reluctant to use the smallpox vaccine.

From the *Papers of George Washington*. Revolutionary War Series. Vol. 9. March–June 1777, 1999, page 587. Note that I have not added [*sic*] to the editor's work to indicate misspellings or capitalization inconsistencies, and I removed a footnote number.

middle-class women, partly because of cultural and language issues. Thus, their firsthand accounts that survive in your family are valuable to historians.

Remember, too, that some of the most famous or treasured published diaries are those of individuals who were unknown until after the publication of their diaries. Anne Frank, whose diaries form the text of a revered book and the script of a play and a film, would have remained unknown to the world if her father and friends had not cherished her diaries and shared them through publication. Historian Laurel Thatcher Ulrich introduced us to Martha Ballard, an eighteenth-century midwife whose journal Ulrich analyzed and reproduced with annotation. Like Anne Frank's words, Ballard's words became the text of a book and a film. Both media explore the experiences of the editor, Ulrich, intermingled with the events of Ballard's life. The whole project has occasioned so much interest—as an avenue into formerly unpublished aspects of women's lives—that there are interactive Web sites and teachers' aids so that students may learn history and historical method from Ballard and Ulrich.

Reminder

Documentary editing is a way that historians, editors, and archivists can present these records to the historical community for its use in developing the bigger picture of history. By producing the papers of a president in a multivolume set, editors have made those papers available to hundreds of libraries and thousands of researchers. On a given day, researchers across the country might look in the same set of papers for information on hundreds of different subjects. (See "More Than Just George Washington" on page 9.)

Thus, our historical primary documents have immense value. By using the methods of documentary editing, you can preserve and prepare your family heirloom documents for publication or dissemination in some form, too. By understanding the social history approach and using social history research, you can recognize the value, audience, and possible publishers for your heirloom documents. You can also use social history to flesh out those documents into readable accounts.

THE BASIC STEPS

My purpose is to summarize, interpret, and, where necessary, augment the guidelines of professional documentary editing projects so that they suit our typical family collections and projects. We will start "from scratch" and try to consider every step in dealing with heirloom documents. Again, the first and best step would be to contact professionals at your historical society and determine whether the trained staff might take on your documents. **If you are going to "do it yourself," however, please follow these guidelines and those available in the previous sources.**

Important

STEPS TO CONSIDER
- ☐ locating family documents
- ☐ acquiring family documents
- ☐ selecting documents for the project
- ☐ caring for the documents
- ☐ transcribing the documents
- ☐ organizing the documents
- ☐ annotating the documents
- ☐ illustrating the documents
- ☐ indexing the documents
- ☐ introducing the documents
- ☐ epiloging the documents
- ☐ researching the documents
- ☐ archiving the documents
- ☐ publishing a documentary volume
- ☐ publishing a documentary article
- ☐ publishing documents online

This book attempts to introduce you to and advise you about documentary editing methods and related systems and models. You might also investigate whether there is a college course near you that would assist with your family documentary projects. Many leading documentary editors teach courses on the practice, or they travel and lecture. There are even whole college programs, usually under the rubric "public history," for students who want to go into editing and publishing. Although these programs are usually for graduate students, you could check how open they are to community enrollments. See the National Council for Public History at <http://ncph.org>. If there is no such program nearby, you might find a history professor who knows documentary editing and would be willing to supervise you in an independent-study format or even online. Of course, the best documentary editing training would be the NHPRC Institute for the Editing of Historical Documents, available to applicants with Master's degrees (see <www.nara.gov/nhprc/edprog.html#ins>). This institute has been annual for more than thirty years, and it is held at the University of Wisconsin, Madison. In one week, about fifteen to eighteen interns attend presentations by and study with leaders in documentary editing. A first step that you can take right now, however, is to declare your family papers as a documentary editing project.

THE PAPERS OF YOUR FAMILY

You can take a professional approach to the entire accumulation of old family papers that you have and build. **You are its archivist as well as its documentary editor.** Taking this approach will help you obtain serious attention and respect for your heirloom documents. If they are archivally organized and preserved, they will survive better and serve you better. Repositories such as historical societies and museums may be more interested in caring for your documents after you are finished with them. Always remember that your historical society is likely to have better, safer storage conditions than you do. You cannot set up a research facility and circulating library in your own home. Only when the papers are in a public facility and/or published will others have access to them.

Reminder

Meanwhile, as long as you are the repository for your family papers, it is best to adopt professional standards. If you believe your collection of heirloom documents is substantial and varied, then as you organize them with proper methods and materials, why not christen the collection as The (Your Surname) Family Papers? Or, if they are papers gathered by or related to one ancestor, call them by the ancestor's name: the John or Jane Doe Papers. This might happen anyway when you approach a local historical society with the collection. For example, my friends Willard and Muriel owned a family printing business that went back many years in Colorado Springs. When they closed the business, many papers and artifacts had accumulated. The Local History Collection in the public library plans to house the collection eventually and so has taken some of it and assisted the family with the rest. The library named the collection after the printing business and the family.

It is important to christen your collection of heirloom documents with a title so you can footnote it as such in your family history writing. Which footnote is better in a family history narrative?

Case Study

\di'fin\ *vb*

Definitions

Ephemera is a catchall term used to describe printed materials, usually brief, of passing interest that thus became period pieces—tourist or political pamphlets, advertising brochures, fliers, posters, sheet music, playbills, event programs, road maps, and ink blotters are examples. In the past, "ephemera" has implied material of lesser historical significance, but with local, social, and popular cultural history on the rise, it has higher interpretive value.

THE FRANK STURDEVANT PAPERS

By being a historian, my husband, Rick, follows in the footsteps of his grandfather Frank Lafayette Sturdevant (1889–1950). Because Frank's mother died when he was small, Frank grew up in the household of his grandfather, John George Lafayette Sturdevant, a Civil War veteran and photographer. These were happy circumstances for the sake of family history. In *Bringing Your Family History to Life Through Social History* (161–162) I explain how Frank was a self-taught but vastly knowledgeable local historian and a "Keeper of Everything."

From his grandfather, Frank inherited stories of the Civil War and of family history, activism as a veteran and community pioneer, and a special appreciation for photographs, tombstones, and other family relics. All of his life Frank did genealogical research. He traveled and wrote letters across the country, taking notes and casually recording details and stories. He also took on the role of a local journalist. During his travels and his World War I service, he wrote accounts of what he saw and sent them back to the town newspaper. Frank collected clippings, cards, printed programs, and any other ephemera. He could hardly stash a photograph or artifact in one of his many boxes without writing an attached note explaining what it represented (thank goodness). Documents from fraternal organizations that no one else wanted, he kept. Naturally, he was often the chapter secretary, so he kept his minute books. In his later career as a letter carrier, he even retained the pro-German propaganda that the government required him to confiscate during World War II.

Frank saved every scrap of paper. He died without organizing them, but his widow was a Keeper of Everything, too. Thus, we have much more than shoe boxes from Frank. He was also parsimonious about paper and pencil. He would write genealogical information on any little misshapen scrap with a pencil worn and sharpened down to shorter than what we call a "golf pencil." His collection includes many accounts that might stand alone with documentary editing. I christened his collection the Frank Sturdevant Papers when I started to cite these as sources of genealogical information in family history. I believe his work was as good as ours is, and his information was usually reliable. Sometimes something he knew about the family does not exist anywhere else, so I cite the Frank Sturdevant Papers with an explanation of what that means. The title does them and him justice and reminds us of the responsibility we owe to both as we pursue the monumental task of organizing and editing it all.

1. From a scrap of paper in the shoe boxes under my bed in the first bedroom on the left. . . .
2. Genealogical notes, file #372, the Frank Sturdevant Papers, in the author's possession.

In some of my presentations on this topic at genealogical conferences, I have had the audience recite the following. Why not try it now? (If you are reading this in a public place, you may want to recite only to yourself.) Place your family name, the one appropriate to the collection, in the blank.

The (Your Surname) Family Papers

Repeat it. Write it down. Start using it for citations. The methods in this book will include ways to organize and care for documents so your collection is more secure and legitimate. Moving from the shoe box to the Hollinger (archival file) box is more than a matter of cardboard; it is a state of mind. Your heirloom documents are the stuff of history, and you are responsible for making the most of them for all of our sakes.

TWO

Being Biographer, Aficionado, Literary Critic

He had by now resumed work on his autobiography as well, Part II, "Travels and Negotiations," though it was still labor he did not relish. "To rummage trunks, letter books, bits of journals and great heaps of bundles of old papers is a dreadful bondage to old age, and an extinguisher of old eyes."

—David McCullough *(prizewinning historian and biographer of presidents), quoting the second president in* John Adams *(New York: Simon & Schuster, 2001), 589*

A good biographer immerses him or herself into the life of the subject person. He takes the responsibility very seriously. Even when the subject is someone unlikable, even an evildoer, the biographer becomes so acutely aware of the inner workings of that person that sensitivity and empathy will develop. Try though we might to be objective in biography, we form an appreciation of our subjects. We should, to some degree. The good biographer unfolds a life story almost as though he lived it himself. We can view our ancestors as writers, the authors of their own documents that we now treasure. Thus, we may be their biographers; as we research and annotate their documents, we can view them as lives in need of biography and their writings as genres of literature.

An aficionado is a passionate and thorough "fan" of someone or something. Aficionados study their beloved topics so intimately and consistently that they know them by heart. If the object of this attention is an author and the author's written work, the aficionado might also become a literary analyst. As an aficionado, however, one is unabashedly fond of the thing one is studying. The aficionado usually also indulges in anything connected with the object of affection. Thus, if you were an aficionado of Charles Dickens and his novels, you might also develop a passion for nineteenth-century England and collect those expensive, irresistible ceramic village pieces loosely based on Dickens's settings.

One of my literature professors was a good example of an aficionado more

\di'fin\ *vb*

Definitions

passionate than may have seemed "normal" to many people. He was a scholar on Mark Twain who knew and analyzed every word of Twain's work. Gradually, the professor started to look like Twain himself. His hair grew long, curly, and outward from his head in an Einstein effect. His moustache thickened under his large nose. His suits became three-piece and his ties became black string or bow. It was eerie. I always thought I should return to see the same man when he was old enough for his hair to turn white to see whether his suit, like Twain's, did also. I haven't yet checked.

I am not suggesting that you alter your appearance, but you might immerse yourself in your author-ancestors enough to think and write as they wrote for purposes of editing them. My father also admired Mark Twain. I grew up immersed in "the adventures of" Huckleberry Finn and Tom Sawyer. Once one of my professors assigned us to write a critical essay in the voice of a "philistine or an ignorant person." I chose Huck and described a famous painting of Mary Magdalene in two pages of Huck's voice; the painting was "a might unseemly." It is possible to do this with your own ancestors' writing, too. Thus, although you would want to clearly distinguish passages written by your ancestor from your own annotation, you could make your passages complementary enough to flow for readers.

FAMILY DOCUMENTS AS LITERATURE

There are documentary editors in literature as in history. They take individual or collected works, letters, and autobiographical writings of literary authors and edit these into volumes. Some of their responsibilities would differ from those of historical editors. For example, a documentary editor on a literary project might have to deal with fiction and literary analysis (textual criticism) of the project—evaluating the writing techniques of the author along with explaining the fictional nuances. You might discover some fiction writing by an ancestor and be in the same situation as a literary editor. You could analyze what your relative composed, or you might use literary criticism's general approach on your family's nonfiction documents—the diaries and letters—too.

Literary criticism refers to analyzing a work of literature in terms of its genre, its period, its structure, the author's style and techniques, and the whole body of the author's work. It often includes evaluating the effectiveness of language use, symbols, characterization, and other literary devices—in effect, any or all of the author's choices. The author's stated and unstated purposes and the effects of the work are part of criticism, too. As a historian, I particularly appreciate literary criticism that traces the historical sources of subjects that an author has fictionalized. I realize this may sound a little heady for our family history purposes, but bear with me.

\di'fin\ *vb*

Definitions

If you have a lengthier, *textual* document in your family—one with substantial paragraphs and pages of exposition, of original writing—think of the ancestor who wrote it as its author. Think of the diary, memoir, manuscript, stories, poems, or collection of letters as an unpublished book or article. The author, your ancestor, wrote the document in order to be read. Oh, some folks would claim otherwise—that diaries, especially, are private. As soon as that ancestor put pen to paper, however, the ancestor was recording thoughts and events for an audience of some kind. The intended audience may even have been the author herself, planning to reread her entries later. Yet she was still conscious of an audience. If you are now the audience and you think the thoughts were private, then you are responsible for handling them with delicacy.

Anne Frank serves as an example again. For all the inspiration many of us have taken from her moving diary, most people do not realize how much Anne thought of herself as an author. She wanted to be a journalist or some kind of published writer someday. She rewrote and revised her diary, which was actually several different diaries and many loose pages of rewrites. She reflected on whether her diary might be published after the war—especially whether the musings of someone as unknown as herself could capture attention. She realized that her unusual experiences of hiding from the Nazis might interest others. Anne prepared fictional names in stories she wrote about her family and the people who stayed with them and helped them. When her father pursued publishing her diaries after the war, he used a combination of authentic names and Anne's fictional names. Thus, a thorough analysis of Anne Frank's documents for a "critical" or "authoritative" edition includes literary analysis and an awareness that she was writing for an audience, even though we think of a diary as private.

If you are working with a family nonfiction document such as a memoir, you can apply a bit of literary analysis to it, especially if you can tell that the author was thinking carefully about the literary qualities of the piece. Often good storytellers, such as my father and grandmother mentioned earlier, had so many years of practice telling their stories to best effect that they couldn't help but do creative writing, carefully choosing words and metaphors.

Try answering the following questions to see whether your family nonfiction document has literary qualities that you can analyze.

- Are there clues that the author of this document wrote it for a larger audience or had ambitions to write for publication? If so, then the author may have made careful choices of technique and style that you can evaluate.
- Does the author state his/her purpose in writing this piece? Are there other purposes that become apparent?
- How does the writing style compare to techniques and language of the time?
- Would this piece have appeal for a larger audience because it uses more literary devices, such as characterizing people rather than just flatly naming them?

Issues of literary criticism will be more important if you have found fictional writing in your family. You can analyze the short stories or poetry of an ancestor the way a literary critic would in order to

- determine the value of these formerly unknown stories or poems as pieces of literature, and thus know more about who might want to archive or publish them
- decipher the hidden meanings and identities of the places, characters, and

THE MARK TWAIN PAPERS AND PROJECT

The Mark Twain Papers and Project at the University of California's Bancroft Library in Berkeley is a major documentary editing project sponsored by the field's leading organizations. (See ADE and NHPRC in chapter three.) The collection includes Twain's letters, organized so you can see all of his exchanges with any individual or all of his letters within a particular time period. They have his notebooks edited, indexed, and on microfilm. You can see his manuscripts at their various stages of incarnation, including his autobiography, and the scrapbooks in which he and his family kept clippings and other papers. You can even find copies of Twain's personal library books with copies of the notes he made in the margins. The collection includes a photograph archive and almost any document that the documentary editors could find relating to Twain. Thus, the Mark Twain Papers and Project is a large-scale model of what one might do with any individual's or family's collection. See <http://library.berkeley.edu/BANC/MTP/>.

Library/Archive Source

events in the stories, as they may pertain to the real lives of your family members (remember, most literary authors, especially beginning novelists, write autobiographical fiction)

- speculate on what these writings reveal about the author, your ancestor or relative

Therefore, with your textual family papers, you can be the biographer or literary expert who finds the unfinished, unpublished manuscripts of these unknown authors and finally achieves *their* goals. Great novelists such as Charles Dickens and Mark Twain left unfinished manuscripts when they died. They may even have been conscious of leaving an unfinished mystery and taken pleasure in it. I have always thought it revealing that Charles Dickens left *The Mystery of Edwin Drood* and Mark Twain left *The Mysterious Stranger*, both unfinished and without definitive clues as to planned solutions. It was as if they meant to tease and torment us with unsolved mysteries after their deaths. Some of their biographers and literary analysts came forward to present these otherwise unknown works to the public. Scholarly standards insisted that the editions make clear which parts were original and which were editorial. The result was to make the manuscripts available, to augment them with explanatory editorial material, to speculate on what else the author might have written, and to thus "complete" the work that the author began.

Experts and fans of Charles Dickens have long debated his intentions with his last unfinished novel, *The Mystery of Edwin Drood*. I solved the mystery in my own way in a graduate seminar paper. Others have written books, plays, and films solving it in their way. Our solutions overlapped in key aspects because we all based them on Dickens's own clues and tendencies. It is a good example of how modern folks can take the unfinished work of a past writer and make it even more interesting and valuable than it might have been had

TYPES OF FAMILY DOCUMENTS FOR WHICH DOCUMENTARY EDITING MIGHT SERVE

memoirs, reminiscences

diaries, journals

travel accounts

collected letters, especially to and from

autograph books

account books

baby books

scrapbooks, especially with original text

collected papers and documents, especially if some have significant text, including

> wills, inventories

> obituaries, newspaper articles

> deeds, maps

artistic collections such as sketches, photographs, paintings, or other representations

individual short pieces, such as a single letter, depending on the significance and audience

collected writings of one person or persons not before put together, such as

> short stories, poetry, music

> accounts of particular experiences

> genealogy and family history papers that can be an archival collection

complete or partial unpublished manuscripts of books, stories, articles, school papers, reports, theses, dissertations

antiquated published books, stories, articles, or pieces that are out of print, scarce, and in the public domain (without copyright issues)

the author completed it. For a sense of how aficionados gather around such a mysterious manuscript, simply do a Web search on "Edwin Drood." The "cult" will be obvious in the first list of hits you receive.

As your family's documentary editor, you will need to be a biographer in the sense that you discover your ancestor's life story as it pertains to the manuscript. You will need to be the aficionado who thrills to every aspect of this precious document. You will need to be the literary editor who dissects even the vocabulary and style of your ancestor. You will need to be the detective who uncovers the meaning of the mysteries your ancestor left unexplained. By following the established standards and methods of documentary editors, you can perform all of these tasks with accuracy and authority. Your resulting piece of work—your ancestor's document as you have edited it—could then be suitable for publication, for distribution to archives, for researchers to use, and for readers to enjoy.

WHICH FAMILY DOCUMENTS TO EDIT?

To determine whether you have documents suitable for documentary editing and publishing, think in terms of what you would want to read from someone else's family collection. Think of what publishers would find most worthy of a publishing gamble. We will discuss many examples throughout this book, but generally family papers most suited to become documentary editing projects would be *textual* documents, lengthy and rich in the amount of writing. Generally, they would be factual, detailed, autobiographical observances of times and places different from ours.

The more our ancestor-authors expanded upon their opinions and feelings, the more they described events, people, places, tasks, and ways folks dealt with things, and the better writers they were, the better the document for public dissemination. **Diaries, letters, and other personal papers, well edited, can also make fascinating reading for a general audience.** Think how readers seek biographies and "true" stories in their pleasure reading and film viewing. Walking a mile in someone else's shoes, reading about what someone else's life was really like, brings history "to life" for us.

Idea Generator

Of course, you may not have the most obvious documentary treasures in your family. You can be creative, however, in which documents you use for this kind of editing and publishing. You might bring an ancestor's account book to life by annotating the significance of every entry. You might string together many shorter documents to form a family history. You can also be creative in how you present briefer documents. Perhaps you have just one letter that has extraordinary historical value. Some singular, visual documents may be good illustrations for transcribed documents. (See Figure 2-1 on page 20.)

Magazines and journals would be likely publishers for shorter original documents of interest that you have edited. For example, say you have in your family a single travel account or letter of several pages describing frontier California during the Gold Rush of 1849 to 1850. After you transcribe, edit, introduce, and annotate the original, you could submit it to the California Historical Society or other California historical periodicals for publication. Although historical periodicals rarely pay for articles, such a publication would bring your ancestor's document to light, as it deserves, and it would benefit other researchers. If you're ambitious to write and publish more, your late relative has just helped you gain a publication under your belt.

Try answering the following questions to see whether you have family documents suitable for documentary editing.

Figure 2-1 Old stock certificates are artistically and historically interesting and can make good illustrations for your documents. John Harper's collection of certificates, for example, reveals how fruitlessly he was always trying to "get rich quick." Texas Petroleum Company stock certificate, 14 February 1933. Harper Family Papers, in author's possession.

- What do I know exists in my family from the list of document types on page 18?
- Do I have those items in my possession, and do I have legal rights to use them? (See pages 36–39.)
- I know of special documents that are in others' possession. Can I obtain these documents and permission to use them?
- Do my documents have extensive descriptive text in them?
- Did my ancestor-author describe historically interesting events, people, or places?
- Was my ancestor-author the sort of person whose observations would be especially valuable because of fame, uniqueness, rarity, or typicality?
- Did my ancestor-author describe reactions and thoughts about historical events and people that would offer quotable opinions for historians to use?
- Did my ancestor-author compose literature such as stories, poems, or plays that are good enough for publication yet have never seen the light of day?
- Do I have access to additional information or illustrations to accompany the documents?

Be creative when considering what you might do with your documents.

THREE

Professional Field +
Personal Element

People edit and publish historical documents because they believe these materials have enough significance to merit the time, energy, and money needed to make them accessible to a wider audience.

—*Michael E. Stevens and Steven B. Burg,* Editing Historical Documents: A Handbook of
   Practice, *25*

Archival collections and edited volumes of people's papers have followed trends in the last half century that are parallel to the trends of how we study history. The first and most dominant documentary editing projects have been the collected papers of "great white men"—the presidents, or political and military men of equal stature, such as Washington, Adams, Jefferson, Madison, Hamilton, and Franklin. The papers would reflect these men's greatness. They were men aware of their roles in history who therefore kept many documents. Often being presidents and being wealthy men meant that they left behind them boxes of papers that needed homes, as presidents still do. An archive, library, or documentary editing project sometimes grows up around presidential papers because something has to.

Most experts trace the documentary editing field to Jared Sparks, who produced the twelve-volume *The Writings of George Washington* in 1837. Sparks did what was normal for his day: He corrected Washington's spelling, grammar, and rare human frailties. Today editors see this as unprofessional and as an almost sacrilegious tampering with originals. Over the next century, professional standards rose to an exacting level, but the subject matter, like that of history itself, tended to remain great men and their government. Even the great men's private papers about personal life sometimes gathered dust while public papers appeared in print.

Since the 1960s, more documentary editing collections have centered on women and ethnic minorities. Of course, like the writing and teaching of history, this focus first was a shift to great individual women and minorities,

Notes

> ## THE WASHINGTON PAPERS' MISTREATMENT
>
> The history of abuse that the Washington Papers have undergone is interesting and inspirational in the sense that so much has survived in spite of the best efforts to lose it. Editor Jared Sparks liked to cut the papers into scraps for gifts. He cut out signatures and whole pages as relics for friends. Even when he returned the papers to the family, he kept enough so he could continue this practice. Martha Washington burned their personal letters, dooming herself and her husband to the probably inaccurate historical impression that they lacked passion and romance. Bushrod Washington, the nephew, gave away whole diaries to esteemed friends, although many of these documents later rejoined the collection. See <http://rs6.loc.gov/ammem/gwhtml/6gwintro.html>.

particularly political figures, while literary critics were editing the papers of their heroes and heroines. In the last couple of decades, though, there have been more projects about previously neglected subjects that are now popular: lesser known people, collective groups of people or sections of society, and people whose relevance is more to remote western regions and smaller local spheres. Social reform movements for the rights of women, slaves, and the poor have become popular subjects for editing projects.

In other words, documentary editing has followed the paths of history into social history, antielitism, and diverse approaches. The great men's papers are still important, but even their once-less-significant sections about private lives have come more into the limelight. Literary editing ran somewhat parallel to these trends, moving from the greatest male authors to lesser lights and females, with the purpose usually being to produce authoritative editions of authors' works. Of course part of the impetus to move in these directions is finding more material. Each generation of graduate students or new editors needs to work on something that its predecessors did not already exhaust—a happy circumstance for all of us wanting more resources about more people.

YOUR PERSONAL ELEMENT

Idea Generator

To you and me, a natural extension of documentary editing could be editing our own family documents. We care with a personal element beyond what a professional might (although goodness knows editors and archivists can be passionate about historical documents that are not their own). We have or can find our family documents. They may not yet be in a state that an archive would want them. Most importantly, we may have family knowledge, family tradition, family oral history, family artifacts, family photographs, and many of the resources a documentary editor needs for annotation. The typical editor may have to hunt harder than we do because we are working on our own families' documents.

Professional documentary editors and archivists do become attached to their documents, as mentioned earlier in the case of biographers. In a group of archivists recently, one member asked, "Why do we do this?" meaning, Why do we work in archives? One after another, archivists reminisced about their first experiences seeing or handling some original documents that represented sea changes in history. Simply holding those documents and contemplating their importance filled these future archivists with awe and excitement, often causing them to determine their career goals at that moment. Only one or two of the professionals in the group insisted upon a more dispassionate, records-management approach. You probably understand both how the passionate people felt and how extravagant their raptures seemed to the dispassionate records managers.

If archivists' passion (open or suppressed) makes them dedicated professionals, then we can also let ourselves feel some of the emotions that inevitably become attached to our family histories. I recommend objectivity but also empathy. Think what your personal knowledge can do for annotating documents. See what important layers of intergenerational contact, continuity, completeness, complexity, and depth you can bring to editing your family documents. Also note that you can work with different types of documents: a bureaucratic report, reminiscences, or a letter.

EDITORS HAVE STYLE

You should know about several professional organizations important to documentary editing. They have informative Web sites and publications from which you may discover more guidelines useful to your particular project, and perhaps even professional or financial support for an especially worthy project.

Sources

The Association for Documentary Editing (ADE), <http://etext.virginia.edu/ade/>, is the professional association for those who practice in this field. The ADE was created in 1978 to 1979 to promote documentary editing "through the cooperation and exchange of ideas among the community of editors." There are now more than 450 members. Perhaps most useful to ordinary family historians are the indexes on the ADE Web site, which list all of the past articles in its periodical, *Documentary Editing*. Most of the articles evaluate or report about documentary editing projects, but some offer practical advice or news of important issues that affect documentary editing, such as changes in copyright law. The ADE has been fundamental to professionalizing the field of documentary editing. Its members deserve much of the credit for the standards I am trying to impart.

The National Historical Publications and Records Commission (NHPRC), <www.nara.gov/nhprc/>, is an arm of the National Archives and Records Administration (NARA), both created in 1934. While the National Archives protects federal records, NHPRC is the government agency that sponsors nonfederal institutions in their efforts to preserve and publish any other records of historical value. The NHPRC does this primarily through grants and training for state and local archives and historical societies, libraries, and colleges. The NHPRC is the sponsor of papers from the likes of George Washington, Thomas Jefferson, Benjamin Franklin, John Adams, James Madison, Elizabeth Cady Stanton, Susan B. Anthony, Frederick Douglass, Eleanor Roosevelt, and General George Catlett Marshall. The NHPRC has also supported papers collected on topical themes: the First Supreme Court, First Federal Congress, Ratification

PERSONAL KNOWLEDGE AS ANNOTATION

Here are examples of how one might use personal knowledge when editing a document. The personal knowledge may be the focus with passages from the document used to make a point; or, the document may be the focus with personal knowledge as a source for annotation. On the other hand, the two may appear in equal, interspersed doses or mixed with additional documents and resources. The editor must make sure that readers can recognize each passage and its source.

Michelle loved her adoptive parents and viewed them as her mother and father. She knew she was adopted; they raised her to think it was something special to have been "chosen." Only a few thoughts of her biological heritage followed her with any consistency: Why did her biological mother give her away, and did it bother her mother to do so? Did she care?[1] Imagine Michelle's feelings when she acquired the original social worker's report about her mother. First, it outlined the hardships of being an unwed mother in the 1950s, when the girl had nowhere to turn, and then it included this moment:

"Client said she would like to see the baby and then to sign the papers. . . . She did spend about 20 minutes with the baby . . . for the first time some tears gathered in her eyes."[2]

[1] Personal knowledge of author, Michelle . . .

[2] Social worker's report . . .

Excerpt from Carol Sturdevant's reminiscence of living on an Iowa farm, "Childhood Memories of 1930s [by] Mom Sturdevant," in editor's possession. See Figure 3-1 on page 26.

I decided to take a short cut across the fields instead of taking the country road—I forgot about the old bull that roamed in that field—and when I saw it, I had just a short way to make it to Grandma's, but I became frightened and began singing Jesus Loves Me to the top of my voice—and sang it till I got into the country lane—"Home place." To this day when I'm frightened or in a tense situation—I sing Jesus Loves Me.[1]

[1] This, and several other "Jesus Loves Me" stories, became part of Carol's memorial services and eulogies when she died in 2001. Her daughter, Pam DeFranza, noted that Carol always sang it in a "tiny, little girl voice." In her funeral instructions, Carol requested that the family sing this song, and the family met her wishes.

Rick and I pored over the old family letters that we had found in the box. When I was momentarily distracted, I looked up to find him crying over one letter he held in his hand. He said, "I never knew my grandfather wrote this to me." I knew how important his grandfather, Frank, was to him. I also realized that Frank was writing this when he could not yet see his first grandchild because Rick was born in California. Rick read the letter aloud to me with tears sparkling in his eyes.

Waverly, Iowa

2-12-47

Dear Wendell—Carol—Rick(ie)

Well Rick you are now two weeks old—Just think a long two weeks of age. By being admitted to this world on January 28th you beat by 5 days the birthday of your Great Grandpa Chandler. Your name, that is your middle name of Willard was given to you in honor of Grandpa Willard Wellman Chandler who is now 84 years of age and the name Willard also stands for a baby uncle of yours who was born to your Grandpa and Grandma Sturdevant on Feb 26— 1921 but didn't live to grow up like your Daddy—Friendship is a great thing in life and to be named 'Rick' after a friend and Buddie of your daddy is by no means anything but a great honor also. . . . [He continues about family naming patterns, explaining several generations.]

Now Sonny, this is too deep for you now to understand, but as you get older and grow up to maturity you are going to wonder about these names and about your family. In order to keep history straight it might be nice to remember these facts. This is your first letter from your Grandpa Sturdevant. We want you to grow big and strong and to be a fine lad. Anxiously waiting the time when we may see you—I am your Grandpa

Frank Sturdevant

Frank Sturdevant died when Rick was only three years old. We reflected on what a wonderful irony it was, but not a coincidence, that Rick not only became a historian, but the family historian. Frank was also right about how remembering these facts (or having Frank's letter stating them) would "keep history straight." Several of the naming decisions he stated in this letter were not recorded elsewhere or had been forgotten, and yet they helped solve genealogical mysteries.

of the Constitution, and Black Abolitionist Papers, to name a few.

The NHPRC has sponsored hundreds of documentary editing projects. Many are family papers of individuals who were either prominent in American history or informative about their own times. The latter criterion could include any of our families. Many genealogists might also be familiar with the NHPRC-funded projects as research treasures. For example, the projects have included family papers held by different state historical societies such as diaries and journals, the Draper Manuscripts, the Susquehannah Company

Figure 3-1 When using photographs of your ancestors to illustrate documents, choose portraits from the time period described in the documents. Here is Carol Sturdevant, the little girl who ran from the bull (see page 24), circa 1930. Sturdevant Family Papers, with permission of Rick W. and Wendell F. Sturdevant, in author's possession.

Papers, and books such as *Mary Chesnut's Civil War* or *"Dear Master": Letters of a Slave Family*.

Thus, the activities of the NHPRC may help ordinary family historians and would-be documentary editors indirectly or directly. There is also reason to consider whether at some point your documents might earn NHPRC support. Your project might fare better as part of an institutional proposal from a library or an archive, but that is possible if the documents are of enough historical interest. Now individuals also can apply to the NHPRC. Keep it in mind.

The Modern Language Association (MLA), <www.mla.org/>, began in 1883 and is the largest umbrella organization for teachers, writers, and practitioners of English and literature. The MLA used to oversee literary editions in a way similar to NHPRC for historical editions. English professors teach composition students that the MLA handbook is the bible of technical style. Using "MLA style" means following the guidelines in *MLA Handbook for Writers of Research Papers* and *MLA Style Manual and Guide to Scholarly Publishing*. When academic people go on about "style" in this context, they are referring to the mechanics of writing, such as punctuation, quotation, and documentation of sources.

Be aware: MLA style is *not* the style most used in history—*The Chicago Manual of Style* is. The three most popular sources of style in academic circles are MLA, *The Chicago Manual of Style*, and that of the American Psychological Associa-

Warning

tion (APA style). Journalism also has its own style bibles such as *The Associated Press Stylebook* (AP style). MLA is probably used most widely of the three leading styles, especially in colleges and by editors of literary periodicals and books. So, if I were going to write an article or book about my family history for a *literary* press, and especially if I wanted to publish a relative's literary writings, I would rely on the MLA style. Usually both book and periodicals publishers will tell you in their printed guidelines what style guide to follow before you submit the work.

The Chicago Manual of Style (fourteenth edition, fifteenth coming) rather than the MLA style guidelines, remains the style guide for the historical, documentary editing, and genealogical professions. It has set professional guidelines since 1906. Every few years, the University of Chicago Press tantalizes its fans with when the next edition will appear—perhaps even this year. Meanwhile, should you have questions, visit its FAQ page at <www.press.uch icago.edu/Misc/Chicago/cmosfaq.html>. Even an old edition of *Chicago*, available at used bookstores, is better than none, although it does change with the times. Have this big orange book by your side if you plan to undertake a documentary editing project or any kind of publishing in history. As a professional writer in history, I speak of "Chicago style" the way my English faculty colleagues speak of MLA.

Reminder

Remember, however, that a "style guide" is one that will answer technical editing and proofreading questions about matters such as punctuation, capitalization, and documentation (footnotes). It is not a guide to the practices of documentary editing. For the latter, see Mary-Jo Kline's *A Guide to Documentary Editing*, Stevens and Burg's *Editing Historical Documents*, and the book you currently have in your hands.

DOCUMENTARY EDITING GUIDEBOOKS

Until now, there has been no book on documentary editing directed at family historians. My article "Documentary Editing for Family Historians" appeared ten years ago. Both beginning and professional genealogists have commented that these methods are exactly what they have been looking for, exactly what they needed to deal with their own family documents.

Even for the professional or scholarly documentary editor, there have been only a few handbooks published and none written in a lay voice specifically for a genealogical audience. Every piece written on the subject has taken on a precious quality for people in the profession because there are so few guides. **Any of these might be helpful to you in your own documentary editing efforts.**

Some of the path-breaking explanations of documentary editing practices have been brief introductions to major edited volumes such as:

Sources

Julian P. Boyd, "Editorial Method," *The Papers of Thomas Jefferson*

Oscar Handlin et al, "The Editing and Printing of Manuscripts," *Harvard Guide to American History*

As for separate publications on documentary editing, until the 1980s there were only scholarly booklets such as:

Clarence E. Carter, *Historical Editing*

G. Thomas Tanselle, *The Editing of Historical Documents*

Editors have especially used bibliographies to locate the various booklets and articles, notably:

Beth Luey, *Editing Documents and Texts: An Annotated Bibliography*

David F. Trask and Robert W. Pomeroy III, *The Craft of Public History: An Annotated Select Bibliography*

The Association for Documentary Editing endorsed two full-length guidebooks, published ten years apart:

Mary-Jo Kline, *A Guide to Documentary Editing,* 1987, 1998

Michael E. Stevens and Steven B. Burg, *Editing Historical Documents: A Handbook of Practice,* 1997

Both guidebooks are directed at professional editors of institutional collections. Kline's is a scholarly synthesis of the field, and the Stevens and Burg book is a practical guide or manual modeled somewhat on *The Chicago Manual of Style.* It has numbered sections of advice directed at specific editorial questions. Stevens and Burg's book particularly reveals the trend toward projects at the state and local levels since it is a product of the American Association for State and Local History (AASLH), a major state historical society (Wisconsin), and leading staff from that society. Stevens has published several volumes of collected firsthand accounts from ordinary families, too. His handbook relies heavily on useful examples. It could be the *Chicago Manual* for documentary editing.

It is worthwhile to investigate some of the major documentary editing projects and see what their practices have been. Some of the best examples that are accessible online and that provide statements of editorial method are the following:

Internet Source

The Papers of George Washington

<www.virginia.edu/gwpapers/stylemanual/>

The Papers of Elizabeth Cady Stanton and Susan B. Anthony

<http://mep.cla.sc.edu/sa/sa-table.html>

The Papers of James Madison

<www.virginia.edu/pjm/editing.html>

FOUR

Locating Family Heirloom Documents

Mrs. Prest knew nothing about the [Aspern] papers, . . . She was amused by my infatuation, the way my interest in the papers had become a fixed idea. 'One would think you expected to find in them the answer to the riddle of the universe,' she said . . . if I had to choose between that precious solution and a bundle of Jeffrey Aspern's letters I knew indeed which would appear to me the greater boon.

—Henry James, The Aspern Papers, *New York: Macmillan and Co., 1888, 3*

Locating and acquiring your family documents can be an exciting, suspenseful, frustrating, and gratifying treasure hunt. It can even become a passion or an obsession. Perhaps you do not yet have any suitable documents for a publishing project. Then your exciting search may be to discover whether substantial documents exist somewhere in your family—that is, a home sources search, a search through households, asking questions of yourself and your relatives, in person, by telephone, or by e-mail and old-fashioned correspondence.

For your general construction of a family archive, ask relatives whether they have old letters, diaries, and other documents in their possession. Explain to them the necessity of transcription and duplication. Even when you find treasures, you may experience the strain of having to convince others to share. I joke in my lectures on this subject: "Cooperate in any way, sell your soul or your body" to gain access to cherished documents. Seriously, you can offer relatives copies of what you produce or of other family history materials. You should offer them (and anyone who assists you) full credit in your publications. Make sure folks understand the importance of permanent security through publication and archiving—that the materials need to be "out there" for historians to use in research and that publishing them honors the ancestors.

You may already have or think you have the complete documents that you

Idea Generator

wish to edit and publish, especially if it is a singular document such as a diary or memoir manuscript. Even in those cases, however, **you would do well to determine whether there are missing pieces, related accounts, other versions or transcriptions, and additional documents that might fit well with your project.** Documentary editors will tell you that one of your first steps is a thorough search through any and all repositories that might contain something relevant.

If your project is a collection of documents such as letters or the entire "papers of" someone, then you must be exhaustive in your search for more documents to include. With letters, you may have both the "from" and "to" when both writer/recipients were in your immediate family, such as your parents' love letters. If one of the writer/recipients was outside of your immediate family, however, you will need to check whether the mates to the letters you have still exist in someone else's hands.

For your annotation (see chapter eleven) of the documents you possess, you will need to locate other documents as sources of information, even if you don't reprint their text as part of your documentary editing project. You will need to quote and cite many different kinds of sources to write your introduction, conclusion, explanatory text, and footnotes. As you investigate repositories near your family home places, you may find original documents that you did not know existed, even diaries or memoirs. Thus, this kind of painstaking research has many purposes and rewards.

Early on you may also want to begin your search of the published literature relevant or comparable to your documents. In a large, public documentary editing project, say about Thomas Jefferson, this would mean locating every other edition of his papers ever published in any way. Certainly, you need to determine whether your documents have ever been published anywhere before. Then, you might investigate comparable projects. For example, I would want my grandmother's memoir about growing up in the West to fit into the body of published accounts of women in the West. So, I would research and read what others have already done with firsthand accounts on that topic, which, by the way, would be quite an undertaking in itself. Diaries, journals, memoirs, and letters of historical women, particularly frontier women, have been the subjects of much publishing recently.

WHERE TO FIND DOCUMENTS

Like all home sources, you could find documents anywhere, from your own home to an abandoned family barn to a public or private repository. Start with yourself and your home, move to nearby family homes, and then correspond with e-mail, or telephone distant relatives. Ask outright: Did so-and-so, or did anyone in the family, ever keep a diary or letters or write a memoir? It is best if you can travel to a location that may harbor documents and offer to search for yourself. If people are reluctant to part with original documents, be prepared to photocopy or photograph with a digital camera. **If you must be satisfied with copies, consider several aspects while you still have access to the originals.**

Tip

- Did your copies reproduce everything legibly? If not, recopy or take notes.
- Are there accompanying materials you need to copy or photograph before

ARE YOUR FAMILY PAPERS IN PRINT OR IN ARCHIVES?

It is unlikely that there are already manuscript collections or printed versions of your family documents unless the papers belonged or related to prominent individuals in history. If you wish to determine whether such collections exist, see Mary-Jo Kline's *A Guide to Documentary Editing*, 1st ed., 32–40, for advice. Kline suggests searching in the following guides that I list also in my bibliography: the Hamer guide (*A Guide to Archives and Manuscripts in the United States*), NUCMC (the *National Union Catalog of Manuscript Collections*), *American Literary Manuscripts*, the NHPRC directory, the *Harvard Guide to American History*, and the spectrum of American history bibliographies that may exist for any specific period or subtopic.

you leave, such as taking a picture of how the original documents (the cover of a diary, for example) actually appear?

- Can you get your relatives to sign permissions for use while you are with them face-to-face?
- Can you interview the relatives for information related to the documents?

There may also be family documents worthy of editing and publication waiting for you in public repositories, especially in the local areas where the family lived. For example, I inquired of the Kentucky Historical Society whether it held anything on my mother's Revolutionary War ancestors, Basil Williams and his son Jarrett. The society responded that it held applications that Jarrett and his brother Lawrence made for pensions in 1832. To prove their military service, the two men presented detailed narratives about their dramatic experiences on the Pennsylvania frontier. They also provided the pages from their family Bibles to prove the names and births of their heirs. Copies of these were exciting family history resources. See Figure 4-1 on page 32. The narrative accounts could make good articles for publication. I would have to investigate copyright and credit the repository that holds the originals.

A similar situation occurred for different reasons. I asked my mother's cousins whether they had any documents or memorabilia from their father, Frank Dickey, who served in the Spanish-American War. At first I was disappointed to learn that they did have them earlier but gave them away. It turned out they had responded to a call from the Army Military History Institute in Carlisle Barracks, Pennsylvania. They had sent in Frank Dickey's diary, letters, photographs, and bugle. Again, this means I would need to discuss with the repository, as well as with Frank's heirs, any plan to publish his materials. It was good news, though, that these items were safe in an archive. The institute was also generous about sending me copies of all the materials.

Thus, as you do your research, always investigate libraries, museums, and records repositories for possible documents from your family. Use the directories recommended in chapter one to locate these institutions. Approach local historical societies and libraries for any collections they may have relevant to your family,

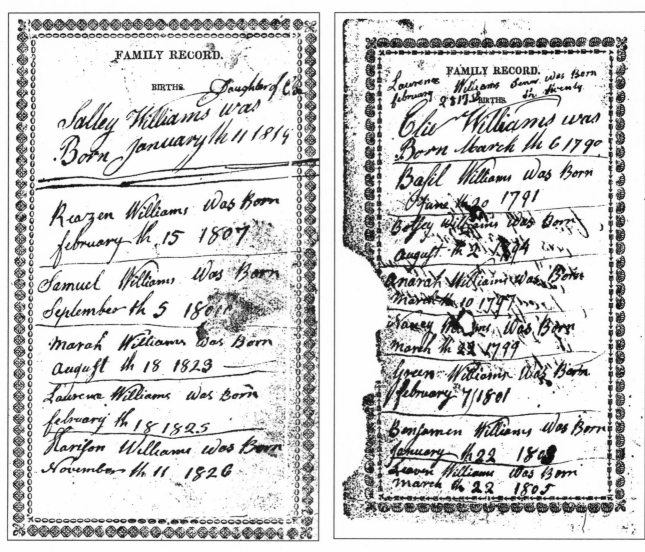

Figure 4-1 You may find reproducible copies of original family documents in a repository. These are pages from a Williams family Bible, circa 1790–1826, which the Kentucky Historical Society copied for me. Williams Family Papers, copies in author's possession.

their time period, or a special experience in their lives such as war service. Consider specialized archives such as military centers, local or regional libraries, or colleges that your ancestors may have attended. Watch for lists of family documents online. Relatives may post their transcriptions on Web sites. Some agencies post lists of the diaries and similar documents in their collections, and some genealogical sites will post these lists for agencies.

Scan the local newspapers from your ancestors' small towns, as well. Of course these are wonderful resources for historical context and family news. Sometimes your relative may have written a letter that was printed in the newspaper. It might be a letter to the editor, but even more common in rural areas would be newsy letters about travels, neighbors, family, and war experiences. You will need to research copyright before you transcribe and reprint any of these into your own collection, but they may be the missing links in your family correspondence.

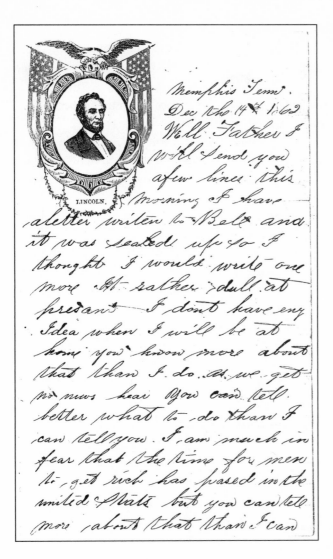

Figure 4-2 Civil War letters often include historical letterhead designs that make them even better illustrations for your transcribed documents. This letter is from Ira P. Withers to James Withers, 14 December 1862. Withers Family Papers, in author's possession.

SERENDIPITOUS DISCOVERIES

Some professional genealogists call serendipitous genealogical discoveries "Hank Jones moments," because the author Henry Z Jones Jr. has published collections of such experiences titled *Psychic Roots* and *More Psychic Roots*. You may have Hank Jones moments in your search for documents, too. The more stones you turn over, the more likely this becomes. In many cases, what seems like serendipity happens because we have been doggedly pursuing our research and making all the contacts that we could.

In *Bringing Your Family History to Life Through Social History*, I introduced Marion C. Parker of Goodland, Kansas (115, 147, 162–163). He gave me several Hank Jones moments. As my contact in my family's old hometown and as the local history expert, he received a retiring lawyer's file containing my family's documents and photographs, circa 1855–1890. This file presented the Withers family story as told through documents that had belonged to Kate Withers Leonard, my grandmother's great-aunt. The documents, in chronological order, were

- an 1839 promissory note signed by my great-great-grandfather, James

Withers, for whom debt seemed perpetual

- a letter from my great-great-grandmother Martha to her mother in 1855; the letter was written after she arrived in frontier Illinois, and it described her life there

- an 1861 chattel mortgage listing all of the family's Illinois property in detail so that they could go deeper into debt

- three Civil War letters from the oldest Withers son, Ira, before he died of disease in 1863; Ira was worried about the state of the farm in his absence; we did not know he had existed until we received these letters (see Figure 4-2 on page 33)

- a photograph of Martha Withers, widow, who took her surviving children into town after losing her husband and eldest son

- a funeral card from 1875 attesting to the death of a baby girl born to Otho and Fannie Withers Dickey, six years before they had their second daughter, my grandmother Kate; we had not known about this first, dead baby (see Figure 4-3 below)

- a funeral card from 1882 for Martha Withers. Martha died in town, leaving her grown daughters to follow their own husbands; Kate and Fannie followed to Kansas

- a reminiscence of early Goodland, typed by my Great-Great-Aunt Kate

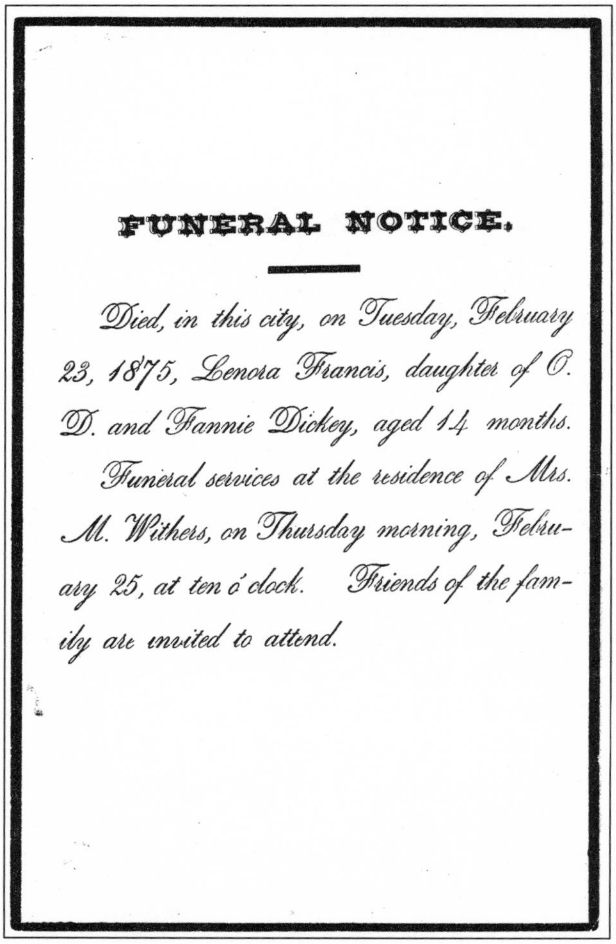

Figure 4-3 Funeral cards are a type of ephemera that serve well for illustrating family history documents. Funeral notice of Lenora Francis Dickey, 23 February 1875. Dickey Family Papers, in author's possession.

FUNERAL NOTICE.

Died, in this city, on Tuesday, February 23, 1875, Lenora Francis, daughter of O. D. and Fannie Dickey, aged 14 months. Funeral services at the residence of Mrs. M. Withers, on Thursday morning, February 25, at ten o'clock. Friends of the family are invited to attend.

Figure 4-4 Thomas P. Leonard and Kate Withers Leonard in his office in the "Leonard Brick" in Goodland, Kansas, circa 1905. Note how the decor offers many clues to regional business. Courtesy of Marion C. Parker and the Sherman County Historical Society. Copy in author's possession.

Leonard in the early 1900s; of Martha's daughters, Kate Leonard was last to be with her and, thus, carried off these family documents (see Figure 4-4 above)

The lawyer's file could have been lost to me and everyone, because my great-great-uncle, widower Thomas P. Leonard's only heir, was an unknown nephew from his side of the family. My grandmother Kate, niece of the Leonards, always lamented that her Aunt Kate's things went off with this stranger, but she was referring to "such nice things" as family silver or crystal. See Figure 4-5 on page 36. I doubt she even knew about these precious documents from her family. She would be so pleased, though, could she have heard that they survived and I received them. **By putting out all of the "feelers" that we can, we position ourselves as clearinghouses for family history materials.** Also note how a simple collection of documents begins to tell a family story even as we just put them into chronological order and start to editorialize about them.

Tip

ACQUIRING DOCUMENTS FROM OTHERS

Although you need to ask direct questions to obtain what may be available from family or repositories, there is an art to cultivating relationships for the best results. In *Bringing Your Family History to Life Through Social History*, there is a chapter about correspondence and several sections about how best to approach librarians and archivists. **A few essentials about this kind of contact are necessary here.**

- Do your homework first. Research which people, places, or agencies would be best to contact, the size of the staff or town, and the best method to contact them. Use the AASLH directory or similar guides to determine

Notes

Figure 4-5 This enlarged photograph of the Goodland parlor and dining room at the Thomas P. Leonard house hints of the heirloom "things" that Kate Dickey Harper wished to inherit from her Aunt Kate Leonard. Thus, a period interior picture can illustrate many aspects of life. Dickey Family Papers, in author's possession.

how best to approach agencies.

- Unless you have reason to believe there are diaries, memoirs, or letters from particular ancestors awaiting you in a home or an archive, begin with general research questions rather than appear to be coveting something in particular.
- When writing to family or other private individuals in their towns, consider that they may respond best to warm old-fashioned letters that give them some individual attention, rather than to brusque, typed inquiries.
- When contacting an agency, keep your explanations brief and to the point.
- With professional research institutions, avoid stating that you are a genealogist or doing genealogical research. Instead, state that you are doing historical research.
- With agencies, offer a year or a time period and place that you are researching rather than the names of individuals and families.
- Send along self-addressed, stamped envelopes and offer to help pay any expenses of transmitting documents to you, such as fax, photocopy, and additional postage.
- Discourage people from mailing or shipping one-of-a-kind family documents to you if there is any more secure way. Encourage them to copy one-of-a-kind items before mailing.
- Be courteous, patient, grateful, and calmly enthusiastic.

CHECK COPYRIGHT

It may seem as though you wouldn't have to worry about copyright issues in your documentary editing projects. If you "own" the original diary, letters, or memoir—having them in your possession—you might think you also own the rights to them, especially if they were so old that no one would care or if you are an heir of the document's author. **It is important that you get this straight now, early in this project, before you waste time on a publishing idea that you cannot legally pursue.**

Important

In the case of unpublished diaries, letters, memoirs, or other original documents, someone else may own the piece of paper, but the author has strong rights to the words. The legal copyright to an unpublished, unregistered original document remains with its author (or the legal heirs of that author) until the rules of copyright law change that situation. Here are summary points of current copyright law.

- If a document was created before 1 January 1978, the copyright remains with the author of it (or the legal heirs of that author) for the author's lifetime plus seventy years after the death of the author. If the author has already been dead more than seventy years, his/her copyright protection ends on 1 January 2003.
- A document originating before 1 January 1978, if published before 1 January 2003, would have a copyright to 31 December 2047.
- If a document was created after 1 January 1978, the copyright belongs to the author or author's heir(s) for the author's lifetime plus seventy years.
- If a document from before 1978 remains unpublished, its copyright is protected until 1 January 2003.
- You are the sole legal heir if you were named such in the will and/or legally recognized as such during the legal disposal of the deceased's property. You share the copyright if you shared the role as heir.
- If the document physically "belongs" to, or is housed in, a repository such as a library, the library can control your access to it but does not own

HENRY JAMES'S *THE ASPERN PAPERS*

Beware your passionate desire to acquire precious documents. It could become a dangerous obsession! Perhaps the most memorable example of this is a fictional editor/publisher in Henry James's story *The Aspern Papers*. In this story, the publisher desperately wants to locate the missing love letters and relics of a legendary poet, Jeffrey Aspern. He believes they are in the possession of Aspern's elderly former lover, Juliana Bordereau, who lives with her niece, Tita, in Venice. This story first captured my imagination on television in a romanticized Hollywood film version called *The Lost Moment* (1947), starring Robert Cummings, Susan Hayward, and Agnes Moorehead as the elderly aunt. You may read an electronic version of Henry James's original text from the University of Virginia Library by searching at <http://etext.lib.virginia.edu/>. In *The Aspern Papers*, the editor/publisher is so anxious to obtain and publish the missing documents that he travels to Venice, deceives the two women, and brings disaster to the precious papers. In the end, Miss Tita informs him, she burned them "one by one."

Warning

BE CAREFUL WITH PARAPHRASING

A warning about paraphrasing: If you choose to summarize the contents of an existing letter or document because you could not obtain permission to reprint it, take care. The more someone restricts a document's use, the more cautious you should be. Do not paraphrase it closely. Do not state the unique aspects of the document, even in your own words, if those unique thoughts or pieces of information are key to the copyright holder's precious rights to the document's contents. In such circumstances, find the minimal way to indicate only the most essential information to assist your readers in comprehending the string of documents.

---

copyright unless the author transferred it to the repository. To publish, you would need permission of the author or heirs and permission of the repository.

- If you share copyright with another heir or if you do not own the copyright at all, you need written permission to publish from the rightful owner(s).
- Obtain the permission for use, in writing, from the copyright holder(s).
- If you cannot obtain copyright permission to publish a document, but you want to include its contents in your published series of documents, you can summarize that document in your own words. For example, you might have copyright to the letters your ancestor wrote but not to all of the letters he received. So the series makes sense to readers, you can summarize the letters for which you could not obtain release to print, or you can even speculate in your annotations what the missing letters might have contained.
- If any part of what you would like to publish was previously published, you need to research the publisher and author. If it was published before 1922 and not reprinted or reregistered since, it is probably in the public domain and thus free from copyright restrictions.
- If you want to quote from a published work that is not in the public domain, you may need permission to quote depending on fair use laws. For our purposes, fair use usually means that you can quote brief passages from published sources in a way that enhances people's appreciation of those other works rather than infringing on the integrity or success of those works by "stealing their thunder." The longer or more important the passage is to the original work, or the shorter and more dependent upon that passage the work is, the riskier it is to quote much from it in your own work.
- If you want to quote more substantial passages from a published source, seek written permission from the publisher and/or author.
- You can include on the backside of the title page of your published book the statement of your own copyright and of how others might obtain your permission to quote from the documents. See page 221 of *Editing Historical Documents* for examples.

- See the sources by Fishman and Stim in the Bibliography for more information.
- Copyright laws change regularly as cases reach court decisions. Therefore, before you go too far in a project where you will need copyright, check the latest sources available.
- When in doubt or in complex cases, seek the advice of a copyright attorney. Although legal fees can be expensive, I do not feel confident without an attorney's advice.

CREATE "NEW" FAMILY DOCUMENTS

Think like a documentary editor about your own papers, too. Your memories, or the oral traditions passed on to you by others that are now gone, are yours alone to record. **Why not now create the documents about yourself that you wish your ancestors had left behind about themselves?** Your stories will be a gift to your descendants, but even if you have no descendants, your writings will be a gift to the historical record. You can write diaries, journals, letters, and other documents of a high quality, with plenty of descriptive text and storytelling to preserve what would otherwise be lost. Creating your own documents requires some discipline, especially to make daily or regular entries, but it does not need to be as demanding as you might fear.

Idea Generator

- Keep a diary, a journal, an account book, a baby book, or any other appropriate account of your life. Write your memoir or reminiscences.
- Set realistic goals for yourself in writing family or autobiographical stories. For example:
  1. If you have been unable to keep a daily diary, then write at length only when events make it worthwhile. Do not make diary writing burdensome.
  2. Set aside a quiet, private time of the day to do your writing, even if it is brief.
  3. Make it a project to keep a journal of a trip or move, when you might be unable or unwilling to work on your required everyday tasks anyway.
  4. As reminders, make lists or files of stories that you intend to record.
  5. Talk stories into a tape recorder for later transcription.
  6. Interview your immediate family members, and have them interview you on tape for later transcription.
  7. If you are lucky enough to have patient friends as I do, use your daily e-mails as an opportunity to document family or autobiographical events and your thoughts about them as they happen. Then, print out the e-mails and save them in binders, or at least save them to floppy disks.
- Make each family letter that you write useful as a document for the present-and-future files of the family papers.
- If you write annual letters to all, such as during the holidays, turn them into family history documents. Some of us hate receiving annual, impersonal, sometimes-self-centered recaps of the doings of a family. If, however, the annual letter contained an interesting, nostalgic reminiscence

along with the necessary catch-up information, we would read and keep the letter.

- As you correspond with family members or about family subjects, in addition to keeping both "to" and "from" letters, keep a sheet or journal of your reactions to those letters. For example, you might write your versions of the same stories or clarify mysteries in the letters.

- Use your own calendars, account books, checkbooks, receipts, tax records, and other records as places to note important family events with as much description as you can squeeze in.

- Scrapbooking is becoming popular again. Include as much explanatory text as you can for family memorabilia in the scrapbooks. Label the scrapbook itself and the scrapbook textual entries with the author's name and date, making the scrapbook an identifiable document.

- As you accumulate business, legal, vital, or news documents, record your own comments about them on separate sheets of paper. For example, if there is a family history story to tell about an obituary, certificate, will, deed, mortgage, clipping, or diploma, write that information and file it with the document.

- If there is an artistic or artifact collection developing in the family, record the accompanying stories and explanations on paper. If you cannot store the paper with the artifact, then have a small indicator with one as to where to find the other.

- Put your name, date, and place on everything that you write and keep.

- Keep your own "new" family papers well organized to inspire others to preserve them.

ORAL HISTORIES AS DOCUMENTS

Oral History

One way to create "documents" for your family history is through taped oral history interviewing. I offered guidelines for how best to interview in *Bringing Your Family History to Life Through Social History*. Once you have interviewed someone, you can transcribe the interview. You can then edit the transcript, because it has become a document. Remember that it is a jointly owned document between interviewer and interviewee. Ideally, you would have full permission to retain and publish all parts of the interview. If you did want to publish it, consider parting from the traditional script format of presentation.

Of course you should not alter the original words in any unethical or misleading way. It is possible, however, to condense them into full, successive paragraphs of monologue so that the interview becomes the one person telling his or her story without your prompting. A good example of this is Susan Tucker's *Telling Memories Among Southern Women*. As long as you make your decisions and steps clear and distinctive so that researchers can tell your words from the interviewee's, you could also integrate passages of narrative to flesh out areas not covered in the interview. Consider the topics, themes, and length of the interview to determine what agencies, such as state or local historical societies, or which publishers might be interested.

You might also have the opportunity to do an oral history volume of the type historians usually create. This would involve grouping several interviews with people whose stories cover common ground with a common theme or topic. I have listed examples in the Bibliography. If you combined your interviews into a group on a specific theme, you might have a book. Or, if you saw themes of general historical interest in the one interview, consider whether it could become an article in a state or local history periodical. At least this would get it into print, help save it, and make it available to other researchers.

FOR THE GOOD OF THE CAUSE

Remember that you can solicit the creation of new documents from other family members, too. I have my grandmother's and my father's memoirs because their children asked them to write down their stories.

- Encourage a relative to keep a diary. Give a blank diary as a gift.
- Encourage a relative, especially an older, experienced one, to write reminiscences. Give as gifts notebooks, computer equipment, or whatever might foster memoir writing.
- Encourage new parents to keep a baby book and use it for stories and anecdotes. Encourage others to do so. Give baby books as gifts, and ask recipients to write descriptively in them.
- Encourage the rediscovery of autograph albums. Give them as gifts. Use them not only for teenage purposes but also for accumulating special messages from family members upon special events. Encourage people to write useful information such as their fondest memories of the recipient. A good example would be for all children and grandchildren to write an album for a grandparent, or vice versa. Utilize blank journal books to offer more space.
- Encourage family to keep scrapbooks. Certainly there are more supplies and support groups for this hobby than ever!

Locating, acquiring, selecting, and even creating documents is a worthy cause for all of us family historians. We may find ways to publish some of them. We may create archival collections from which future researchers might draw the bases for their books and articles. We may answer our genealogical questions. Whatever the results, using the methods of documentary editors and archivists will help us preserve and share the value of the extraordinarily precious words our families left behind.

FIVE

Preserving Original
Documents

*The Conclusion of your Letter makes my Heart throb, more than a
Cannonade watch. You bid me burn your letters. But I must forget you
first.*

—*John Adams to Abigail Adams, 28 April 1776, from L.H. Butterfield, ed.,* Adams Family
Correspondence, vol. 1, 400

S he burned them, as I said in chapter two. Oh, not Abigail Adams,
praised be, but my mother. She burned the love letters that she and
Daddy had written during World War II. She thought they were too
personal for anyone else to read, and she had not even anticipated my existence,
let alone that I would be a family historian and documentary editor. I understand and do not blame her so much as I regret the loss. When I was a teenager,
though, I blamed her, as teenagers do with parents anyway. It would have
meant a lot to me to read about the passion and affection between them and
to know what that was like for two "real" people, not just in the movies. See
Figure 5-1 on page 43.

The "real" quality of our original documents is important before, during,
and after transcription. Handling them as relics of the past, reading the original
ink on the original paper, transports many of us to the times and feelings of
past people. "Identifying the Real Thing," a paper by Diane van der Reyden,
observed that an artifact can have "symbolic and visual power" for any of us,
but "only 'the real thing' contains the evidence to support its symbolic and
visual importance." If you transcribe and edit your family documents for publication, probably no expert will challenge whether what you have transcribed
is "real." Only the originals, however, stand as proof if needed. They hold the
power to inspire us as relics but also the power to verify our work.

Therefore, before traveling further into documentary editing projects, **we
need to stop and consider the best treatment of the rare, fragile, original documents
we are handling.** Transcribing them means we might eventually put them away

Warning

Figure 5-1 James A. Scott Jr. and Barbara Harper early in their relationship, circa 1941. When lacking documents that portray people's affections, photographs serve an added function. Scott Family Papers, in author's possession.

and handle them less, but meanwhile we want them to survive. Imagine your horror if you found the documents, put them away for later transcription, and then came back to find them disintegrated or illegible. Cherishing them with archival methods will also preserve them for others to enjoy and use "the real thing."

WHY DOCUMENTS DETERIORATE

Sometimes the language used in discussion of archival supplies and methods seems too technical. Reading about acid and alkaline paper and pH percentages can be off-putting. For a long time I knew what supplies were needed to properly protect documents and I even knew what could happen to documents not so protected, but I did not really know why. History (in my opinion) always helps explain mysteries. Important documents from before the mid-nineteenth century were on parchment—not parchment paper—but real parchment. **True parchment was animal skin—calf, sheep, or goat—made by stripping, scraping, stretching, wetting, and drying. Vellum was a fine quality parchment from calfskin.** Parchment paper is imitation parchment made from plant fibers such as cotton, flax, or cellulose from fir trees. Our ancestors reserved real parchment for important documents such as the Declaration of Independence or the Constitution.

\di'fin\ *vb*

Definitions

Real parchment can survive for centuries, with just a few enemies wanting to chew on it.

Most paper that our ancestors used before the mid-nineteenth century was partially or entirely "rag" paper. It contained fibers such as cotton, hemp, linen (flax), and some wood fibers such as mulberry, and most of it was handmade. Rag paper will last in high and attractive quality for centuries. Late-nineteenth-century manufacturers, however, turned to wood pulp for mass-producing cheaper American paper. Wood-based paper contains lignin, which over time breaks down into acids. The acids cause disintegration of paper—yellowing, crumbling, and even "acid migration." The cheapest, highest-acid paper—newsprint—is the best example of these effects. Have you seen how newspaper changes character even when left in the weather for a few days, or how brown and fragile an old newspaper becomes? Have you seen the brown stain a news clipping leaves on white materials when it has pressed next to them in storage? **Newsprint has the shortest life of any paper. When its acids contaminate neighboring documents (acid migration), they not only leave a brown stain, but they start the process of acid disintegration in the neighboring documents as well.**

Since most of our documents are high-acid, wood-pulp paper, they are already handicapped. Fortunately, the paper used for some special documents such as high-quality stationery was still partially rag paper; unfortunately, the paper commonly used for mass-produced scrapbooks and photograph albums was high-acid paper. To compound the problem, the documents are mixed with the news clippings. In our ignorance, many of us have been comedies of errors as conservators. We stored our heirloom documents in basements, attics, and garages, not realizing that heat and humidity cause them to deteriorate more rapidly. Warm, damp conditions also encourage mold and insects. We left the boxes of documents on the floor of the basement waiting for the next flood. When we appreciated a document, we framed it and hung it on a wall for all to admire—in acidic framing materials, facing the sun's ultraviolet rays, which faded it quickly. Maybe we laminated it, permanently dooming it to heat and chemical damage. Or, we tied the precious love letters with a pretty ribbon, never realizing that by leaving them tightly folded we caused future tears at the creases. When we damaged our documents, we tried to tape and glue them, unknowingly adding new destructive chemicals. Perhaps we even loved having our documents out so much that they gathered dust, we spilled coffee on them, or the children filled in the letter *o*'s with crayons. We all need help with our documents.

Definitions

Paper is an organic artifact, as are textiles, whereas stone or metal are inorganic. Being organic means that the artifact is more susceptible to environment and infestation.

HANDLING DOCUMENTS

There is nothing quite so inspirational about doing historical research as holding the original document that a predecessor held and perhaps wrote or signed. **You do not want to handle documents to their own detriment, however.** Look thoughtfully at your old heirloom documents to judge how best to handle them with care. Copy, transcribe, or preserve them soon to minimize handling the originals. When you do handle them, wear white cotton gloves to protect documents from your skin's oils and dirt. White gloves are less liable to contain

Warning

HAZARDS TO DOCUMENTS

improper handling by people, either handling the documents roughly or by having them come into contact with the natural dirt and oils in skin

fluctuating or extreme temperatures

fluctuating or extreme humidity levels, especially high humidity

high levels of or frequent exposure to light, especially ultraviolet rays

pollutants such as tobacco, fireplace, or cooking smoke; dirt and dust; urban air pollution

proximity to high-acid documents that "migrate" like newspaper clippings

introduction of harmful fasteners, metal or rubber, and adhesives

storage in folded, creased, or rolled condition

storage in acidic containers or adhesive albums

storage or transport in positions that cause falling, bending, breakage, or pressing

mold, mildew, rodents, and insects

lamination

static electricity

improper labeling, framing, or packaging

spillage of food, beverages, or other contaminants near documents

natural disasters such as floods, fire, and leaks

theft, vandalism, unwanted sale or dispersal, or abuse by children

chemical dyes than colored gloves are. Archival and photographic supply stores and catalogs sell cheap gloves for this purpose. As with all archival supplies, these are cheaper by a higher volume. If you can buy a dozen pairs cheaper than one pair, perhaps you can share the cost with friends who also need them. **If you do not have gloves, at least wash your hands carefully before touching a document.** You will wash your hands more often than ever when you start handling precious documents. Wait until later for the lotion, too; the idea is to minimize oils.

When you can plan in advance, try not to open and handle fragile old documents on the spur of the moment. Instead, prepare a location and the equipment you will need. Locate a safe, clean, flat surface where there will be no spills, catching, or bending on other objects. Follow these additional steps:

- Wash hands thoroughly.
- Wear white cotton gloves.

Tip

- Do not eat, drink, or smoke near the documents.
- Use a flat, clean work space at least twice as large as the documents.
- Do not lift or carry a fragile document without stiff support underneath it.
- Try not to slide or stack documents in ways that may cause abrasion.
- Lift documents one at a time.
- When you pick up a document, lift it by strong diagonal corners rather than just the top, middle, bottom, or one side.
- Do not grasp a document tightly enough to pinch it.
- Do not set anything on top of documents.
- Use the advice below to unfold or unroll documents.
- Label archivally, as described on pages 47–48.
- Avoid using any adhesives or fasteners on documents.
- Do not laminate, but consider encapsulation for frequently handled documents.
- Clean documents carefully, following the advice on pages 48–49.
- Check originals periodically to guard against hazards.

Flattening folded or rolled documents is best before handling or storing them, but do this with care. If letters unfold easily, for example, simply start keeping them flat in archival file folders. Remember to keep the accompanying envelope, if there is one, together with the right letter in the same folder, especially if the envelope carries any identifying information. Use legal-sized folders for legal-size documents rather than leaving some parts of the documents folded. If the document does not unfold and flatten easily, do not force it. Do not try weighting the document at this stage.

Professionals have ways to humidify and "relax" folded or rolled documents. First, carefully consider whether your documents are suited for humidification. If the documents are rare, valuable, and questionable candidates for this process, consult a conservator. Before trying humidification, do surface cleaning of the documents (see page 48). Never humidify documents that have water-soluble aspects, such as watercolor paintings or some inks; layered or textured items such as oil paintings or certain kinds of photographs; or "friable" art with charcoal, chalk, pastels, or certain kinds of pencil that easily lifts off. The best instructions I have seen for flattening by humidification are from the National Park Service and are available on the Colorado Preservation Alliance site at <www.archives.state.co.us/cpa/articles/paper/flatten.htm>. The better method involves using an ultrasonic humidifier, like the ones many of us in the West keep in our dry-climate homes. There is also a hot steam method. In either case, great care is necessary to avoid accidental wetting of the documents. I have not used the methods myself yet and so would recommend contacting a conservator if you are uncertain of your ability to follow the National Park Service instructions.

Encapsulation (not lamination) is a good way to protect an original document if you need to handle and examine it repeatedly, as you may when transcribing it. **When you encapsulate a document, you encase it in polyethylene or polypropylene sheets (Mylar) that have acid-free adhesive (double-sided tape) around the edges.** The document "floats" securely inside, away from the edges.

\di'fin\ *vb*

Definitions

Figure 5-2 Moses Margam, Welshman, circa 1880. This is a photograph of a charcoal overpainting, here described as "friable" media. Having a photographic copy like this prevents handling the valuable original. Harper Family Papers, in author's possession.

This allows you to handle it safely. If necessary, you could remove it by carefully cutting the plastic edges away from the document. Do not laminate an original document, because the heat and plastic permanently alter it and it is virtually impossible to remove.

To encapsulate you can purchase the plastic and adhesive strips separately, or you can purchase encapsulation units premade in standard sizes. All of these products come in a wide range of sizes. If you are going to cut your own plastic and tape, you will also need a workspace, grid paper, a utility knife, and a brayer or squeegee for pressing. Do not allow the adhesive strips to touch the document. Encapsulation is not suitable for "friable" media, documents with chalk, charcoal, or other dry-dust materials. Since static electricity is what floats the document in the encapsulation envelope, the same charge could lift the chalk or pencil particles off the page. See Figure 5-2 above. Dirty items need cleaning before encapsulation. Some high-acid papers seem to age faster in encapsulation. In these cases, place a sheet of buffered paper the same size as the document behind your document in the encapsulation. The buffered paper will slow the deterioration.

Labeling is another way to minimize harmful handling. If you label the envelope, folder, or protective sleeve in which you store a document, then you do not need to open and handle the artifact to see which one it is. Use a no. 2 pencil to label containers, keeping inks away from documents. Or, you can buy sheets of acid-free, self-adhesive labels and print them out. Do not write on the

> ## CHARCOAL OVERPAINTINGS
>
> In a charcoal overpainting, the photographer/artist drew or painted over the outlines of a poor-quality enlarged photograph, making the charcoal representation look very accurate. These are usually sixteen-by-twenty-inch, black-and-white portraits, although sometimes smaller and sometimes hand-colored. They make excellent illustrations for relevant documents, and their clear lines and light backgrounds make them easy to reproduce for publication, either photographically or by photocopying. Charcoal overpaintings are friable media, meaning that the charcoal could come off the paper if it is not handled carefully.

documents. With photographs, label the container and then use light pencil or a preprinted label on the back of a photographic copy. If you must mark documents, do so lightly in a back corner. Write on the backside of the unused margins of photographs. Archival supply houses sell many kinds of safe labels and pens. If you're labeling a document that you have specially treated, such as through encapsulation, assist future conservators by indicating what you have done and when.

Books, particularly heirloom volumes, deserve special treatment, too. If they are on bookshelves, don't stack them so tight as to make it difficult to remove one. When you do reach for a book, do not pull it by its head cap. Instead, push the books on either side of it back so you can grab its back edge or spine. Try not to bend or break the spine of a book, turn down its page corners, mark in it, or use bookplates. Mylar covers are good, or you might place a fragile book in an archival box where it would lie flat.

CLEANING AND RESTORING DOCUMENTS

Surface cleaning is relatively safe and easy. Some documents bear dirt that can cause them further harm or that obscures your view of the contents. These are valid reasons to find a way to clean the document superficially. Conservators usually state that simple, dry surface cleaning with a soft, camel's hair brush or an erasing compound is safe for us to do ourselves. Even these simple methods are too risky for newspapers, books, photographs, friable media, hand-colored items, or anything extremely fragile or heavily damaged.

With either a brush or an erasing compound, gently brush the document from the center outward. As you reach its edges, keep using straight, outward strokes to avoid tearing. If there is already a tear, brush *with* it, not against it. Erasing compounds such as Opaline or Skum-X Powder come as granules in canisters. Lightly shake the granules on the document (on a test corner first), then gently rub or brush them over the document. Finally, brush them completely away. Residual granules can cause more harm than would be caused by leaving the dirt where it was. Only brush off the easiest dirt; leave the rest for an expert. Deeper cleaning and stain removal are best for a professional conservator to do. Remember to clean with any degree of pressure over the edges and not directly over the printed words of the document. You do not want to accidentally harm the printing. The same brushing technique works for removing mold as well. Brush the document outside on a sunny, dry day. Then, store it in better conditions for the future.

Mending documents is also work for a conservator. Adding tape or glue can be a disaster. Conservators struggle to remove what is left of old tape on documents. Then, they can mend a tear with Japanese tissue and a special glue or with heat-set tissue and an iron. Standard tapes, even those marked "archival," may only last ten years and then leave a sticky, discolored residue.

Newsprint (such as your clippings) is so acidic that you may want to "wash" it before encapsulation. Washing means rinsing in distilled water and then allowing to thoroughly dry flat. There are also deacidifying sprays in archival supply catalogs. If your clippings seem too fragile to wash, you may wish to encapsulate them with a sheet of buffered paper as a backing. Some archivists photocopy and then discard newspapers and clippings rather than risk contaminating a collection.

To clean the surrounding area where you store documents, or books on a shelf, some archivists recommend One-Wipe Dust Cloth, Stretch and Dust, and Dust Bunny as the safest and most effective ways to dust around documents, books, and artifacts without chemicals or roughness that might hurt them. These cleaning supplies are also available in archival supply catalogs. Conservators point out that frequent vacuuming and dusting of your home will help preserve documents, too.

THE STORAGE ENVIRONMENT

Like museum curators and archivists, we need to think of our documents and artifacts as requiring a safe environment for their prolonged lives. **Documents survive best at moderate temperatures and low humidity comparable to normal human comfort levels.** Regulate temperature, as fluctuations can do the most harm to paper. The ideal temperature range for storage is 65 to 71 degrees Fahrenheit, with 68 degrees being the best. Basements are too cool and moist; attics are too hot. Experts usually say 45 to 50 percent humidity is fine, but some prefer 30 to 35 percent. Extreme fluctuations are more harmful than a steady high or low. Mold or foxing (small brown spots) on documents are signs of too much humidity. Basements—where most family historians might store things—are probably the worst storage places, in terms of humidity. Do not store documents near windows that you keep open, water pipes, air conditioners, or any other source of moisture. Place packets of silica gel (like the ones you sometimes find in new shoe boxes) inside containers to reduce humidity. Perhaps your room or house needs a dehumidifier.

Conservators suggest that an interior closet, such as a bedroom closet, might be the best storage location for heirloom paper. Interior walls carry less humidity and temperature fluctuation than exterior walls. Also, your bedroom closet is liable to reflect your preferences for temperature through your use of heating and air conditioning. The best temperature and humidity levels for documents are the ones most people find healthy and comfortable. Your closet for heirloom

Quotes

"The basic tenet of conservation is above all to do no harm."
—Konstanze Bachmann, ed., *Conservation Concerns: A Guide for Collectors and Curators* (2).

Important

For More Info

For detailed advice on testing and controlling humidity, see Arthur W. Schultz, gen. ed., *Caring for Your Collections* (25–28).

documents should be one that you can keep closed most of the time. Do not store documents on the floor, especially in a basement or ground level. Use platforms or shelves to get boxes a minimum of four to six inches off the floor.

When choosing places to store documents, avoid any transition zone of the house such as entryways, atriums, mudrooms, or vestibules. These are meant to be different in temperature and humidity than the parts of your house where you and your documents can live comfortably. When you avoid storing against outside walls, remember that the worst walls are ones where winter winds prevail from that direction. Thus, do not store next to a west or north wall. The same would be true with hot climates and southern exposures.

Keep documents away from light. Store them in the dark. If you frame or display originals, keep them away from both sunlight and artificial light, especially fluorescent lighting. Draw drapes, get ultraviolet shields for windows and lights, turn off lights when not needed, or frame and display only copies. If you must display originals where they receive light, then rotate your displays as museums do so that each item gets minimal exposure. Once the damage is done, it's done. Protect documents also from pollutants such as fireplace, cooking, or cigarette smoke and any kind of spillage or dirt. Keep them in archivally sound, protective containers.

Of course many of us, and our ancestors, have stored our precious documents in exactly the wrong containers: our special, hand-carved wooden boxes, trunks, and antique dresser drawers. Wherever you store documents, remember that the materials surrounding them can be unfriendly to their long-term survival. Acid-free folders and boxes, and steel file cabinets with baked-on enamel finishes are safe. Avoid wood boxes or drawers because they contain chemicals that can affect documents. For containers such as boxes, binders, envelopes, and albums, use acid-free, archival materials available through supply catalogs (see Appendix A). **For covering, displaying, or storing in plastic, use Mylar Type D, polyethylene, or polypropylene. Do not use polyvinyl chloride (PVC) or polyvinyl acetate (PVA).** These unwanted plastics chemically degrade and can take your materials with them. Remember to separate out high-acid documents such as newspaper clippings and telegrams so their acid doesn't "migrate" to other documents. If there are strong historical or sentimental reasons to keep these items integrated with your other documents, then photocopy the high-acid documents onto archival paper, keep the copies with the document collection, and isolate the original acidic documents.

Archival supply houses offer a large variety of folders, envelopes, protective sleeves, and boxes. Buy from reputable archival supply houses, because advertising terms such as "archival," "acid-free," or "museum quality" appear on inappropriate products. Popularity has made these terms similar to "low fat" or "all natural." Most of us will use simple, acid-free, letter-size manila folders. When selecting folders for your documents, use the following guidelines:

- To avoid cramping, make sure the folder is slightly larger than the documents.
- Put no more than about ten to twenty pages of older documents in one standard folder.
- If some documents going into these folders are of odd, smaller sizes or are

particularly fragile or damaged, first slip them into their own envelopes of paper or clear polyester, then put them into the folders.

- To keep documents from harming each other, use buffered twenty-pound paper as interleaving sheets.
- Keep folders in strong and reinforced archival storage boxes made for this purpose.
- Keep enough folders in one box so that they hold each other upright but not so many as to crush one another.

Infestations happen. Discourage mold, mildew, and fungi from staining paper and other items by maintaining proper temperature and humidity. Discourage rodents or insects through temperature and humidity control, frequent checking, cleaning, and sometimes pest controls. Mice will nest in a long-undisturbed box or drawer of papers that they can shred. Silverfish, small but longish gray insects that skitter out of sight quickly, love high humidity and dark spaces. They nibble lacy holes in documents, although what they really relish are the starchy adhesives and coatings. If you use pest controls, avoid any chemical contact with the artifacts. Moth crystals may keep them away but, as you probably know, could contaminate your documents as well as introduce an all-too-familiar smell.

Generally, prevention is the best method. Keep the doors and windows screened. Clean the house regularly. Maintain the documents at recommended heat and humidity levels. If you need to set traps, try Frank Sturdevant's method: Keep plugs of tobacco on shelves and in drawers to discourage silverfish. I can't say it works, because I've only tried it in Colorado, where it's dry and silverfish are not much of a problem. Indeed, moving to save your documents could be your last resort, extreme though it seems. All of my Iowa artifacts and documents were subject to mildew and infestations until we moved them to Colorado where it is so dry that glue dries out and furniture falls apart!

Notes

PRESERVATION OR SECURITY COPYING

More and more archivists recommend photocopying in a systematic way that they call preservation or security copying. The Library of Congress recommends that archives dedicate separate machines for this copying so the quality remains high. Of course, you cannot afford this scale. Also, copies will not offer the excitement of handling original documents. There will be times when you must return to the original for practical reasons such as deciphering handwriting. Copying your documents is essential, however. Usually you can work from copies, even for most transcription. Preserving copies in different locations from the originals may mean that at least one survives fire or theft. Copying makes it possible to share documents with archival institutions or other relatives. Sometimes copying even makes it easier to read words obscured in the original.

How to Copy

- It is best to minimize your photocopying of rare documents because they might suffer from repeated handling and light exposure. Try to copy them once and make these good copies.

- Use 100 percent rag content paper. Acid-free and buffered papers have a pH balance of 7.0–7.5 and 8.5, respectively. Acid-free paper is neutral and sufficient for copying documents.
- Use a photocopying machine that uses powdered, carbon-based black pigment toner for permanence.
- Test how well the machine makes the image adhere to the paper. Place a piece of tape over some lines of copied text. Good adherence would mean none of the copied text peels off when you slowly lift the tape from the document.
- Compare the quality of the copy with the original for legibility and completeness.
- Identify the copy you have made as a copy and include the name and date, without defacing the text.
- Note on the copy if the original was poor so someone doesn't assume she has to make another copy.

When to Copy

- Copy any document that you intend to handle frequently.
- Copy documents to share them.
- Make quality copies to frame or display instead of originals.
- Copy rare documents to keep spares in other locations.
- Copy disintegrating or harmful documents like news clippings to keep the copies among the other documents.
- Copy a document that you are transcribing. This will darken fading ink or enlarge illegible passages for easier reading.
- Copy documents out of books—such as pages out of Bibles, scrapbooks, or baby books—when you want to work with the documents without handling the books. Handle the books gently while photocopying. Do not break the spines. Some facilities offer special machines for book copying.

With good paper and ink, you can create a copy for research or display that is a fine document itself and thus protect the original from exposure or frequent handling. Distributing copies can alleviate some ruffled feathers if anyone resents or resists your efforts to accumulate the family documents. Scanning documents into your computer makes it possible to send them to family members electronically, too, although I would hesitate to make accessible to just anyone the documents that I wanted to edit.

SPECIAL-NEEDS DOCUMENTS

Certain documents or documentary artifacts have special problems that need special attention. If the paper is highly acidic, such as the telegram on page 67, then the items need isolation similar to newspaper clippings. Sometimes ink is fading, which I find makes oral transcribing all the more worthwhile (see pages 120–122).

SCRAPBOOKS AND MIXED MEDIA

Scrapbooks are extremely popular today, both as new hobbies and as old arti-facts. They have a special set of characteristics that bother archivists. The main problem: A wide variety of stuff is thrown together without regard for the preservation of each item. Thus, advice for dealing with your scrapbooks would also apply to other family books (account books, Bibles, etc.) when a relative used them for eclectic collecting. A Bible or account book may have all manners of ephemera between the pages where your ancestor stashed keepsakes. Some of our ancestors even damaged published books by pasting their scraps and clippings onto the printed pages. That book would be a scrapbook whether someone meant it for that or not!

Some archivists view scrapbooks as annoyances. The memorabilia inside may be worthy of preservation to them, but the bad habit of pasting it all willy-nilly with harmful adhesives onto harmful paper, is anathema to some archivists. They would rather remove the scraps of memorabilia and discard the scrapbook. Another typical scrapbook problem is that the hinges were not made to hold the double thickness of memorabilia that people chose to keep.

If you have an oversized scrapbook, account book, baby book, or similar item to store, archival supply houses sell flat storage boxes for just such items. A box is also a good solution for a scrapbook that is bulging or already broken at the seams. If the book is oddly shaped, you may wish to wrap it with acid-free paper and use loose string or Velcro closures (on the paper, not the book) to close it.

Tip

Some archivists recommend re-creating the scrapbook by first placing the memorabilia in enclosures, then in a new, archivally sound scrapbook or three-ring binder. My suggestion is to keep the original intact, with the possible alteration that you photocopy loose news clippings and keep the copies with

---

DOCUMENTS AT SPECIAL RISK

newspaper clippings

high-acid papers such as telegrams, and scrapbook and photo album pages

charcoal, pastel, chalk, or heavily applied pencil drawings or writings

scrapbooks, baby books, and other mixed-media albums

rare published books

photographs

folded or rolled documents

documents with fading ink

ephemera between the pages of a Bible, cookbook, account book, or other holder

documentary material recorded on other media (tapes, disks, etc.)

the original album. If the clippings are firmly attached to the pages, however, I would leave them and use interleaving paper to protect from acidity. You should also remove any metal fasteners such as paper clips, staples, or pins that are rusting in and staining the scrapbook.

As a historian, I see inherent value in many of these mixed-media artifacts that our ancestors left. Folks were doing their best to piece together documentary volumes of what mattered to them. Often, by mating two different types of items, and especially by labeling them, they left much more family historical information than we would have had otherwise. See Figure 5-3 below and 5-4 and on page 55. Photographing the photographs and pages of an old album can provide good copies for a new album, if you wish. Note that Figure 5-3 is a traditional photocopy while Figure 5-4 is a digital, photographic copy (such as Kodak's Picturemaker). How you make copies will obviously affect quality.

If you insist on using old family documents and memorabilia in a new or re-created scrapbook, here are suggestions based on those reluctantly offered by today's archivists:

- Use copies rather than original documents, photographs, and artifacts.
- Don't cut photographs or memorabilia into different shapes or "pink" the edges. This lowers the value of each item.

Figure 5-3 Hair samples were popular family relics during the late Victorian era, circa 1850–1900. Fortunate, indeed, if the original keeper sewed them to a calendar page and then recorded the exact ages of the family members! In terms of conservation, however, hair is an organic material and requires special protection from pests. Hair samples of Birdie, Aunt Lill, Aunt Mary [Sturdevant], and Opal Lovejoy, circa 1884–1885. Sturdevant Family Papers, with permission of Rick W. and Wendell F. Sturdevant, in author's possession.

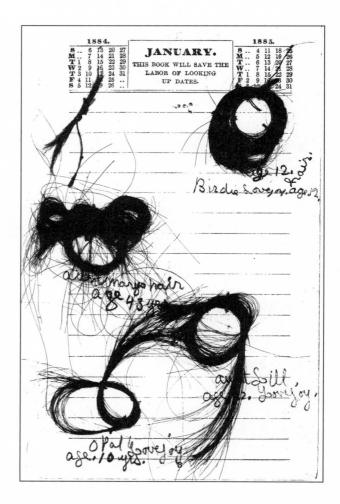

Figure 5-4 This page from Kate Dickey Harper's baby book for John Leonard Harper, circa 1909, shows how an entire page can make a good illustration, especially if it reflects the way the ancestor-author organized materials. Although mixed media is a challenge to preserve, making this baby book caused Kate to note historical information and preserve photographs that reveal time, place, and people. Harper Family Papers, in author's possession.

- Use acid-free paper corners rather than tape or adhesives to attach things to pages.
- Use archivally safe albums and pages from a bona fide archival supply house.
- To prevent bulging, get an album whose pages are much less thick than

the binding can hold. Or, cut out every other page of the album to make room, only use one side of each page, or use loose-leaf binders.

- Separate the materials by type, grouping together documents and memorabilia that will not harm one another.
- Label everything so that making the album doesn't erase context of where the originals came from, to whom they belonged, their time periods, etc.

DISPLAYING

Supplies

For framing family or antique documents, pictures, or memorabilia, use archival, safe materials. **Archival supply catalogs have substantial sections of framing supplies:** acid-free mounting board and foamboard, precut archival mats, ultraviolet glass or Plexiglas, safe aluminum and wood frames, archival backing, adhesives, and hanging materials. You can do it yourself if you wish. This will save some money, although the archival supplies are substantially more expensive than ordinary picture frames. The elements are those I just mentioned. Use acid-free, 100 percent rag mounting board for both the backing and the matting. Nothing else is safe. Attaching the artifact requires special photo corners or paper hinges because adhesives or tape will stain or damage the original. The glass or Plexiglas should be "UV," or resistant to ultraviolet light, if the artifact will be seriously exposed to light. The original document should not touch the glass for fear of moisture buildup, so make sure the window mat is sufficiently thick or use a safe spacer. Remember to take special care with friable media such as charcoal and chalk pictures, which need special matting to avoid static contact with the glass. Glass is safer for them than Plexiglas. Seal the back of all framed documents with acid-free paper to keep out dust and pollution. Do not expose your framed document to much light, especially sunlight or fluorescent light, or to extremes of temperature or humidity.

Tip

I could list much more advice, too. Or, you could take your document to an expert to frame. Have I made it sound difficult? I hope so, because the better solution is to photocopy the document and frame the copy. You may think a photocopy rarely looks worthy of framing, but try this: **Even if your document is black ink on white paper, use a color copier to make your copy. It will pick up or even enhance the nuances of ink tones and ivory paper.** I had my framing expert frame a 1940s magazine cover, and when she was done even she was surprised to learn it was a color photocopy, not an original. By making and framing copies, you can enjoy and share your documents safely, while preserving copies and originals for posterity.

WHEN DISASTER STRIKES

Have you experienced a flood yet? We did. Our house sits atop an almost imperceptible little ridge in dry Colorado. The appraisers had observed that we had the best drainage decline they had ever seen, with our yard sloping down from the house to carry away water. The basement (or unfinished level) was dry, not humid, with a black plastic moisture barrier on the floor. We never had water in there, until about fifteen years after the house was built. Heavy

BEFORE DISASTER STRIKES: HOW TO HELP PREVENT DAMAGE

- Do not store materials directly on the floor. Put your boxes of documents, heirlooms, or books on a raised surface such as a shelf or even a pallet. Getting things a few inches above the floor is usually adequate. If there is five feet of water in your book stacks or living room, rescuing your collection will probably be low on your list of priorities!

- If an area is prone to leaks after storms or is near a water pipe, store materials somewhere else. Is the storage area beneath an upstairs restroom? If a leak is possible, it will probably occur.

- Make sure windows are sealed properly. Weather stripping not only prevents rain from entering, it also saves on heating and cooling costs. Duct tape makes an effective, if unsightly, patch.

- Make sure your electrical system, lights, and appliances are in good working order. Do not convert a two-plug outlet into a six-plug outlet with little plastic adapters—they are electrical hazards. If extra outlets are necessary, surge suppressors, often used with computers, offer a safer alternative.

- Know what your insurance carrier will and will not cover. You may treasure a run of *Arizona Highways* magazines, but your carrier may classify them as expendable. It's better to know before disaster strikes than to discover afterward that your insurance will not pay as you had assumed.

- Set some salvage priorities before you're faced with a room of wet materials. Although everything may be important to you, some items are more important than others. Only you can make that decision. It's better to make those choices when you have time than during a panicked response.

- While setting salvage priorities, make a list of your most valuable possessions. Monetary value does not have to be the only criteria. A treasure may be almost entirely without monetary value and still be cherished by you and your family. Consider storing such items together in the safest place available.

- Do not wait for ten days to seek help! In most cases, wet materials must be stabilized within seventy-two hours. After that period, permanent damage is probable and total loss becomes a serious threat. If you can't find a knowledgeable person locally, the State Preservation Officer may be available for consultations.

Adapted with permission from Michael McColgin, preservation officer, Arizona State Archives, at <www.dlapr.lib.az.us/archives/g-preserve3.htm>.

TEN TIPS FOR THE CARE OF WATER-DAMAGED FAMILY HEIRLOOMS

The American Institute for Conservation of Historic and Artistic Works (AIC) and the Heritage Preservation (HP) offer the following general recommendations for homeowners who have had family heirlooms and other valuables damaged by severe flooding. These recommendations are intended as guidance only. Neither AIC or HP assume responsibility or liability for treatment of water-damaged objects.

Ten Tips for the Homeowner

1. If the object is still wet, rinse with clear water or a fine hose spray. Clean off dry silt and debris from your belongings with soft brushes, or dab with damp cloths. Try not to grind into objects; overly energetic cleaning will cause scratching. Dry with a clean, soft cloth. Use plastic or rubber gloves for your own protection.

2. Air-dry objects indoors if possible. Sunlight and heat may dry certain materials too quickly, causing splits, warpage, and buckling. If possible, remove contents from wet objects and furniture prior to drying. Storing damp items in sealed plastic bags will cause mold to develop. If objects are to be transported in plastic bags, keep bags open and air circulating.

3. The best way to inhibit the growth of mold and mildew is to reduce humidity. Increase airflow with fans, open windows, air conditioners, and dehumidifiers. Moderate light exposure (open shades, leave basement lights on) can also reduce mold and mildew.

4. Remove heavy deposits of mold growth from walls, baseboards, floors, and other household surfaces with commercially available disinfectants. Avoid the use of disinfectants on historic wallpapers. Follow manufacturer's instructions, but avoid splattering or contact with objects and wallpapers, as disinfectants may damage objects. Note: Exposure to molds can have serious health consequences such as respiratory problems, skin and eye irritation, and infections. The use of protective gear, including a respirator with a particulate filter, disposable plastic gloves, goggles or protective eyewear, and coveralls or a lab coat, is therefore essential.

5. If objects are broken or begin to fall apart, place all broken pieces, bits of veneer, and detached parts in clearly labeled, open containers. Do not attempt to repair objects until completely dry or, in the case of important materials, until you have consulted with a professional conservator.

6. Documents, books, photographs, and works of art on paper may be extremely fragile when wet; use caution when handling. Free the edges of prints and paper objects in mats and frames, if possible. These should be allowed to air-dry. Rinse mud off wet photographs with clear water, but

do not touch surfaces. A professional conservator should treat sodden books and papers.

7. Textiles, leather, and other organic materials will also be severely affected by exposure to water and should be allowed to air-dry. Shaped objects such as garments or baskets should be supported by gently padding them with toweling or unlinked, uncoated paper. Renew padding when it becomes saturated with water. Dry-clean or launder textiles and carpets as you normally would.

8. Remove wet paintings from the frame but not the stretcher. Air-dry, face up, away from direct sunlight.

9. Furniture finishes and painting surfaces may develop a white haze or bloom from contact with water and humidity. These problems do not require immediate attention. Consult a professional conservator for treatment.

10. Rinse metal objects exposed to flood waters, mud, or silt with clear water, and dry immediately with a clean, soft cloth. Allow heavy mud deposits on large metal objects, such as sculpture, to dry. Caked mud can be removed later. Consult a professional conservator for further treatment.

As noted previously, these guidelines are general in nature. It is strongly recommended that a professional conservator be consulted as to the appropriate method of treatment for household objects. Professional conservators may be contacted through the free Guide to Conservation Services of the AIC, 1717 K Street, NW, Suite 301, Washington, DC 20006, telephone (202) 452-9545, fax (202) 452-9328, <info@aic-faic.org>. Based on a complete description of the artifact, a computer-generated list of conservators will be compiled and grouped geographically, by specialization, and by type of service provided. Guidelines for Selecting a Conservator, enclosed with the listing, will explain the guide, provide information on how to select a conservator, and outline general business procedures.

Guidelines for Selecting a Conservator (brochure), Caring for Your Treasures: Books to Help You (bibliography), and Basic Guidelines for Care of Special Collections (brochure) are also available from AIC. "Emergency Preparedness and Response: Federal Aid for Cultural Institutions During an Emergency" is available from HP (see Appendix A or page 209.)

rain fell for enough consecutive days that several neighborhood houses had water just seep up, even bubble up, through the sandy soil.

We were lucky. Rick had propped our boxes (mostly of books) on boards. The water barely touched the bottoms of a few boxes before we discovered the problem and rescued them. Rick used the wet-vac and portable fans for days to dry out the basement. Some neighbors used pumps. Next door, Denise found

REMOVING ODOR

There are no magic sprays or powders to remove odors from water damage, mold, and mildew. Although visible mold may be cleaned from dry materials, permanent stains and structural damage usually occur. Mold-damaged materials will always be prone to additional infestation, so they must be maintained in relatively dry areas.

Bad odors, on the other hand, may be eliminated or greatly reduced by sealing materials in an airtight enclosure with baking soda or unscented kitty litter. Materials must be dry or they will develop mold. The container may be anything from a clean oven to a cardboard box or nonworking refrigerator. Fan books open and set them in the container, place a dish or plate of odor-absorbing material in the bottom of the enclosure, and seal it up or close the door for several days. The baking soda or kitty litter will absorb odors. You may treat individual documents similarly.

Adapted with permission from Michael McColgin, preservation officer, Arizona State Archives, at <www.dlapr.lib.az.us/archives/g-preserve3.htm>.

all of her old family photographs soaked and put them out with the trash. By the time I heard this, it was too late to advise her otherwise.

Flooding in Houston has at times been disastrous. One article from the *Houston Chronicle* said it all for family historians, too: "Why So Much in So Many Basements?" (13 June 2001). We all should know better, but even major institutions in Houston did not. The only good outcome of all of this flooding, archivally speaking, may be that literature is proliferating on how to deal with disaster when it hits your family documents.

See the Bibliography for other sites and guidelines. No longer should we assume our documents, photographs, or heirlooms are gone forever just because they got wet. See "Ten Tips for the Care of Water-Damaged Family Heirlooms" on page 58 for more advice from the experts.

See Also

FINDING A CONSERVATOR

The AIC (American Institute for Conservation of Historic and Artistic Works) offers advice for contacting conservators (see page 59). If the AIC service does not turn up a conservator that suits your needs, ask nearby museums and archives. Your state historical society or state preservation office may house conservators. **Or, ask other local collectors, art galleries, or antiquarian bookstores.** No recommendation is better than word-of-mouth based on experience. Your conservator should be someone who can demonstrate professional training (with references upon request), experience (with satisfied clients to attest to success), ethics (through AIC membership and adherence to its code of ethics and standards of practice), and community activities in the field (as evidenced by reputation).

Tip

Conservation is growing as almost a "movement," and many societies have conservation information on their Web sites. Unfortunately, Congress threatens government funding for conservation in the same way it has for documentary editing projects. The Smithsonian Center for Materials Research and Education (SCMRE) provided many useful conservation pages for the public online but closed by December 2001 because the Smithsonian Institution had to reallocate tight funds. So, as you learn the value of these techniques for your own purposes, consider supporting this dedicated field.

THE SHELF LIFE OF ORIGINALS

Preservation of your original documents is important partly because paper documents, for all of their fragility, will live longer than electronic substitutes. Studies show that the traditional media have much longer shelf lives. Paper will survive hundreds of years. Microfilm might survive about 130 years. A compact disc might last dozens of years, but not hundreds. Audio and videotapes could last only ten to twenty years. A floppy disk might last three years. So, as you preserve your paper and do preservation copying, you are already working with the most "advanced" format for preserving documents!

Warning

Some of the most visible damage to documents comes from past framing. Paper absorbs, so acid migration occurs from the wood-pulp mats, adhesives, tapes, cardboard, and unsealed backs of old framing jobs.

SIX

Your Selection Process

I never travel without my diary. One should always have something sensational to read in the train.

—*Oscar Wilde in* The Importance of Being Earnest, *1895, act I*

Important

O nce you have the papers you might want to use, your next step may be a selection process for the documentary editing project. **You need to determine, at least initially, the extent of your project.** You can always change your mind as you learn more. Documentary editors on large-scale projects spend much of their time sorting and winnowing.

Is the project going to be a complete, book-length document (even multivolume), a set of documents, a series of excerpts, or a shorter publication based on a brief item such as one letter or an excerpt? Is it going to be "comprehensive" or "selective"? See Stevens and Burg's *Editing Historical Documents*, pages 39–40, for the norms of big projects. Your edition will undoubtedly be selective, as you cannot publish it all. To be selective and professional about it, then, you need to develop standards for your project. Using the Project Development Form on page 214 may force you to think like a documentary editor who is proposing a project to an agency, say, for grant support, or to a publisher.

Expert documentary editors use some standard selection criteria. Once you have determined your themes, it should be easier to apply these criteria. Assuming you may have more documents than would make a good volume or project, you will need to cull some from those you will feature. In his classic *Historical Editing* (14–15), Clarence E. Carter listed the following criteria for selection:

- "fiscal limitation"
- "previous publication"
- "triviality"
- "routine nature"
- "duplication"
- "priority"

PROJECT DEVELOPMENT FORM

Name of Project _Memoir of Kate Dickey Harper_

Documentary Editor _Katherine Scott Sturdevant_

Date Commenced/Planned Completion _June 2002/June 2004_

Historical Time Period Represented by Document(s) _1881–1942_

Other Documents to Include _Leonard Harper's baby book, family letters from period, newspaper accounts of events_

Themes Developed in Project _westward migration; homesteading; impacts of Rev. War and Civil War; women in the West; boosterism; 1900 courtship and youth; mining politics; progressive reform; Spanish-American War; immigrant trains; tuberculosis; frontier KS, CO, AZ_

Examples of Comparable Projects/Models _Janet Lecompte, ed., Emily: The Diary of a Hard-Worked Woman_

Research _census, local histories, directories, military records, school records, newspapers, histories of courtship and youth, time periods, TB, women, mining, regions_

Attach an outline of the proposed contents of the project.

Although Carter directed these standards at public projects with public or major private funding, and, thus, with larger imperatives than most family historians face, they are still adaptable standards. To achieve a worthwhile goal such as publication of the best documents in a family, the family editor needs to recognize the limitations of time, energy, and finances. If one's family documents are already well published, then there is no point to repeating the effort. If, on the other hand, you found previously unknown documents or the existing publications were faulty or inadequate, Carter would agree these are exceptions to the rule.

If you need to reduce the number of your documents, then drop the trivial, routine, or redundant ones. However, if dropping them threatens the integrity of a whole document or collection, think twice. For example, imagine that your ancestor wrote virtually the same letter to two different relatives, reporting the same information in the same way or with minor variations. You could transcribe only the more important of the two and make a footnote about the existence and variations of the other. Yet if the entries in a single diary are trivial, routine, or redundant, an editor would normally transcribe all of them anyway rather than interfere with the integrity of that diary.

Priority may be the most difficult means or standard of determining what to put in or leave out when you are editing documents. This is where you most need to know the whole potential collection and what themes or aspects you wish to include or emphasize. Here is a case in point. You might intend to prepare your grandparents' wartime letters for publication. You have letters that they wrote before, during, and after the war. Some are about the war or its effects, and some run far afield. You will be submitting the transcribed and edited collection for publication as a book. Setting your priorities for the war-related themes will mean that you can set aside irrelevant letters. When you do this, of course, your introductions and annotations need to make clear that this collection contains *selected* letters, not all. For a sampling of different editors' selection processes, see pages 41–54 of Stevens and Burg's, *Editing Historical Documents*. Your standards and priorities are largely up to you when you are the editor of your own project. Your critics will look most for whether you state and reasonably explain what those standards and priorities are and whether you apply them consistently.

DOCUMENTS TO EDIT
Diaries and Journals

If you asked professional documentary editors and historians to prioritize which of your family documents they might like most for you to present for publication, they might list diaries, journals, and letters first. We see these as slightly more precious than memoirs and reminiscences because people compiled them contemporaneously—at the time of the event—rather than from memory. **A diary is usually a daily or regular account that emphasizes personal thoughts and feelings about anything. A journal is more properly a regular account of events and observations about them, often with a theme of its own, such as a journal about a trip or a journal compiled during a particular experience.** Whichever term we use, diaries and journals are valuable as firsthand, "eyewitness" records. A detailed, observant, or revealing historical diary or travel journal, say, from the Civil War or the Oregon Trail, could easily have publishable value, depending on its length and how unique or descriptive its entries are. A diary from the Revolutionary War or a travel account from the Great Wagon Road of the 1770s might be even more publishable because it is rare.

Another examination of the issue of diary privacy might be in order. Lynn Z. Bloom made interesting distinctions in " 'I Write for Myself and Strangers': Private Diaries as Public Documents," a chapter of Bunkers and Huff's *Inscribing the Daily* (23–37). Bloom wrote that we err to think that the presence of personal information means a diarist was writing without an audience in mind. On the contrary, she explained, the diary truly intended for no audience was more likely the pedestrian diary, which simply recorded "bare-bones" facts of daily life. Using Martha Ballard's diary as one example, Bloom noted that a person who kept track of such information was the person who was not thinking of an audience. The entries "are so terse they seem coded." The contents would be weather, accountings, and comings and goings. The order is day-by-day chronology. Such a diary does not stand alone for publication, because there is no context or characterization. Meanwhile, Bloom viewed the diaries with more built-in interpretive text as "freestanding public documents." The

\di'fin\ *vb*

Definitions

"public private" diary is the more fully written diary, with reflections, interpretation, characterization, and explanatory context. These diaries are literary and can become "classics" beyond our own families' interest.

The trends in publishing diaries, or in publicizing their availability in archives or online, reveal some of your opportunities. Of course, a great man or woman's firsthand account, or a great "classic" diary, if you happened to run across one that no one else knew about, would be of value. For social history of everyday folks, however, the history of women and minorities has relied heavily on diaries and individual accounts to build enough literature before a synthesis is possible. For example, Kenneth Holmes's *Covered Wagon Women*, a multivolume accumulation of Oregon Trail diaries and accounts, made many Oregon Trail diaries available for historical study and comparison. The series has gone into paperback volumes because they are fascinating to read. Some of the accounts would've been too short for individual publication. Some were in private hands and would've been unavailable to most of us.

Sometimes diaries may seem so pedestrian or sparse in their entries that one is not sure of their value. A common piece of information that many diarists recorded each day was the weather. Wow, you think, how fascinating! If your relatives did this, they are in good company: so did George Washington, John Adams, and Thomas Jefferson, to name a few. **If the diary is worthy of publication for other reasons, however, your annotation can make up for these dry spells.** As an editor might do for these great men, you can analyze why weather was so important in your relatives' daily lives, how it dictated their work and affected their safety. How meticulously accurate were they? What does this say about them?

Tip

Historian Janet Lecompte published *Emily: The Diary of a Hard-Worked Woman*, a diary that on first glance might have seemed pedestrian. Emily French was a rather ordinary, poor woman who lived in Denver, Colorado, circa 1890. Lecompte found Emily's diary in the Special Collections Department of the Tutt Library at The Colorado College in Colorado Springs. Historians have been trying to uncover and record the lives of poorer classes, so we could use a published Emily. Emily had fallen from middling classes after a divorce and spent the rest of her life, as her diary records, struggling to work for her keep and her family. Women's limited options became clear in Emily's story, as did society's tendency to suspect women's morals when they were making it on their own. Thus, Emily's diary revealed much of use to social history. To make it a readable, understandable account, Lecompte did genealogical research—in censuses, land records, city directories, vital records, and newspapers—so her annotations could explain everything and everyone that Emily mentioned. Lecompte, of course, also researched in history books—on women's work, divorce, medical care, farming, and communities—to place Emily in the larger context of her times, through the editor's contributions to the volume. Thus, your apparently unexciting family diary may just need something extra—you: its editor.

Letters

Collected letters form the bases for many major documentary editing projects. With letters you may have the greatest need for the selection processes, standards, and priorities on page 62. If you have both "to" and "from" letters that represent a time period, event, or theme, you are fortunate. Because people usually kept such bundles only from defined moments, such as wartime, courtship, or some dramatic period of separation, the parameters of your project may already be clearly defined. You may not have the letters of both writers and recipients, however. That does not necessarily make them less worthy of preservation or publication.

Individual letters, or pairs or small groups of letters, can make valid smaller-scale documentary editing projects. John Kaminski, director of the Center for the Study of the American Constitution at the history department of the University of Wisconsin, Madison, told me that "ancillary publications" from these, such as articles in periodicals, are topics of current discussion amongst documentary editors. A person who holds or has access to an important single letter, for example, might write a page of introduction and a page of annotation or narrative explanation to go with the original letter, thereby making an article.

Earlier, when discussing serendipitous discoveries, I listed Ira Powell Withers's Civil War letters. I have only three—he died so soon in his military service. Nevertheless, I can follow these steps to make his three letters suitable for publication in a periodical:

- Transcribe the letters.
- Intersperse or footnote them with explanations of his cryptic references.
- Include a partial transcription of his Civil War record, noting his death.
- Introduce the letters with his family background and the context of his times.
- Epilogue them with what happened to Ira's family after his death.
- Conclude them with what was typical for young men leaving farms for the Civil War and what was typical in their letters home.
- Illustrate them.

Remember, too, that people wrote other kinds of letters during wartime and remarkable events: correspondence in newspapers, telegrams, and World War II "V-mail" are examples. **(V-mail was correspondence sent by American soldiers to loved ones back home. A soldier's letter form was photographed, reduced, and transmitted overseas to be enlarged and delivered.)** Look in newspapers from small towns where your ancestors lived to see whether they (or their families) submitted letters to serve as reports from a war front or even from travels elsewhere. Frank Sturdevant was one who served as this sort of de facto newspaper correspondent. He would write to his family in Waverly, Iowa, about his cross-country trips or his National Guard mobilization to the Mexican border. Family members in Waverly, or Frank himself, submitted the newsiest letters to the local newspaper. Thus, when we go to transcribe and edit together Frank's correspondence or "journals," we will seek out newspaper accounts (and permission to use them) to intersperse chronologically (or conflate) with the handwritten ones in the family.

It is unlikely that a telegram or a piece of V-mail would stand alone as a documentary editing project. Yet it might be the perfect punctuation for a collection of standard letters or a diary, allowing original documents to tell even

\di'fin\ *vb*

Definitions

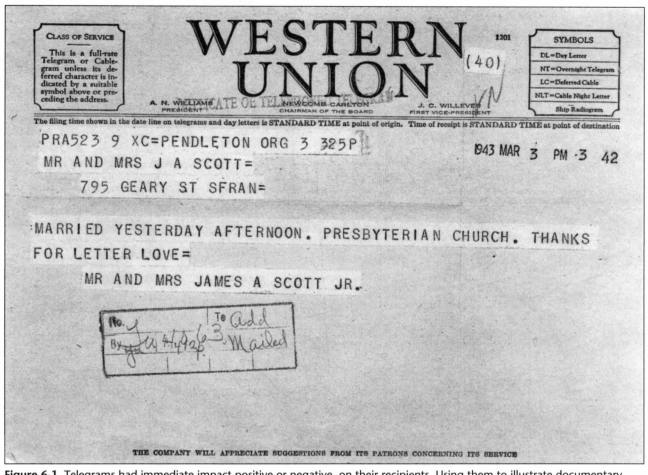

Figure 6-1 Telegrams had immediate impact positive or negative, on their recipients. Using them to illustrate documentary volumes can re-create the impact. Telegram from Mr. and Mrs. James A. Scott Jr. (my parents) to Mr. and Mrs. J. A. Scott [Sr.] (my father's parents), 3 March 1943. Scott Family Papers, in author's possession.

Tip

more of the story. **Rather than announce the information they contain in your own footnote, use the telegrams and V-mail themselves.** Even better than transcribing them, why not reproduce them as they appeared? In Figure 6-1 (above), a telegram delivers happy news. One can imagine what the recipients thought when they opened it. That pleasure would turn to dramatic shock had this been the classic wartime telegram notifying a family of a soldier's death or status as missing in action. If you have a photograph or postcard to further illustrate an occasion, use it to set the scene. See Figure 6-2 on page 68.

Then, too, V-mail almost cries out for a photocopied reproduction in your printed collection. See Figure 6-3 on page 69. Why transcribe and describe its unusual appearance when you can display it so easily? The telegram and V-mail in Figure 6-3 are from my father's documents. Although my mother burned the more private letters, she did label photographs and keep telegrams and V-mail better than many folks would. All would make good illustrations for my father's memoir.

Memoirs

Did anyone in your family write memoirs? If so, you are fortunate, as am I. Your answer may have been "Yes, well, so-and-so started them but never fin-

Figure 6-2 Postcard from Pendleton, Oregon, March 1943, labeled by Barbara Scott on the back to indicate the hotel where they spent their wedding night. The telegram plus this photograph illustrate the family documents or narrative, especially in the absence of a wedding picture. Scott Family Papers, in author's possession.

Definitions

Definitions

ished." Then, you are fortunate, but you also bear extra responsibility. If you're reading this book, you already know you can transcribe, edit, annotate, and publish those memoirs. The extra responsibility is that these activities can finish a project that your relative meant to finish someday. Our family members who kept diaries, wrote letters, pasted in scrapbooks, or accumulated documents did not necessarily plan for those items to someday become published historical books. Those who wrote memoirs had something different in mind. **Memoir writing is creative nonfiction writing.** Memoir writers usually did have larger audiences in mind. They often dreamt of publication. They meant the memoirs to have conclusions, to be completed.

It would be dubious to suggest that you literally "finish" someone else's memoir. That would be ghostwriting if you did not make clear where his writing left off and yours began, and it would be fiction. A memoir can remain somewhat unfinished, however, and still be publishable. This fact limits the burden on the editor of someone else's memoirs. A memoir is not an autobiography. It doesn't have to be authoritative, complete in all its detail, or heavily researched and processed by the author. **A memoir is a set of reminiscences, often impressionistic, that are often told as a storyteller or as family oral tradition would tell them.** There can be, and usually are, gaps. The good memoirist has already

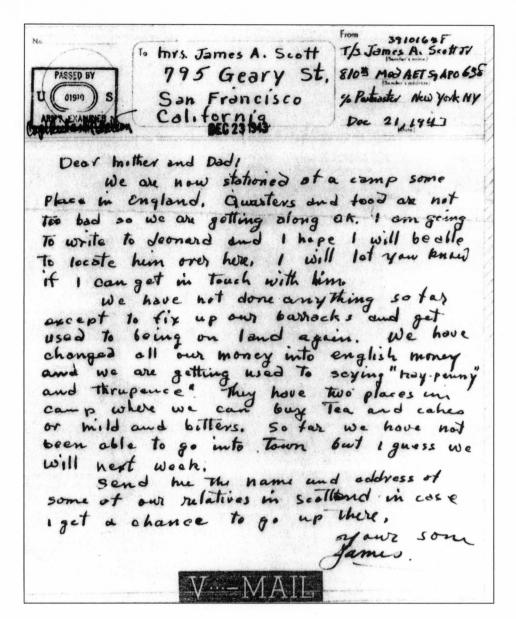

Figure 6-3 V-mail was another form of communication best portrayed by an illustration. Enlarged and lightened V-mail letter from James A. Scott Jr. to Mr. and Mrs. J. A. Scott [Sr.], 21 December 1943. Scott Family Papers, in author's possession.

culled out the routine, the trivial, and the redundant by choosing not to write about them. He or she may have died, become incapacitated, or lost interest before achieving the intended goal of completion. That incomplete part, then, becomes part of your editorial responsibilities along with identifying the names and places or explaining the little mysteries and inside remarks. You can complete the volume, though, with your own editorial annotations and conclusions, without necessarily completing the memoirs as the author would have done.

If the memoir in your possession is too brief to become book length, it might be a candidate for publication as an article in a periodical. You might even combine two brief memoirs. My great-grandfather Archibald Naismith was a country doctor in Stratford, Ontario. I wish that he, like so many horse-and-buggy doctors, had written his memoirs. Instead, I do have a copy of "Reminiscences" by him from a local newspaper in 1932. Transcribed, this becomes only about five to six pages. My father, who loved this grandfather as a character, wrote

Idea Generator

one of his own memoir stories about the country doctor as he remembered him. It is about the same length. Thus, the two might edit together nicely for a brief publication.

Another way to "complete" a brief or truncated memoir is to transcribe it together with multiple other documents and connective annotation. My grandmother Kate Dickey Harper's memoir, as mentioned in chapter one, will be this kind of project. A special challenge with her memoir is that she wrote autobiographically in her first son's baby book. Her memoir, written in 1941 to 1942, ended with her early life in Arizona before her first son was born, circa 1907–1908. The baby book, written in 1909 to 1915 (ending with the birth of her second child), therefore, takes up where the memoir would later leave off, in terms of chronologically reporting her life events. Thus, I want to edit them together consecutively in the same volume. But baby books can present an "itty bitty" challenge of their own, you know.

Baby Books

Who kept a baby book? The author was usually a doting, new, first mother. She kept the book religiously for the first or only child. Someone gave her a new baby book for the second child, and she wrote the first few entries in it. Then, she fell off the wagon. No more baby books. There was no more time and even less enthusiasm, especially if, like my mother-in-law, she had several children in diapers at any given time. Middle-class women of the 1880s to 1910s, according to historian Josephine Gear in "The Baby's Picture: Woman as Image Maker in Small-Town America" (438–439), inspired businesses to produce baby books because women had an "almost obsessive" need to record the first two years of this idealized function of motherhood. Baby books from that period tended to have more interpretive text than modern ones might. Some women who lost their babies even completed the books with mourning memorabilia.

Many baby books are not suitable for full transcription and editing into publishable projects; they are treasures nonetheless. Portions will fit well into narratives and documentary collections. Although fill-in-the-blank formats usually limited creativity, even that information is useful. Parents sentimentally kept baby gifts, for example, and listed in the books who presented what precious little item to Baby. Most of the books also had pages of blank space for storytelling. The printer might have encouraged those stories to be about first steps, words, and teeth, but Mother may have ventured into narrative. I hope, if she did, she did not wax too sappy for transcription.

If you have a baby book that has narrative storytelling in it, consider transcribing, annotating, and including that in your documentary project. My grandmother wrote about the family's adventures during baby Leonard's first years as though she were writing through baby Leonard's eyes and vocabulary. Aye, there's the rub. I want the stories and descriptions, but here will be a distinctive change of voice when my volume switches from Kate's memoir to Leonard's baby book. At least she did not use too much baby talk, except when she recorded the exact way Leonard said things: "Mama, you get me a little bittie boat. . . ." Otherwise, Kate recorded where the family moved and what happened in each place, fo-

Idea Generator

cused on Leonard. Thus, when a violent controversy drove Leonard's Papa from his career, placing Kate and little Leonard in physical danger, Kate wrote, "Lots of fearful and wonderful things happened there." Yes, baby books can be a challenge for a documentary editor, but you "wuv" a challenge. (See Figure 5-4 on page 55 for a photographed page from this baby book.)

Account Books

Account books, where people have listed their personal or business income and expenditures with regular entries, usually in a columnar format, are treasures of information but may seem awkward as documentary editing projects. The challenges are to find and rescue them, care for them if they are old and decrepit, transcribe them if necessary, and determine how to use their contents. People sometimes cherished their account books but very often did not. One kept an old, out-of-date, or filled-up account book in the same way we keep tax receipts. We think we might need that information someday, but we usually do not. So, the account book might stay in the building or on the property somewhere, but with perhaps less care than letters or a diary would receive. We found Rick's ancestors' account books, crumbling and yellowing, in a dark and musty woodshed. Note from the woodshed story on page 72 that even the account of how you located your family documents can become an interesting editorial contribution to your documents, or part of your family history narrative.

Nineteenth- and early-twentieth-century folks tended to keep accounts in tall books with gray or brown, leather or canvas covers. These books often bear preprinted labels in big lettering: "Ledger," "Record," "Accounts," "Journal," "Day," or "Day Book." Anyone who was used to keeping accounts, however, might use whatever notebook was at hand. **A true account-book keeper who lived a longer life would probably switch from one book to another over time. So, in a household where there is one book, look for more stashed somewhere dark and dusty.** These ancestral accountants may have been secretarial enough to identify their books with names, places, and dates in the front inside covers. If not, they would at least date some of the entries, and minimal detective work could probably identify the owner.

Hidden Treasures

Men were more liable to keep business and farm account books than women, except during wartime. Indeed, bookkeeping was one of the tasks women would learn during a war. Historians have noted that some women bristled at the returning husband reasserting his authority. It becomes more likely that a female ancestor kept account books if she became a widow or if her adult life postdates the 1910s and 1920s. It is good that men kept the early account books, because you may have your male ancestors' account books and your female ancestors' diaries—documentary clues to both sexes. Either way, accountants who kept good books sometimes treated their account books the way others treated Bibles and recipe books: as catchalls. So, you may find in the account book clippings, receipts, recipes, letters, addresses, birthdays, licenses, bills, calling cards, and even pressed flowers. These contents may also help identify the owner. Maybelle Sturdevant began an account book of the 1920s halfway through an ordinary notebook that she began as "Baptist Cradle Roll," listing babies, mothers, and birth dates.

WHAT'S IN THE WOODSHED?

Rick and I were sorting and packing our way through Grandma Sturdevant's house, gathering family history documents and memorabilia. Without any human inhabitants for years, critters had started to view the house and property as their own. Crows and jack squirrels would shout warnings from the treetops when we entered the yard. This was a comfortable fall day, so we decided to work outside in spite of them. Rick taught me how to hull and wash the black walnuts that covered the ground, so we could dry them for later cracking. I was conducting that operation on my own, raking them through a galvanized washtub of blackening water, when Rick decided it was time to excavate the contents of the old woodshed.

It was about an eight-by-ten-foot white frame shed, perhaps sixty to eighty years old, with a door kept latched shut. We knew at least the top layer of what was in there: old furniture, long ago relegated to storage when some damage or problem developed; gilded, plaster picture frames that had become too fancy for modern tastes; garden tools and supplies; tubs, washboards, and burners from old-fashioned wash days; baskets and buckets for nuts and berries; storm shutters for winter and window screens for summer; and, of course, firewood for Grandma's cookstove. This shed was where Rick's grandparents had stashed old account books.

It was also where animals reigned. The chipmunk that lived underneath the little building was a pleasant critter. A nightmarish critter discovery occurred, however, because of an account book. Rick was excited to see one such book, lying inside an old cabinet atop a bench. He opened the cabinet door, lifted the account book, and there, underneath it, was a busy army of huge, black ants that had eaten through the bench, through the cabinet base, and into the cover and some pages of the ledger book. Their combined efforts produced a strange hissing sound. Rick saturated them with old bug-killer spray and saved the account book and furniture despite the damage.

On this walnut-washing day, however, Rick had overcome ant phobia and ventured back into the woodshed. Suddenly, I heard a ruckus. It sounded as though a fight was going on in the woodshed, buckets clanging, wood falling, and general chaos. As I turned, I saw a large, long, orange tabby tomcat dash lickety-split from the woodshed, across the yard, and disappear. "What was that?!" Rick screamed from the dark interior. I had to laugh. Now we knew why the woodshed smelled the way it did.

Transcribing an account book may seem to be a daunting and even useless task. It may be unnecessary with a legible, more recent account book unless you plan to publish one or sections of one. My father-in-law's account books, circa 1950–present, are useful for research without transcription because he printed so clearly. See Figure 6-4 on page 73. The older ones, from the nineteenth century

16			17
— DECEMBER -1956-(CONTINUED) —		= DECEMBER -1956-(CONTINUED) =	

12-13-56	GEORGE COWGER (SHOES+SEALER)	$5.41	12-28-56(CONT)	PARKA COAT (RICK)	$9.10
12-14-56	PAY CHECK	$91.98	12-29-56	PAY CHECK	$85.97
	GROCERY BILL	$30.00		GROCERY BILL	$30.00
	MILK BILL	$19.86		HAIR CUTS	3.00
	FUEL OIL (DILLAVOU)	$13.42		SHOE REPAIR	2.80
	GEORGE COWGER (SHOES+SEALER)	$5.00		SLIPPERS (CAROL)	3.05
	CHRISTMAS TREE	2.91			
	GIFTS	6.03		= JANUARY -1957 =	
12-18-56	STAMPS -ETC,	5.00			
12-20-56	GAS	2.00	1-2-57	GAS	$1.00
12-22-56	PAY CHECK	$91.88		FUEL OIL (DILLAVOU)	$11.37
	GROCERY BILL	$30.00	1-5-57	PAY CHECK	$79.53
	CHRISTMAS GIFTS	$5.00		GROCERY BILL	$30.00
	SEARS-ROEBUCK (ON WEATHER)	10.00	1-7-57	GAS	2.50
	STAMPS	1.00		ELECTRIC BILL	$20.39
	MISC,	3.00		MILK BILL	21.02
	GEORGE COWGER (SEALING SHOES) FINAL	6.00	1-8-57	CREAM	3.25
12-24-56	CREAM	3.25		MISC,	1.00
	GAS	3.00	1-11-57	GAS	4.00
	MISC,	3.00	1-12-57	PAY CHECK	$88.23
	GIFTS	6.10		GROCERY BILL	$30.00
12-28-56	TELEPHONE BILL	3.38		FUEL OIL (DILLAVOU)	$13.74
	MISC,	1.00		MISC,	4.00

Figure 6-4 Twentieth-century handwriting, such as the printing on these account book pages, can be legible. Note also how account book entries can reveal social history information such as a family's household expenses and holiday traditions. Account book of Wendell F. Sturdevant, Waverly, Iowa, circa 1950s. Sturdevant Family Papers, with permission of Rick W. and Wendell F. Sturdevant, in author's possession.

or earlier, may require transcription for convenient reading and safe handling. All of the men who kept old account books (that I have seen) wrote as though they never expected us to read their writing, because they didn't. If an account book is old and illegible, I would transcribe it to have a usable copy. Once immersed in the day-to-day business of the author, you will see so much from transcription or careful reading that you would miss otherwise. Account books reveal what it took to establish and sustain a household or business, and they show the intricate relationships within a family and community.

One can transcribe and annotate account books. (See the example on pages 142–143.) They do not literally tell a story by themselves, however, the way that a diary or memoir can. So while I would transcribe old account books to make the information accessible, I would probably not attempt to publish them alone unless they were very rare or unusual. Instead, **I would use sections of them in a narrative or in documentary editing annotation for other sources.** If you do transcribe and edit an account book, consider substantial annotation and interspersing other documents to make a community or business study take shape. As with all documents, remember, too, that you may research other people's

Idea Generator

account books for information about your family. For instance, the State Archives of Michigan lists its collection of account books and ledgers online. See <www.sos.state.mi.us/history/archive/circular/c63.html>. If your family lived in a Michigan town for which someone kept account books, you might have a resource.

In the case of Frank and Maybelle Sturdevant's 1920s account book, one can analyze their feelings from their posttraumatic expenditures. For years after World War I, Frank kept up his "War Risk Insurance," monthly donations to the Red Cross, and dues to the American Legion. After their first child, Willard, died in 1921, they had funeral expenses, and when their son Wendell was born in 1924, they took out Prudential Insurance on him and maintained it every month. One wonders what they were thinking: perhaps not that money would replace a second lost child but that money would cover funeral expenses? In either case, the insurance attests to their natural fear of another loss. I would transcribe the appropriate sections to integrate them with the information from other sources.

Cookbooks and Recipe Collections

Many families have ancestral cookbooks, recipe collections, or at least some recipes written or memorized. The last case brings the first reminder: If your family recipes are only part of oral tradition and memory, write them down and solicit them from others. Think how frustrating the cryptic recipe can be, where Grandma listed ingredients with vague measurements and no instructions. You could write yours down, or get the appropriate relatives to do so. If there are foodways stories of customs and beliefs associated with the recipes, record those, too.

For More Info

The heirloom recipe collection is a precious resource for more than cooking tips. **In *Bringing Your Family History to Life Through Social History* (31–37), I analyzed how one might treat a recipe collection as a material culture artifact and extrapolate family social history from it.** You may also use your family cookbook or recipe collection as part of a documentary editing project. Surely it is a precious document to preserve in the family archive. For publishing documents, there are several directions to take.

Many families publish their own cookbooks, collections of recipes from family members, some or all of which are handed down across generations. If this is your only goal, it is not necessarily a documentary editing project in the classic or scholarly definition of the term. There are many opportunities for self-publication through printers, presses, online publishers, and fund-raising cookbook publishers. Consider your cookbook(s) carefully. Can your recipes form a documentary editing project—a family history cookbook? Ask yourself the following questions:

- Is the cookbook of book length?
- Are the recipes unique enough to the family that they would not duplicate too many other books currently available?
- Can you convert the old recipes to modern, useful ones?
- Do the recipes have a historical character related to time periods, ethnicity, regional location, etc.?

- Does the cookbook contain additional domestic information such as home remedies or personal notations?
- Does the cookbook contain any paragraphs of text about family foodways or domestic life?
- Most importantly, do the recipes invite family history annotation, and do you have the materials and anecdotes to write these annotations?
- Can you make such annotation rich and serious, with family foodways, holiday customs, farming and gardening traditions, folklore, etc.?

With the annotative material indicated in the last two points, you might make a good documentary volume of a particularly historical family cookbook. Of course, sections of the cookbook or recipe collection might transcribe well into the documentary volume that uses many varied family documents.

Janet Theophano's book *Eat My Words: Reading Women's Lives Through the Cookbooks They Wrote* is an excellent example of how a historical analysis can help us place ancestral documents in context. Theophano interprets cookbooks as communities, collective memory and identity, family legacies, autobiographies, and commentaries on women's roles in society. She bases her analysis on the "trail of clues" that ordinary women left in their own cookbooks. You can reverse this resource to help analyze your family cookbook within the appropriate conceptual framework.

Scrapbooks and Photograph Albums

The bulk of scrapbooks and photograph albums are visual, graphic images and even tactile objects, none of which lend themselves easily to a documentary editing project. Both types of albums were a creative response to mass-produced materials and photography. They also came from the same desire to document ourselves and our families that causes people to create Web sites today. The classic, late-Victorian scrapbook, circa 1880–1900, reflected the meaning of its name: It contained "scrap," the colorful cutouts from catalogs and tradesmen made especially to feed the scrapbook fad. Our ancestors cut them out and pasted them on album pages with other memorabilia. The personalized memorabilia in many scrapbooks tells stories of social life, schooling, or career. The scrapbook or photo album, interpreted and annotated, may serve as autobiography.

The classic photograph album of the same era offered pages made just for cabinet cards, cartes de visite, postcards, or, by the 1920s and 1930s, held black pages for snapshots. Between 1880 and 1920, as amateur and inexpensive photography made picture taking more casual, it was common for women and men to compile and annotate thematic photograph albums. These books are all excellent sources of information and appropriate for your archive, as well as offering illustrations for your other documentary editing projects. (See chapter twelve.) Some may have bits of text suitable for documentary editing, such as school and play programs or captions under the photographs. Some ancestors kept clippings or handwritten pieces in their scrapbooks, and these are better sources of documentary text. **A family editor could start with a particularly well-organized and annotated photograph album and, with juxtaposed text, make it a documentary volume.**

Idea Generator

I bought a family. Well, I bought the memorabilia of a family in a consignment antiques store. I will alter the family name and call them the Parkers, in case they prefer anonymity. I will be using examples from their heirlooms in several parts of this book. The treasure included photographs (tintypes and cabinet cards), a scrapbook, autograph albums, calling cards, a school primer, a recipe book, an 1849 pocket calendar book used as an account book and a recipe book, and a teacher's school bell. The collection dated from about 1850 to 1935. I bought the memorabilia to use in family history classes, where we determined much about the Parker family in our exercises. The story of how the family sold these items is sad, ironic, and all too common. The heirs, two daughters who were now grandmothers themselves, had to empty two houses at once when their aunt died and their mother went into a nursing home. They sorted and disseminated. Among the photographs and family history papers, they kept "only those items that were about their immediate family," the antique dealer explained to me. "These items that they're selling belonged to remote relatives," she said, and were not part of their "close" family history.

The scrapbook alone taught me the Parker's direct family line in America, from the Irish immigrants in the 1840s through the era of the memorabilia in rural Illinois (circa 1850s–1930s) to Colorado Springs. The clippings in the scrapbook mainly gave all the clues. The sellers' mother had pasted in the scrapbook obituaries, wedding descriptions, family reunion articles, and any other newspaper columns from Illinois that summarized family events. See pages 141–146 for an example of how to edit such clippings into a documentary project. Thus, even the clippings and memorabilia in a scrapbook might serve as documents for your project. My antique-store purchase is also a reminder that we all may have "close" family history in our homes without realizing how "close."

Autograph Albums

Typically, autograph albums were wide (about seven inches across) and short (about four inches tall), with blank pages of ivory, white, or alternating pastel colors. Their covers were leather, velvet, or imitations, sometimes prettily embossed, and usually titled "Autographs." I remember when my mother gave me an autograph book to use at the end of grammar school (circa 1966), just before junior high, because the other kids had them. Otherwise autograph books were a passe custom during my lifetime, at least in my San Francisco schools. But I noticed how the other children thought themselves clever when they wrote little poems and sayings that they did not make up themselves, sometimes duplicating one another. I even remember one signature. I was so pleased that the prettiest, most popular girl, Jan Headlee, was willing to write in my book. She even indicated her approval of me! (I was so far "out" I was not even in an out group.) Jan was not a good speller, nor calculator of age, so she wrote: "To a real sweat woman."

The quaint nineteenth-century, Victorian custom of keeping autograph books among friends and family left behind a useful set of documents. Historians use them occasionally for research purposes. For example, Princeton University has a collection of 196 books from 170 members of graduating classes

---

EARLY-TWENTIETH-CENTURY AUTOGRAPH MESSAGES

When you get old and ugly
As young folks often do
Remember that you have a friend
Who's old and ugly too.

Love many, trust few
But always paddle your own canoe.

Your heart isn't a play thing,
Your heart isn't a toy,
But if you want it broken,
Just give it to a boy.

I like the tulips that grow in the park
You like the two-lips that meet in the dark.

From an autograph book labeled "Barbara Harper, 7B-1, Junior High School, Vallejo, Calif.," circa 1930, in the author's possession.

---

between 1825 and 1884. The university library has listed them online and recommends them for evidence of college life, particularly noting the references in the 1850s and 1860s to Civil War and sectional feeling. They note that autograph books at the college level became less popular with the growing trend in the mid-to-late-1800s of producing college yearbooks. See <http://libweb.princeton.edu:2003/libraries/firestone/rbsc/finding_aids/autograph.html>.

Generally, a transcribed autograph book would not be a publishable document unless there was something unusual about the entries or the people involved. You can use sections and information from an autograph book, however, for your narrative family history, for annotation of other documents, or for interspersal with other documents. In an autograph book, one might find customs, associations, relationships, names and dates, nicknames, places, games and puzzles, explanations, school and teacher information, and photographs and memorabilia. The messages reveal friendship and love, but perhaps modern generations need a word of caution. It was common to use romantic, even suggestive messages between same-sex friends or brother and sister without implying anything untoward. What additional social history messages might you extract from the bits of doggerel verse featured above and on page 78?

The family whose memorabilia I bought (see page 75 under "Scrapbooks and Photograph Albums" and the index entry "Parker") had included in the sale four autograph books, circa 1880–1918. Relatives wrote to each other identifying themselves as Cousin Clara, Uncle Charles, or "Your Father, Matthew Parker." Clearly the autograph albums could answer genealogical questions, and some entries would be worthy of transcription into a narrative or documentary account. Now we can compare the autograph messages from different eras.

LATE NINETEENTH-CENTURY AUTOGRAPH MESSAGES

Love many, trust few,
And always paddle your own canoe.
[This one lasted 1880 to 1930!]

Remember me till death shall close
My eyelids in their last repose
And the green willows gently wave
O're the tomb of your schoolmate's grave.

If wisdom's ways you wisely seek
Five things observe with care
Of whom you speak to whom you speak
And how and when and where.

[The above verse is also the one that Caroline Ingalls wrote in her daughter Laura's first autograph album in 1881, as related in Laura Ingalls Wilder's *Little Town on the Prairie* (New York: HarperCollins Publishers, 1941, 1981, 183–184).]

The older the tree
The tougher the bark
The taller the girl
The harder to spark.
Beware.

[This was to an album holder, Emma, who, through photographs, was obviously taller than her sisters were. Ironically, however, she was the only one who married.]

When you are married and settled in life
You must love and obey like a good little wife.
May heaven protect you and guard you through life
And may the one prosper that calls you dear wife.
[This was to sister Mettie Parker who never married.]

From the Parker collection, circa 1880–1918, in the author's possession.

Do you see a trend of differences between the 1930 poems and the 1880s poems? Analyzing even the vocabulary, the use of imagery, the meaning of the sentiments, the attitudes toward women's roles, and the sources of the quotes—as in literary analysis—can tell us about our ancestors' societies. The older albums have more messages on the serious subjects of religion, marriage, and eventual death. Interestingly, the older albums also contain some messages in Morse code and shorthand. The older ones have much finer handwriting and more courteous salutations and signatures. **A family documentary editor could make visual aspects such as these (and the lovely covers of some autograph albums) apparent by using photographed or photocopied representations of them in the edited volume.**

Idea Generator

SIGNATURE QUILTS: AN 1840s AND 1850s PHENOMENON

The autograph album gave way to the school yearbook, but what came before the autograph album? One answer is the signature quilt. Also known as the friendship quilt, its heyday was actually in between waves of popularity for autograph albums, in the 1840s and 1850s. Indelible inks made a difference. Friends would sign (or sometimes embroider) comments similar to the verses in albums. If you have a signature quilt in your family, consider it as both a textile artifact for preservation purposes and a document for transcription. Like an account book or an autograph album, it might reveal your relatives' social circles and communities. It might contain quotable passages for a documentary editing project.

From Old School Papers to Literary Compositions

Among family documents you may find school notebooks and papers. These can range from treasures of original composition to ho-hum recopying of assigned readings and lectures. Although all would be worth keeping and analyzing as part of our relatives' educational experiences, few would be original and interesting enough for transcription into a documentary editing project. So make that your litmus test: Is it original, creative, or thoughtful writing? A childish poem, the story of a summer vacation, or a valedictory address might all reveal our ancestors and make good additions to collections of transcribed documents; what Grandma copied out of her science textbook about amoebas might not. If, on the other hand, she copied from her home economics text about how a wife should behave, then that lesson might be worthy of transcription and analysis as evidence of the prescriptive literature that affected her life.

As discussed in chapter two, your ancestor may have been a literary writer who left unpublished poems, stories, plays, or a novel. Bringing these to light may be another special responsibility for you. One litmus test might be: Are they good? If you like them but are uncertain of your ability to judge, consult with a literature professor at a nearby university. Don't let the originals out of your hands just yet. If you have something of literary significance, you need some expertise to edit it for publication. Study the literature of its time period, region, gender, and genre. This will give you a basis for comparison and the names of some experts in that area of literature.

Long-lost literary manuscripts have often seen posthumous publication by family members. Perhaps the best example is Emily Dickinson's poetry. She lived like a hermit, cloistered in her family home, passionately writing more than 1,770 poems. Only after her death did her work see the light of day, and then in dribs and drabs, eked out as different relatives and editors released some and fought about the rest. So, even some of our great literary figures lived in obscurity, owing their publication to posthumous editing. Let's hope that the family feuding is not an inevitable side effect.

SEVEN

Organizing Your Documents

Don't waste time mourning. Organize!

—*Reportedly the dying words of labor union activist, songwriter, and Swedish immigrant
Joe Hill, executed in Salt Lake City 19 November 1915*

en and women have died, gone to jail, been deported, and suffered all
manner of unfair treatment for the sake of that one goal: organizing.
Of course, they were organizing laborers to better their working conditions, not organizing a family history or documentary editing project. Sometimes organizing your family papers may seem that daunting, however. At least
it is not as burdensome as jail or execution, although many genealogists think
there would be no better way to go than in Salt Lake City, researching, of
course.

Seriously, organizing your family documents is a productive alternative to
prolonged mourning. Joe Hill's last words work for us family documentary
editors. Many of you share with me the sad awareness that grandparents, parents, the "greatest generation," and many others are gone or going. In the
seventeen years that Rick and I have been married, we lost three of his grandparents (World War I generation) and, in the last two years, three of our parents
(World War II generation). Beyond a certain point, simply mourning them does
no long-term good. If, however, we can "bring them to life" with family history
and complete some of their lifelong goals by publishing their life stories, then
we have organized their legacies for them.

PLAN FIRST

Warning

**Stop! Do not reorganize your documents from the order in which you found them,
yet.** When I speak to genealogical conferences on how to organize documents
for publication, I "demand" something that I can't regulate here: "It is good
that I am holding you captive in this room before I send you out to follow my

instructions," I say. So please, stay in your seat and read the rest of this chapter *before* you start to reorganize your documents. The foremost reason for this is you should keep the documents, at least temporarily, in the original order in which you found them. The order itself might reveal important information. Make a record of that original order. Perhaps you can photocopy, scan, or transcribe the documents so that you rearrange the order of your *copies* and never your originals. If kept as they were, the originals can be your record of how they were. Here's why it can matter.

Suppose you have a bundle of wartime love letters. As was so common, the lovers wrote every day and sometimes multiple times a day. Whether they correctly marked times and dates on their letters is problem enough. The conditions of war, censorship, and overseas posting added new dimensions. There were months when he did not hear from her or she from him. Sometimes he would receive a reply to his third letter of the week or month before she would receive his first and second. As their thoughts and responses crossed in the mails, they may have bundled the letters in order of receipt, not date. Knowing that order of receipt could be critical to understanding their reactions to one another and to events. **So before you reorganize those letters chronologically, document the order in which you found them.**

Another example is Kate Dickey Harper's memoir of homesteading days. As stated in chapter one, she wrote in changing pencil and ink on folded brown paper. She folded it so the sheets appeared to be pages in a book, and she wrote across each half sheet, so one would turn the pages book-style. She numbered the first nine pages consecutively, then did not number all the rest, then numbered the additional loose sheets that continue the memoir starting with "1." Her storytelling would switch from one story or period of her life to another as she recalled (by free association) another event she wanted to include. Some are out of chronological order. Some of these switches occur in the middle of a page. Occasionally, she labeled the switching passage "Insert," but she did not label it by an identifying date or topic and she did not mark a place to insert it. Indeed, the memoir pages have the appearance of a rough draft, with scratch-outs, erasures, revised words, and blank pages. I believe she intended to write more and to polish its appearance, or perhaps have her secretary-daughter type it all up.

A secretarial relative other than her daughter set out to transcribe the memoirs and apparently shuffled the pages. Then, she tried to type them in what she thought was chronological order. She made mistakes, creating a typescript of misplaced puzzle pieces with no editorial marks to differentiate her work from Kate's. Thank goodness the original came back with the typescript, intact though shuffled.

Holding the original order of documents may be even more important when someone found the documents with a group of diverse artifacts. For example, you may accumulate many family documents as the recognized Keeper of Everything. Here is a hypothetical case:

- Relative Number 1 sent you some of Uncle Jake's World War II letters to Grandma, a set of poems and stories written by a little boy, and a Victorian scrapbook with no name in it.

Important

- Relative Number 2 sent you Uncle Jake's war letters to his wife, her letters back to him, an unidentified handwritten recipe book, and a 1930s scrapbook with no name in it.
- Relative Number 3 sent you Uncle Jake's war letters to his brother, a collection of war medals and souvenirs, and a wartime scrapbook with no name in it.
- Relative Number 4 sent you Uncle Jake's war letters to Great-Aunt Bess, an unidentified handwritten recipe book, and a Victorian scrapbook with no name in it.

In your enthusiasm to organize all of Uncle Jake's war letters into a documentary editing volume suitable for publication, you pulled the letters in order to shuffle them into chronological order. You put everything else in the same, hopefully archival, box. You set about transcribing the letters. Later, you returned to the artifacts and realized what you had done.

First, when transcribing, you discovered problems with the letters. Placing them in simple chronological order destroyed the order in which the letters arrived. Then, too, Uncle Jake liked to use 1940s trendy terms such as "swell" and "Baby." He called his wife, his mother, and Great-Aunt Bess "Baby," because he thought they were all so "swell." So, you can't always tell to whom he was writing without carefully reading and comparing. You also no longer have an easy way of knowing what little boy wrote the childish poems, who made which scrapbook or recipe book, or which brother earned the war medals. What could you do?

- Analyze the content of the letters to surmise their intended recipients.
- See if the letters refer to any of the other artifacts.
- See if you retained cover letters that came with the artifacts, identifying them.
- Embarrass yourself by contacting the surviving relatives for help.
- Guess the authors of the scrapbooks and recipe books by era and content.
- Obtain military records that indicate which brother won these medals.

If Grandma, Great-Aunt Bess, and the World War II generation were already dead or were foggy in their recollections, and the letters and other records offered no clues, you might never absolutely know who created which artifacts.

ORGANIZING YOUR TIME

If you were the family historian in the previous scenario, even if you did recapture all the information you had lost, you could not recapture one precious commodity: the time you wasted. I rarely use the word "hate," but I will say I "hate" discovering that I wasted a large chunk of time, especially through my own momentary lapse of vision. How frustrating that is when one has so much family history to do! So, to avoid destroying research evidence and wasting time, we want to organize our efforts as much as we organize our documents.

You thought genealogy was time-consuming? A documentary editing project will consume even more time than that. Take heart; at least a documentary editing project, like a published genealogy, has a final product, and you control its scope. Typically, the big projects that are most comparable to a big private family project may take one to ten years and more, depending on the editor's other commitments. On the other hand, annotating a single letter for magazine publication could take a day or two, depending upon the research needed. As any writer might tell you, the publisher will also add months for magazine-article publication and years to progress from book-length manuscript to published book.

Witness some other "family-style" documentary editing projects. Mary Clay Berry edited her family letters into *Voices From the Century Before: The Odyssey of a Nineteenth-Century Kentucky Family*. She began her acknowledgments with the sentence, "Years ago, I started to edit these letters but got sidetracked into doing something else." She had to "start the project all over again" (xiii). Sherry Smith discovered her great-great-grandfather's diary in about 1980, experimented with the material in her college classroom, and published *Sagebrush Soldier: Private William Earl Smith's View of the Sioux War of 1878* in 1989 (xi–xii). Jane Jacobs started to help her Great-Aunt Hannah put together her memoir when Jane was twenty-one and "lacked sufficient craftsmanship." With Hannah long dead, the project still "had hooked" Jacobs. In her introduction to *A Schoolteacher in Old Alaska: The Story of Hannah Breece*, Jacobs spoke for many family historians and editors: "To complete a project hanging about in one's head is good. But to dally more than fifty years? Well, it is more leeway than one has a right to expect" (xiv–xv).

Of course, each of these family editors built careers and private lives during those years. One does have a tendency to postpone editing original family documents, based partly on the knowledge that hardly anyone else will "beat you to it" if it is your family. Being a combination editor-writer-archivist is a large task, and one wants the ultimate product to "do justice" to admired ancestors. Historians who have edited family papers that were not their own also have taken similar amounts of time. Byrd Gibbens heard about the Charles A. Brown Collection from his professor Lillian Schlissel who suggested he edit the letters. Schlissel first discovered them in 1981. Gibbens's book, *This Is a Strange Country: Letters of a Westering Family, 1880–1906*, appeared in 1988 (vii–viii).

John Rozier knew of the Baxter-Bird-Smith Family Papers before they came to the University of Georgia Libraries in 1982. He waited for the staff to catalog them, then spent five years transcribing and researching. The book, *The Granite Farm Letters: The Civil War Correspondence of Edgeworth and Sallie Bird*, was published in 1988 (xxxi). Miriam DeCosta-Willis learned of Ida B. Wells's diary in 1984, ordered a photocopy in 1989, started transcribing in 1990, and her book, *The Memphis Diary of Ida B. Wells*, appeared in 1995 (xix–xx). You should know, however, that some editors use excerpts and information from the papers for shorter projects in the meantime. Each editor wanted to "do justice" to the documents that they held somewhat in awe.

I should confess, in case you haven't already done the math about my projects yet, that my mother first asked me to publish her mother's memoir when I was a child and not yet qualified. I presented it as a proposed project at the NHPRC Institute in 1982. I have picked it up and put it down regularly ever since, giving

DOCUMENTARY EDITING PROJECT LOG

Name of Project	Date of Entry	Event	Result/Comment								
Kate Dickey Harper memoir	30 April 2004	completed revised transcription	compared with all versions								
James Scott memoir	15 November 2002	got old disks converted	need to compare these versions with printed								
Frank Sturdevant Mexican border article	12 March 2002	submitted to NM periodical	expect response in thirty to sixty days								

more time to teaching, speaking, dissertation, writing contracted books like this one, and all varieties of family business. As Miriam DeCosta-Willis wrote, "I always begin a research project convinced that I can finish it in a summer, but, inevitably, the summer stretches into three years" (xxi). Thus, if your project is a full documentary volume, it will probably take years. Perhaps it should take years, in order for you to locate the best materials and do the best job. **To complete it at all, however, you will need to organize your time and your priorities.**

Tip

- Create your own prospectus for each documentary editing project. See the form on page 63.
- Estimate the time each aspect will take, particularly transcribing (which is tedious and time-consuming) and research (which is addictive and will fill as much space as you give it).
- Separate the different kinds of document projects—locating, selecting, preserving, editing, etc.
- Prioritize which document projects may be most urgent, such as making preservation copies of rare originals, properly storing fragile originals, obtaining originals from family members, or interviewing elderly relatives.
- If the project will involve travel, which this kind of research rightfully does, consider when that will fit in your schedule.
- Determine where the documentary editing projects fit among your life's priorities.
- If the larger projects must wait, examine how you might use pieces to conduct smaller projects in the interim.

JOURNALING THE PROJECT

Some editors keep a journal about the steps and discoveries of the project. To others this is just another time-consuming task. There are compromises in between daily journaling and none at all. **Keeping an organized record of your experiences, realizations, hypotheses, and conclusions can be a time-saver compared to trying to recall or find evidence of them later.** The longer the project lasts, the more you may need a record to remind you of your editorial discussions. A journal about experiencing the writings of an admired personage could be rewarding. For example, Miriam DeCosta-Willis enjoyed realizing that she was simultaneously "a reader of [Ida B. Wells's] diary and the writer of a diary in which she appears" (xxi).

Idea Generator

If you keep a journal of the project, you could later quote it as another document in the project, say, to explain a choice you made as editor. If you prefer not to keep a journal, you could at least keep a modified research and correspondence log to document the particulars along the way. See the Documentary Editing Project Log on page 84. This form is intended for those of us juggling several projects at once, although you could create a separate form for each project.

JUST A BIG MESS?

At this point some of you may be saying, "Wait a minute. I'm not even there yet. I just have a box, room, or house full of family papers and can't even consider an editing project until I get these under control." Perhaps to you the first issue of organizing is that all of your family papers are just a mess. Are they stuffed or stacked or boxed willy-nilly, scattered hither and yon, overwhelming you and your surroundings? Mine have been, and some still are, so I know one can survive it. Amongst all of those papers, however, are treasures—the original documents you want to transcribe, edit, and preserve. The answer to your problems with your papers may be in two fields: the field of archival management and the field of documentary editing.

ARCHIVAL METHOD AT HOME

\di'fin\ *vb*

Definitions

Let's call the organization of the documents as artifacts, into files and containers, *external* organizing. This phase of organizing is external, about the physical handling of the documents, compared to internally organizing them into a selected documentary volume or project. If you live in a big mess of family papers, if they arrive on your doorstep when someone sends them to you, or if you find them in a family home after a death, you need help. You first need to tackle this external part of organizing the masses of documents and artifacts. The *internal* organizing of a special project, such as creating a documentary editing volume, will have to wait.

You need to organize the family document collection externally before you develop specific projects from it for several reasons. If you have the family papers, even if it is not already a large collection, you're liable to become the Keeper of Everything. You'll locate other documents and relatives may send them to you, like it or not. For your own sake, then, to keep them straight and easily accessible, you need to organize the papers. Professional archivists would tell you that their leading purposes for organizing documents are (1) to preserve and (2) to facilitate easy access for research.

Professional archivists don't necessarily want or expect you to use all of their methods for organizing documents. Whether you do will not make or break your opportunities to someday place your documents with a professional archive. Certainly, some organization or some aspects of organization could make a collection easier to process when donated to an archive. Organization also might make it easier to determine a collection's value and easier for the archive to know whether or not to accept the donation. Don't assume, however, that you need to follow archival methods strictly or in detail. That is the archivist's job when your donation arrives, and most of us would make mistakes trying to imitate it. If you're going to follow archival methods and standards with an eye toward future placement of your collection in an archive, concentrate on the methods where you can do the most good: preservation, provenance, and family research to build the collection. **Otherwise, organize your papers on two principles: retaining original order and providing a clear and practical filing system for your own use.**

Tip

So, your archival methods should include good conservation techniques and thorough recording of provenance information (See "Provenance in Archivists' Terms" on page 86). How did the documents come into your hands? Write that down and keep explanatory correspondence. Who created the documents? When, where, and why? What was the history of their ownership in between their creation and your acquisition of them? You will be glad you kept track of provenance when you go to publish some documents. You can quote your records as you tell the documents' history. Often we can put provenance in human-interest narrative forms. Archivists also will be glad you kept track of provenance when they receive your collection. For example, it is important to the story of Kate Dickey Harper's memoir that she wrote it from her mourning bed, at her surviving children's request, after her eldest child had died. There would be no record of that fact if I had not written it down, just now. The story of Mr. Parker finding the Withers family documents in an attorney's file (see page 33) is a great story that is key to the provenance of those documents. Again, I wrote it down. Also, I have the correspondence about it between Mr. Parker and me. The stories of my father trying to rewrite his memoir repeatedly during the onset of senile dementia is another opportunity for provenance narrative.

In the case of Martha Ballard's diary (Laurel Thatcher Ulrich's *The Midwife's Tale*), there is the wonderful story of Martha's great-great-granddaughter Mary Hobart. Her great-aunts gave the massive diary to Hobart in 1884 because they recognized a family tie between Martha's midwifery skills and Hobart's recent medical school graduation. Thankfully, Hobart donated the diary in 1930 to the Maine State Library. When I teach women's history with Martha Ballard's diary or the film *A Midwife's Tale*, my students want to know the provenance of the diary and how it survived. They are touched to learn the story of Mary Hobart and her great-aunts.

FILING SYSTEMS

You need a filing system for a larger collection of papers. It needs to have a sensible and well-defined way of breaking down the documents into categories so you can find something when you need it. On this score I always think of a particularly unhelpful college secretary I knew. Let's call her Eve. Eve had some endearing qualities, and even her mishaps could be funny. If we asked her for a file on an individual part-time instructor, she would have one file marked "part-timers" where we might find something. If we needed a history course outline or syllabus, she might have a file for all of the social sciences marked "outlines" or "syllabi." Later, she became malicious. If she lost a file and the faculty member was frustrated about the loss, she would accuse another faculty member of stealing that file. When she planned to move on to another position, she destroyed our files. So, see? Vague, useless file designations are the first signs of documentary crime!

In designing your more helpful filing system, remember the key goals:
- preservation or conservation
- retaining original order
- keeping track of provenance
- practical filing for easy access

Tip

To reemphasize preservation, use archival folders and containers, maintain safe environmental conditions, do no irreversible harm to documents, and dress for your handling of originals: cotton gloves, washed hands, pencils rather than pens, and no food or drink.

Retaining original order can be vital to understanding the documents and the history they reveal. It is also related to provenance. If you acquire someone else's collection of papers, you may wish to behave as an archivist and treat that as a separate collection. If Uncle George sends you his boxes of papers, designate it with his name as his papers, organize it internally within itself, but do not integrate it among the other documents. The contents and provenance of separate collections may be important to preserve. This could simply mean that Uncle George has his own box.

To define the nature and name of the collection, ask, Whose collection is or was this? Is it the ＿＿＿＿＿＿ Family Papers? Or, is it the papers of an individual, an organization, or a central theme? If they all came from the same source, then that is probably the appropriate nature and name of the collection. If I donated all of the documents from our married families to an archive, it might start out as the Katherine Scott Sturdevant Papers or the Sturdevant Family Papers. Soon enough the archivists would see distinctive separations that I want to distinguish now: Sturdevant Papers, Scott Papers, Harper Papers, and so forth. So, start out with a broad category and leave yourself room to adjust. You also want the designations to follow and preserve the original order, as explained earlier. If you have multiple collections, you will need an abbreviation for each collection title to place on the series labels of folders, such as "KDH, personal correspondence" for Kate Dickey Harper.

You need an inventory of the documents, even just a rough one that you can improve later. It should list all items, box by box or container by container. You and others will move documents as you use them. An inventory is the safest way to make sure the documents return to their original order. If you use a computer database for the inventory, always keep a hard (paper) copy with the collection, too. Inventories help with preservation. If your inventory lists documents by name and date, sometimes you can refer to the inventory rather

Notes

When complete collections belonged to families or individuals, archivists will usually call them Papers, as in the Papers of Andrew Jackson or the Brown Family Papers. If they were the records of an organization, they become the organization's historical *archives* when they transfer from being the active organizational *records*.

SIMPLE ARCHIVAL STEPS

1. Define the nature and name of the collection.

2. Inventory the contents of the collection.

3. Determine the series within the collection.

4. Document the provenance of the collection.

5. Locate additional contents of the collection.

6. Remove and replace unwanted parts of the collection.

7. Establish the order of the series within the collection.

8. Label the folders according to the series designations.

9. Date and cross-reference folders.

10. Process, store, and label relevant materials such as ephemera and memorabilia.

11. Maintain these systems and procedures.

---

than handling the documents. The inventory should include a key to the abbreviations you are using.

"Series" refers to subdivisions of the collection. Studying the collection, you can determine some general series, categories, subgroups, subseries, or types of documents into which you can break the collection. Again, these should be broad enough to allow for maintaining the original order. Archivists usually list series in descending order of importance. Correspondence, diaries, memoirs, literary works, or any original writings by the document creators rank highest.

TYPICAL SERIES IN COLLECTIONS

correspondence
    business
    family
    general
    personal
    professional
    third-party
diaries and memoirs
ephemera
financial documents
legal documents
literary works
oral history transcripts
photographs
scrapbooks

To read a hot controversy about whether archivists and librarians discard historical resources too freely, read Nicholson Baker's *Double Fold: Libraries and the Assault on Paper* and Richard J. Cox's "Don't Fold Up: Responding to Nicholson Baker's *Double Fold*" on the Society of American Archivists Web site at <www.archivists.org/news/doublefold.html>.

The distinctions in correspondence bear some explaining. Family correspondence means letters between family members. Personal correspondence refers to letters of the lead person(s) of the collection that were not strictly professional. Business correspondence usually means financial business as separate from professional (job related). Third-party correspondence means letters to/from people outside the family or outside the individual after whom you have named the collection. General correspondence could be either the whole category of correspondence or pieces that fit nowhere else. If a catchall file becomes full, however, ask yourself whether its contents justify creating another specific category.

If there is a transcribed oral history from a person deeply relevant to the papers collection, file the transcript with the papers. It is appropriate even though it is a modern addition. If you don't file the transcript with the family papers or if you have not yet made a transcript, file a "see also" cross-reference to the interview tapes with where they are located.

Important

I hesitate to urge anyone to discard anything from a collection. **If we err, we should err on the side of keeping.** When collections become too large for archives, archivists turn to technologically advanced methods of photographing and cataloging them—means beyond most of us. Archivists also "deaccession" documents, which, if you are an instinctive Keeper of Everything, sounds like a euphemism comparable to "putting down" an animal. Professional archivists know what they're doing, discuss it widely among their colleagues, and often make deaccessioned items available to other archives. They do throw things away, as space is always critical. If there are a few items worthy of removal from your collections, replace them with copies.

Remove and Replace
- Newspapers and news clippings that are contaminating the environment for other documents. If you must keep them, keep them separate. If they're attached to something you wish to keep whole (like a scrapbook), interleave acid-free paper. Photocopy on acid-free paper to replace clippings. Make sure the photocopy contains everything of value about each clipping, including important information on the back, such as clues to dating it.
- Whole newspapers that already exist on microfilm in archives.
- Modern documents that are out of place in the historical collection.

To establish the order of the series within the collection, consider three alternatives: order of importance, alphabetical order, and chronological order. Think of what will make the most sense for your use. Generally, you would organize the series (each of which may mean multiple boxes) in order of importance. Within each series or each box, however, you want folder labels to line up in alphabetical order so you can easily find a folder. Inside each folder, say of to/from letters, you might want chronological order to read the documents in order of creation. Remember, again: Always attempt to retain the original order or a record of it.

Tip

As you label your folders, you can follow a few style tips from archival manuals. Most of them are parallel with *The Chicago Manual of Style*, if you wish to be most professionally consistent. Label each folder COLLECTION ABBREVIATION: Series: Specific Folder Name or Number. Normally, you would capitalize the first word of a folder title to make its collection home most prominent. You may wish to create a numbering system for your folders, although I keep mine as simple as possible. If the folder gets full (more than twenty pages), so that there will be more than one folder by that name, then number them "1 of 3," "2 of 3," etc. Or, if you expect the numbers to increase even more, you can break down the categories even further. So, for example, if I were labeling a folder of letters that Frank L. Sturdevant wrote to seek genealogical information, I might label it FLS PAPERS: Correspondence: Genealogical Research, 1 of 3.

There may be some documents whose proper folders are difficult to determine. For example, if more than one person wrote an item together, file it by the dominant or lead author. If one of the authors is a name featured in the collection and the other(s) are third parties, file it by the name that is part of the collection. If a document's author is unidentified, either keep it in its original placement with a notation to yourself to investigate its authorship, or place it in a file for "unidentified letters."

On your file folder labels and in your inventory, offer a span of dates or years for the contents. If the dates are unclear, put your guesses in brackets and use question marks: [28 June 1881–3? October 1965]. You may also use abbreviations such as *c.* or *ca.* ("circa" or "about"), *pre*, *post* or *aft.*, or *n.d.* ("no date"). If you're trying to determine correct dates, the Internet offers many sites where you can use perpetual calendars or convert dates from the old-style calendars.

If you fear that by placing an item or folder in one spot you or a future researcher will not realize its connection with another part of the collection, you need cross-referencing. Place a note in a folder and in your inventory that says "see" or "see also." Use the titles you have given as the cross-referencing information. I also recommend that you cross-reference your documents with artifacts (three-dimensional memorabilia) in your family collection. If a letter mentions a ring given, a gift sent, or a garment worn, and you can't keep the item with the letter, make a notation (on a separate sheet of acid-free paper) in the file that the artifact exists and where to find it.

Ephemera in your family documents needs your oversight in different ways than it may in public archival collections. Usually ephemera is a great resource for general social and popular cultural history. You'll also use it for that kind of history in your project, but you'll be seeking to tie it to specific family members and family events. If the piece of ephemera is with the family documents that are tied to it, I recommend keeping them together. If the ephemera seems to be damaging the documents, surround it with acid-free paper, keep it in an acid-free envelope, or encapsulate it. Ephemera reveals much about our ancestors and should be organized with their things as they left it. It also makes a nice variety of illustrations for our family history projects. See Figures 7-1 and 7-2 on page 92.)

TYPES OF EPHEMERA

advertising on paper	bookplates, bookmarks
badges	broadsides
bills and receipts	brochures
booklets	bumper stickers

Important

Archivists normally file a woman's papers under her official, legal, dominant name—her married name. Genealogists most often identify women by their maiden names on charts. Choose according to your needs. Whichever method you use, be consistent and note it in your inventory and in your introduction to an edited volume.

Tip

When pulling documents from folders or boxes for use, use "check-out sheets" for easier and more accurate refiling of those materials. Colored paper calls attention to the spot, although you would not want to accidentally leave a highly acidic piece of paper in a folder.

For More Info

For general advice on organizing all of your other, nonheirloom papers from family history research, see Sharon DeBartolo Carmack's *Organizing Your Family History Search*.

calendars
campaign souvenirs
cards of all kinds
catalogs
certificates and licenses
charts
cigar and cigarette bands and
    wrappers
comic books
currency
diplomas
ink blotters
labels of all kinds
leaflets (unbound, usually under five
    pages)
maps
matchbooks
military papers
needle packets

pamphlets (paper-cover, single
    printed items of five to fifty pages)
paper dolls
paper napkins
patterns
playing cards
postage stamps
programs and playbills
recipes, especially printed
religious tracts
report cards
school certificates
scrap for scrapbooks
seals and stickers
seed packets
souvenirs, if printed on paper
tickets
timetables
wrappers

Figures 7-1 and 7-2
Sometimes a photograph and a document were meant to go together. James A. Scott as an air raid warden, and his ID card circa 1942, would illustrate the corresponding part of his memoirs. Scott Family Papers, in author's possession.

92

If the ephemera is a collection in itself, you might keep it as its own separate series. Or, if a family member collected ephemera, such as maps, and if that collection is large enough for its own container(s), you might keep it separate within that family's or individual's papers.

CONTROL

If you're a collector, a genealogist, a historian, a Keeper of Everything, or if you've enjoyed reading this section about using archival methods, you probably like some degree of control over your projects. Then, you should enjoy this. Archivists strive for control—physical, intellectual, complete control. Control in collections management means that you have thoroughly organized the collections in every way, created "finding aids" (guides) to help researchers in the collections, updated the conservation methods, and generally maintained the collections at the highest professional levels. So, archival methods may give you control. Surveys show that the greatest stressors in our lives are the areas in which we have no control. Stress-free control of family papers: Are you there yet?

Notes

Thomas Jefferson tried to organize his own papers after disasters struck. In 1770 Shadwell Plantation burned, and he lost many of his papers. In 1780 a raid on Richmond took his gubernatorial letter books. Jefferson set out to get copies of the documents by borrowing letters and letter books from George Washington or Horatio Gates. He also took great care which heir he would trust with his papers, grandson Thomas Jefferson Randolph, who tried valiantly, for his day, to preserve and edit the papers. See <http://rs6.loc.gov/ammem/mtjhtml/mtjprov.html>.

EIGHT

Organizing Your Project

Departure from conventional chronological organization, like departures from any other general editing principle, should be taken only after serious thought.

—Mary-Jo Kline, A Guide to Documentary Editing, 85

\di'fin\ *vb*

Definitions

For the sake of our discussion, "internal organization" will be the name for how you organize the documents within the volume you intend to publish or the special project you are doing with some of your documents. The order in which you arrange transcribed documents for a publishing project will depend on the purpose or goal of the project. Here are some norms. Remember, it is best to put copies, transcriptions, or lists of documents into any new order you create; don't shuffle originals.

TYPICAL DOCUMENT ARRANGEMENTS IN PUBLISHED VOLUMES
- chronological throughout
- topical chapters, chronological within each
- topical separate series or volumes, chronological within each
- chapters by types of documents or genre, chronological within each
- groupings isolated by owner, such as papers of one family member, then another
- to/from letters mixed together chronologically
- to/from letters chronologically but separated in groups by recipients
- narrative based on documents, followed by transcribed text of documents
- topical chapters created from excerpts of many documents
- most important document as body of text, others as appendixes

Whatever your documents for the project, documentary editors advise using chronological order as the norm and diverging from it only with compelling reasons that you explain in your introduction or annotation. **There are two main reasons to wed yourself to chronological order:**

1. Those who study your volume for their own research purposes need to trust your chronological integrity, as they look things up in the book.
2. Those who read your volume as a whole for entertainment and edification need the story to progress as it did in life, as events unfolded, to understand it.

A grand example of the importance of chronology is the Papers of Thomas Edison, housed and published by Rutgers University. There had been a tradition that scientific papers were organized by projects, discoveries, and research, so as to emphasize how each developed. The Edison editors are known for their determination to maintain holistic chronology. Thomas Edison's work was eclectic and his projects simultaneous. To properly document any one strand of thought and experimentation, they would have had to duplicate the same documents from one grouping to the next. They wanted to display Edison accurately, in all of his constant richness and complexity. So, they used a strictly chronological arrangement.

Many large-scale documentary editing projects do diverge from chronology in one major way: When a prominent personage or family accumulated hundreds, thousands, or millions of documents during a career, and when researchers will need access to those documents for a wide variety of reasons, editors seek convenient topical breaking points for volumes or series. The volumes of the *Papers of George Washington*, published by the University Press of Virginia, serve as one example. Note how first the editors separated the diaries and journal as unique types of documents. Then, the rest of the papers are mixed types of documents, presented chronologically and divided by the eras of Washington's career.

PAPERS OF GEORGE WASHINGTON

The Diaries (6 vols. by chronological groups of years, 1748–1799)

The Journal of the Proceedings of the President, 1793–1797

The Colonial Series (10 vols. by chronological groups of years, 1748–1775)

The Revolutionary War Series (presently 12 vols. to 1777, by chronological groupings of months, complete; 1775–1783 in progress)

The Confederation Series (6 vols. by chronological groupings of months and years, 1784–1788)

The Presidential Series (presently 9 vols., by chronological groupings of months, complete; 1788–1797 in progress)

The Retirement Series (4 vols. by chronological groupings of months, 1797–1799)

It's easy to understand why the Revolutionary War Series and the Presidential Series might be the longest in both pages and time to complete. If a researcher were studying one period of George Washington's life, however, she would have

Notes

In this present edition of the *Papers of George Washington*, all documents (except diaries as noted) are mixed chronologically, including to/from correspondence. Earlier editions carried only letters by Washington. The current editors also note whatever they can reconstruct about missing letters based on sources such as auction catalogs.

to know to look in the correct series for the era in question, and to also check the diaries for that era.

It seems highly unlikely (though not impossible) that any of us would find in our families so many documents generated by or dominated by one august ancestor like George Washington. We might, however, trace a single individual's career through documents, where the career breakdown of the Washington papers by series might inform our chapter breakdown. Thus, your father's memoir chapters might become somewhat parallel to Washington's eras . . . well, modestly so.

Youth
The War Years
Starting a Family
The Ad Man
Chief Executive Officer
Retirement and Grandchildren

Not every great man or woman was as exclusively career-focused as Washington was. The second president, John Adams, and his impressive wife spawned a family of prominent and interesting individuals across several generations, including John Quincy Adams, the sixth president. Thus, the editors of *The Adams Papers* developed a more family-oriented organizational scheme to their publishing. Harvard's Belknap Press now publishes *The Adams Papers*. The Massachusetts Historical Society houses the project.

The Adams Papers

Series I: Diaries
Diary and Autobiography of John Adams, 4 vols. (1755–1804)
The Earliest Diary of John Adams, a supplement (1753–1759)
Diary of John Quincy Adams, vols. 1–2 (1779–1788, 3–4 in progress)
Diary of Charles Francis Adams, vols. 1–8 (1820–1840)

Series II: Adams Family Correspondence
Adams Family Correspondence, vols. 1–6 (1761–1785)

Series III: General Correspondence and Other Papers of the Adams Statesmen
Legal Papers of John Adams, 3 vols.
Papers of John Adams, vols. 1–10 (1755–1780)

Series IV: Adams Family Portraits
Portraits of John and Abigail Adams
Portraits of John Quincy Adams and His Wife

Note, though, that *The Adams Papers* editors were selecting prominent documents or groups of documents to publish. They haven't been publishing (in print form) a chronological collection of all of the millions of documents from the whole family. This selectivity will be wise in our families for publishing purposes. "Comparatively few readers would approach the volumes with the intention of studying the Adamses as a family," Mary-Jo Kline stated in *A Guide to Documentary Editing.* While we do think of our own family papers as family papers, valued for that designation, the publishable parts are the ones with the greatest general historical interest.

TO MIX OR NOT TO MIX

Some of our most precious family documents, the singular ones that may seem publishable, cannot stand alone. Perhaps they are even too incomplete for our own annotation to flesh them out. This would make a good instance for combining, mixing, or juxtaposing documents, as long as the reader can always tell one from another.

Wendell Sturdevant, for example, kept a hidden diary in 1944 to 1945 while a prisoner of war of the Nazis after the Battle of the Bulge. He wrote it for daily sanity's sake. Usually the entries appear as substitute letters to the loved ones he could not directly address. Like many soldiers in his predicament, his central focus was food. As he starved, he fantasized about home cooking and about sharing it with his fiancée, Carol, whom he dubbed "Kay." See Figures 8-1 (couple) below, and 8-2 (diary cover), 8-3 ("Tageszettel"), and 8-4 (handwritten page), all on page 98.

Figure 8-1 Wendell Sturdevant and his fiancée, Carol Gates, circa 1944. This photograph presents a strong sense of the attractive young couple and their feelings. The uniform (particularly the polar bear patch) also helps date the photograph as being taken between Wendell's service in the Aleutian Islands and his horrendous experiences in the Battle of the Bulge. Wendell Sturdevant and Carol Gates, 1944. Sturdevant Family Papers, with permission of Rick W. and Wendell F. Sturdevant, in author's possession.

Wed. Feb 21, '45

For supper tonight I'll have a bread soup, It's not bad when one has the sugar to sweeten it. Nothing really but bread and water tho.

Saturday, March 3, 1945.

"Kay", How about a picnic tonight. We'll have hot dogs and buns, mustard, catsup, onions, baked potatoes, cokes, chocolate cake, butterscotch pie. . . .
—Quoted with permission of Wendell Sturdevant.

The diary doesn't tell the stories of danger, hardship, or horror, except between the lines. After all, the diary was his escape, his mock letters home, and a contraband item. He could not be graphic in it. He would not admit his more desperate thoughts, describe ugly sanitary conditions, or recall the maggot-encrusted horse's head that a guard gave the men one day to put some meat into their soup.

How could we, then, publish his treasured diary, yet convey the many more graphic experiences not written in that small document? We could write narrative and annotation, of course, but that would utterly surround his word with ours. Fortunately, there are ways to create additional documents. Wendell described those war experiences, literally step by step, in several hours of oral history interviews. He also wrote a summary account as part of his application

Figures 8-2, 8-3, 8-4 Wendell Sturdevant's World War II POW diary, circa 1945, tells a story that needs annotation to be complete. He created it by folding German factory-labor pay stubs (top left) into a booklet, with cardboard from a K ration package as the cover (above). He kept it inside a pocket Bible and bartered for bits of pencil. Such a document, when transcribed, needs its original form pictured and described as annotation. Sturdevant Family Papers, with permission of Rick W. and Wendell F. Sturdevant, in author's possession.

for a disability pension. **So, we can juxtapose his diary entries with excerpts from his chronological oral history transcripts and other accounts.**

The monumental volume *The Diary of Anne Frank: The Critical Edition*, prepared by the Netherlands State Institute for War Documentation, is more ambitious about one diarist's many versions than most of us would ever be. Nevertheless, we can learn from the editors' interesting methods. On each large-format diary page of the 719-page volume, we see three sections of text presented vertically from the top to the bottom of the page. The top paragraphs, always marked "a," are from Anne Frank's original diaries. The middle paragraphs, with a line between them, are always marked "b." These are from Anne's loose sheets of revisions of her own diaries. The bottom paragraphs on each page, always marked "c," are from the previously published *Anne Frank: The Diary of a Young Girl*, with which most of us are most familiar. This way several approaches to reading are possible. A purist who only wanted to read a particular version could read only a, b, or c by reading across the top, middle, or bottom of each page. It is far more interesting reading, I think, to compare the a, b, and c on each page. One gets a more complete picture of Anne's days and thoughts, but especially how she and others tried to edit her.

Idea Generator

One worthy experiment was in the volume of New England family history, genealogy, and World War I letters that I mentioned on page 3. Editor Sharon Carmack wanted to re-create the emotions she felt when she read the love letters of this family's parents. For the sake of discussion, I will call the father Mr. J and the mother Mrs. J. Sharon's assignment was to write the entire family history narrative, but the letters were the worthiest part. So, Sharon's chapter outline became a documentary editing project surrounded by narrative.

Case Study

Preface: editorial explanations
Introduction: quotes about the Js from their children
One: narrative about the Js' youth and early contact, with some quotes from letters
Two: narrative about Js, with some transcribed letters, as he entered military service
Three: letters showing the developing relationship as he left for war
Four: future Mrs. J's letters as she worried and waited to hear from him
Five: his letters, while he waited to hear from her
Six: narrative, a few letters and quotes, carry through to his return
Seven: narrative about marriage and family
Eight: narrative on family business and son
Nine: narrative on family based on interview with daughter
Epilogue: on the deaths of Mr. and Mrs. J

Reminder

Reminder: You can choose any order for your documents as long as you (1) take into account how potential publishers and audiences will receive it and (2) state and explain good reasons for your choices in your introduction.

Can you see where Sharon diverged from chronological order? In chapters four and five, she grouped the letters of first the woman and then the man. Thus, she maintained the chronology within each group but did not integrate them chronologically. She found that the upheaval of his transport and activities in Europe disrupted their regular communication and delayed their mail. Each was waiting for the other to write with increasing anxiety and frustration, trying to exhibit neither. Sharon wanted to let the suspense build first with the woman, while we readers cannot be certain what she would hear about his safety, and then with the man. Integrating the letters by date would have confused the order in which the couple received them.

Another technique would be to present narrative followed by a variety of transcribed documents. The narrative should summarize the individuals or family who are the documents' subjects, then thoroughly introduce the documents. This is the organization of Miriam DeCosta-Willis's *The Memphis Diary of Ida B. Wells*. Here the editor also located a second Wells diary from Chicago, 1930, and a group of six essays by Wells. With the preliminary narrative, afterword, and annotation, the editor tied all together and the documents complemented each other. She could have integrated them all with her own text, making one chronological edition. Most editors, however, prefer not to interrupt the integrity of a diary that way. With narrative and documents separate, each maintains its own strength, although some readers may skip from one to the other rather than reading a cohesive whole.

Idea Generator

Sometimes a historian has taken a collection of documents, excerpted them into topics discussed, and organized those excerpts into evidence that speaks to those topics. One especially sees this with oral history anthologies. For example, *Voices of American Homemakers*, edited by Eleanor Arnold, contains the results of more than two hundred interviews with rural women. Their names, ages, and locations remain attached to their quoted passages. The editor organized the passages into themes such as childhood, education, courtship, marriage, child raising, foodways, housework, and social clubs. This is also the editorial strategy of Studs Terkel. Julie Jones-Eddy used a similar strategy for *Homesteading Women: An Oral History of Colorado, 1890–1950*. She combined excerpts from interviews with about forty-seven women into chapters on women's history topics.

If you have the appropriate family documents, experiment with this topical approach. Perhaps you have four to ten different descriptions of the same family history events from different family documents and oral histories. Juxtaposing them could be revealing of social history and perspectives. Or, perhaps you could juxtapose accounts from several individuals of different generations. These would be options for briefer, more incomplete documents and for oral history transcripts.

My own favorite plan for my grandmother Kate's memoir is to intersperse the original passages (carefully marked as such) with passages from other documents and "connective tissue" where needed, to create a narrative flow while still keeping the documents clearly designated. Her memoir lends itself to this organization because it is already episodic and anecdotal, with gaps and some lost chronology. This is where I believe in matching the style enough for the sake of flow, too. I shall always be grateful to my weeklong mentor at the NHPRC's Institute for the Editing of Historical Documents, Larry I. Bland, editor of *The Papers of General George Catlett Marshall*. I described this plan for my grandmother's memoir, expecting a professional documentary editor, especially one of such "manly" projects, to be skeptical. Larry said, "Sure, you can do that. You can do it whatever way you want, as long as you follow solid standards and explain your decisions."

BOOKS OUR ANCESTORS WROTE

Some family documents, such as cookbooks, scrapbooks, novels, or complete autobiographies, are already books. However, just because it looks like a book; opens like a book; stands on a shelf like a book; has a beginning, middle, and ending like a book; and even has a title page and dedication like a book, does not mean it is a book. It probably isn't ready for publication and would benefit from documentary editing.

Even though your relative laid this document out as a book and even if the pages are bound, consider its organization realistically. Remember, I am not suggesting you rip out and shuffle the pages of any original documents; just make copies for shuffling. As indicated in chapter two rarely would a scrapbook or account book by itself make a good published volume. Consider the scrapbook full of family obituaries and other clippings, for instance. On page 75, I suggest transcribing those materials into a document-based family history. Certainly there would be excerpts from a scrapbook or account book to intersperse with other materials in a volume. In some cases, with a sophisticated editing approach and lots of historical research, one could annotate a scrapbook or account book into a publishable volume.

If you have a truly complete autobiography, it may need only annotation. The same might be true for a completed novel. In either case, however, and especially in the latter, evaluate the strengths and weaknesses of that "book." Perhaps ask scholars or potential publishers or agents to help with the assessment. Is the autobiography or novel good? Is it marketable? If the novel is not fine literature with a broad appeal, could it be publishable as a period piece or as a regional or local work?

Seriously evaluate that cookbook, too. If it's like those family examples that I've seen, it's full of raw social history that an editor needs to "cook." It could be one of several types of cookbooks or recipe collections: a period piece, ethnic, regional, rural, methods, etc. There are millions of cookbooks, and there are books on how to write and publish cookbooks. See the Theophano book cited on page 75. **Here is what I hope you will do as a documentary editor:**

- Research the family and social history behind the cookbook and build from that narrative and/or annotation.
- Interview family members for more information about foodways.
- Organize the book chronologically if that structure is apparent, such as the cookbook of a new wife who kept adding over the years or a compendium of family foodways over the years.
- Organize the book topically if that is the obvious or pre-existing way. There are many cookbook models of how to organize different types.
- Adapt old recipes to new equipment, foods, and time management.
- Make it more family history and foodways history than "cookbook," but keep it cookbook enough to help you sell it.

Important

General rules: If you present a whole document in its entirety as a published volume, don't change the chronological order of its entries unless they were unnecessarily out of order. If you're pulling excerpts from a document to use elsewhere, then that volume's dominant documents or functions determine the order. In any case, maintain proper source citation for all documents.

Notes

DETERMINING CHRONOLOGY

The accurate chronological order of your documents won't always be obvious. If parts are undated, try to determine dates by original placement in a book or bundle or by historical research into what is said in the documents. In a few cases, such as undated letters, you may never be certain of their placement, in a strict chronological sense. Sometimes you will have multiple documents written on the same date. Then, it's your responsibility as a documentary editor to set a policy of how you will place them and why, and to state it. Other times envelopes and letters have become separated. If you have multiple versions of the same autobiographical stories, you may notice that different details and viewpoints occur after some years. You could follow the example of editor C. Vann Woodward in *Mary Chesnut's Civil War*, and decide what to choose from among several versions.

Our relatives may have organized their writings with numbers and codes of their own. This is similar to the genealogist who was sure she could design a better numbering system than the ones that professionals recommend. Before you ignore or discard what your relative did, however, analyze it. Make charts on paper of how he numbered his pages or subsections to see the method in his madness. I am doing that with my father's memoir. He dated each story by when he wrote or rewrote it (instead of when it happened). His system helps me put them in order. Observing the dates when he switched from one story to the next suggests some of his mental associations and moods as well. Comparing later versions of the same story, I find new information and revealing evidence of life changes.

Tip

Tips for Dating Letters

- Keep them with the collection in which you found them. Look for clues in surrounding documents and artifacts.
- Estimate dates by comparing letters from before and after the letter in question.
- Keep envelopes with letters to study postmarks.
- Estimate dates by details within the letter—who was alive or dead, what events are mentioned, where were folks living at the time, do they mention seasons or seasonal weather?
- Estimate dates by inserted memorabilia such as clippings and photographs.
- Look for gaps in a steady flow of letters, and see if the strays fit there.

Among documents, gaps may truly be gaps. As editor, though, you will need to offer explanations for them in your annotation. Kate Dickey Harper presents a good example. As I mentioned earlier, Kate wrote her memoir in 1941 to 1942, partly as therapy for the depression she experienced after her first son, Leonard's, premature death in 1939. She interrupted the narrative in about 1906 to 1908. Then, as I have indicated, I have Leonard's baby book from 1909 to 1914 to pick up the narrative. What was happening in her life between 1906 and 1909 that might explain the gap of storytelling? While living in Colorado with the near inevitability of following her in-laws to Arizona, she lost her first baby, a girl, before having Leonard in 1909. If, when she was writing her memoir in 1941 to 1942, she was depressed about Leonard's death at age thirty, that may explain why she stopped writing her stories at the 1906 to 1908 juncture, where the next major event to tell was the first loss of a child. So, what happened after 1914 that stopped her from writing any more material similar to the baby book? Why, two more babies, of course, in 1915 and 1917.

Time lines and chronologies are essential at every stage of your documentary editing project. Make and maintain your own from all of the family sources available: the documents, oral history, genealogy, photographs, etc. The time line should include any family events that pertain to the project. This will become an invaluable tool for organizing your materials and, later, for conducting your research. It will become long, so do it on a computer so you can keep adding and altering without making a mess. For each question that arises in your project, such as dating an undated document, see if the chronology can offer clues.

Important

Chronology of Family Events

Put in your chronology the dates of the following events:

- births, marriages, and deaths
- parties, reunions, social occasions
- jobs held, businesses owned
- places lived, property owned
- migrations, moves, travel
- visits between family members
- immigration and naturalization
- military service
- major illness
- natural disasters
- schooling
- membership in churches and organizations
- relevant legal events in court, divorces, adoptions, taxes, mortgages, elections
- letters that first announced important news
- relevant publications
- the span of the documents
- unexplained mysteries and gaps

Use history books in conjunction with family time lines. From the historical sources, add events to your family chronology that are or may be relevant. **A good resource is the *Encyclopedia of American History*, edited by Richard B. and Jeffrey B. Morris.** The bulk of this book is organized as a chronology, but it has far more detail and analysis than a simple time line. When Sharon Carmack was researching Mr. J's World War I experiences, for example, I was able to look up exactly what events were occurring when and where Mr. J was stationed. This information helped Sharon explain his cryptic observations. There are also other historical chronologies listed on pages 229–230.

Organizing documents may simply be a matter of reading how fragments form

Printed Source

a sentence—a sort of grammatical chronology. When the well-meaning secretarial relative shuffled Kate Harper's memoir pages, it was not difficult to read the ending phrase or sentence on the bottom of one page and connect it with its other half at the top of the next page. See if you can match them below as a practice. Remember to match grammar and punctuation. Use common sense about context.

CLOSING LINES FROM BOTTOMS OF PREVIOUS PAGES	OPENING LINES ON NEXT PAGES
many people were frozen to death in the blizzards—sometimes only a few	the age of five years.
boys wore dresses until they were ready for pants at about	where Uncle Doc made the trip to Olathe to be in attendance when I was born
the Rouse family had moved to Springfield, Mo., from	were only about 13 years old.
They seemed so old and grown up to me—but I know now that they	feet from their own doors.
I suppose I slept a lot—Mother never said that I	ever cried or made much fuss. I think I was considered a "good child."
I still wanted my mother. I guess that's something we never get over. We suddenly think we're grown up and	can't he ever learn to behave himself . . ."
Very early in my life I began thinking "Why	do very nicely without her

Before you're finished, check the sentences for subtleties of meaning. The answers are on page 107. Yes, documentary editing can be fun!

DETERMINING AUTHORSHIP AND AUTHENTICITY

Occasionally, it's not immediately obvious who wrote what. Like the approximate date of a letter, figuring out its author may be essential to organizing it among the documents or understanding how it fits.

Tip

WAYS TO DETERMINE FAMILY AUTHORSHIP
- handwriting comparisons
- references in document to people, places, events, and dates
- location and ownership of document
- proximity of other documents
- age and nature of paper and ink
- age and nature of handwriting style
- age and nature of usage and abbreviations
- historical references in document
- researching any specifics in document

- comparing document with new ones found
- showing document to family members
- oral tradition
- common sense

Here is a common-sense example of deducing authorship, adapted from *Bringing Your Family History to Life Through Social History* (31–33). In the family collection, there are two different copies of the identical recipe for Suet Pudding.

> Recipe A is written on a worn, yellow, crumbling scrap of paper in shaky handwriting that you do not recognize.
>
> Recipe B is on one of Great-Grandma's regular pages, in better condition. You recognize that it is in Great-Grandma's handwriting. She gave the recipe a title that it did not have on copy A: "Mother's Suet Pudding."
>
> So who wrote copy A? Logically, Recipe A was the original one, written in the hand of Great-Great-Grandma, and later copied by her daughter in Recipe B. We would not know who wrote Recipe A without also finding Recipe B. Both become precious.

Thus, surrounding documents and deduction can help authenticate an unidentified document. Research can also fill in blanks as you organize family historical events. Another example starts with a typed, unlabeled, undated, unidentified account of a man's Civil War experiences, beginning with Quantrill's Raiders in 1862. It was old paper, old typewriter print, and had gaps marked with blank underlines and question marks as though the typist was copying from a handwritten original and could not read some parts. The account made clear that the author was a Confederate who enlisted from Independence, Missouri, at age eighteen while staying there with "Uncle John." The soldier-author had supposedly fought under General Jo Shelby, from Missouri through Arkansas, Indian Territory, and Texas, dropping the narrative there. It was an amazing account, matter-of-factly reciting, in concise form, each battle, officers by name, and several individual experiences. Whose was it, and was it authentic?

Case Study

- Descendants found it in the trunk made and owned by Otho D. Dickey (1844–1924), along with Dickey family materials dating back to before, during, and after the Civil War. The typescript appeared to be a transcription of a handwritten version, but no earlier version was found.
- Family tradition was that Otho served in the Civil War. When asked, his granddaughter confirmed this but stated that she had always assumed he fought for the Union and never heard details. She was shocked to think he had been a Confederate and said that the family could have kept such a "skeleton" secret.
- In the same trunk was a San Francisco news clipping, circa 1920, recalling General Jo Shelby's 1863 Missouri raid. At the top was handwriting: "I think that you were in this raid and would like to read of it. Frank" Frank Dickey and his family lived near Otho in the last years of his life. Frank could have shared this clipping with him.

- In the same trunk was a set of letters written by Otho's older brother, Thomas Clemens Dickey, from 1867 Illinois. Tom addressed Otho as being in Shreveport, Louisiana, and expressed great relief at having finally heard from the long-lost Otho. Tom congratulated Otho for finally "being out of that miserable country" and told him not to fear coming back to Illinois. He reflected on how they had been so utterly separated by war. He urged Otho to come home to their anxious mother, who had given him up for dead long before. There would be no retribution for a man "from the South . . . if he don't talk too much politics."
- Applying to the National Archives brought Otho D. Dickey's Confederate Civil War record. It showed that Otho D. Dickey had enlisted on 12 August 1862, in Jackson County, Missouri, serving in the 12th Missouri Cavalry, until at least early 1864.
- The National Archives also yielded Civil War records of Thomas Clemens Dickey, who had been a Union officer from Illinois since 31 August 1862. The Dickeys were originally from Kentucky and had moved to southern Illinois just before the war.
- Research in Confederate army histories revealed all of the battles and engagements that a man in Otho's units would have seen. The histories matched the list in the typed diary, even in the same chronological order. Many of Shelby's troops accompanied him into Mexico when the Confederacy collapsed, and some didn't return to the United States until 1867.
- The 1860 Census placed Uncle John near Independence, Missouri, and his young nephew Otho living and working with him on his farm.
- Histories of the Independence area during the war and of Quantrill's Raiders explained that Union troops attacked and burned the town, terrorizing the area, to pursue Quantrill and his supporters.

What would you conclude? Apparently, the brief, typed memoir is authentic. A grown child of Otho's likely typed it from Otho's handwritten version, which may have been disintegrating. With confirmations of so many parts of the account, the other individual experiences are probably true. The clues also suggest that Otho was one of the men who followed Shelby to Mexico, although the typed account stopped short of what happened after Texas. It seems that fleeing to Mexico was almost a taboo subject. More research would probably yield more answers. Unattributed documents can exercise our detective skills.

THE BURDEN OF A LEGACY

Gosh, this is a lot of work! You already knew that about every aspect of doing family history. It is rewarding, though. To deal with your documents takes time and effort. Joe Hill said: "Don't waste time mourning. Organize!" Organizing the documents archivally is a major undertaking but not a waste of time. Organizing them for documentary editing and publishing is another investment of time and effort that is not a waste. If you're a genealogist, you always have "completion" and possible publishing in the back of your mind anyway. With

ANSWERS TO MATCHING QUIZ ON PAGE 104

many people were frozen to death in the blizzards—sometimes only a few feet from their own doors.

boys wore dresses until they were ready for pants at about the age of five years.

the Rouse family had moved to Springfield, Mo., from where Uncle Doc made the trip to Olathe to be in attendance when I was born.

They seemed so old and grown up to me—but I know now that they were only about 13 years old.

I suppose I slept a lot—Mother never said that I ever cried or made much fuss. I think I was considered a "good child."

I still wanted my mother. I guess that's something we never get over. We suddenly think we're grown up and do very nicely without her.

Very early in my life I began thinking "Why can't he ever learn to behave himself . . ."

these methods, the product can be crafted from the writings of your relatives, precious primary sources, with more marketability and research interest than many other genealogical projects you might attempt. The documents are also a legacy. Family historians love to "connect" with their ancestors. How better could you connect with them than to present their writing in its best light?

NINE

Transcribing Your Documents

Transcribing is a demanding and rewarding task that requires far more than typing skill.

—*Willa K. Baum,* Transcribing and Editing Oral History, *25*

\di'fin\ *vb*

Definitions

Y ou need to love what you are doing. You need to love it with a passion, feel driven by a cause, have a whimsical sense of humor, or be compulsively detail-oriented, in order to love transcribing. It can be the most tedious chore of documentary editing and an even more tedious chore of oral history interviewing. Yet you must do it, and you must do it painstakingly well. **Transcribing means reproducing the text of documents (written or oral) into a clear, modern, easily accessible, and readable form.** In both documentary editing and oral history, that reproduction should be so close to the original that scholars can trust and use it in their work, without having to return to the original document itself. If the original disappeared, faded, disintegrated, or was destroyed, the transcribed version should stand as a reliable replacement, although nothing can really replace the original in its intangible values.

If you've ever worked as a copyeditor or proofreader, you know what detailed and precise work it is. Transcribing from older documents, then editing and proofreading what you have transcribed, can be even more challenging. The ordinary editor/proofreader checks the text versions against a lifelong knowledge of English vocabulary, usage, spelling, and punctuation that have become almost second nature to the editor. The editor also uses a good dictionary and a style manual. My favorite everyday dictionary is the *American Heritage Collegiate Dictionary*, and, as I have indicated, history people use *The Chicago Manual of Style*. Only occasionally would ordinary, modern editing and proofreading stymie you or send you all over a library to solve one tiny riddle.

For documentary editing, however, one sometimes needs to develop a second-nature familiarity with writing from the ancestor's time period. To transcribe a seventeenth-century Puritan diary, one needs to know the conventions of seventeenth-century Puritan writing. I don't mean you must already be an expert, but immersing yourself in your documents and relevant sources will help you solve your document's mysteries. The transcriber has to develop an eye for that old script, a means of decoding the cryptic marks, and use resources to explain historical references that are no longer clear. If your family documents are from the nineteenth and twentieth centuries, however, the original writing will be more modern. The vocabulary, the penmanship or typography, and the social references will still include mysteries, though. You can make this fun by thinking of yourself as a detective and priding yourself on how your skills improve.

Reminder

To start, keep in mind a few general approaches. Don't give up on your project if this is scaring you. You don't need to be a trained, experienced editor, transcriber, proofreader, historian, archivist, writer, teacher, or librarian, although any or all of these would help. You need to develop some skills and circumstances for yourself. As Arthur Plotnik put it in *The Elements of Editing*, determine whether you already have or can develop "the editorial personality." For him this meant the compulsive person who is "functional" enough to balance perfectionism with realism and get the work out. The functional editor focuses on the reading audience first. The "dysfunctional" editor slows and stops projects by obsessively fixing on insignificant details beyond any necessity. If there is hope for you, as there is for most family historians who want to transcribe their documents, then work on preparing your environment.

Minimum and Preferred Qualifications

Wanted: A good and happy documentary transcriber, editor, and proofreader. Any applicant for this position should

- be a detail-oriented person, at least in this activity
- have a good, basic sense of correct English/American usage
- have typing skills that emphasize accuracy, not necessarily speed
- have a stake in the documents and the project
- be a culturally literate person, with broad knowledge
- be excited about making historical discoveries
- have a good imagination and an open mind
- be empathetic enough to walk in someone else's shoes
- have patience and what my father called "stick-to-it-tiveness"
- be compulsive about what is most necessary
- have the ability to laugh even when alone
- be able to sit still and concentrate for hours at a time
- have a comfortable chair, desk, and computer station
- have a comfortable, clear work surface several times larger than the documents
- have good eyesight and hearing or good vision aids and hearing aids
- have good lighting, preferably bright natural or incandescent light
- be willing to wash hands often and use pencils
- live alone or have a quiet, private work area with a computer
- have helpful and patient family, friends, or colleagues

- have easy access to good libraries and the World Wide Web
- enjoy word humor, such as wordplay and puns
- really want to do this

TYPES OF TRANSCRIPTION

\di'fin\ *vb*

Definitions

Several types of transcription are highly technical and are used mainly for either critical editions of famous literary works or other specialized purposes. In publishing you have probably seen *facsimile editions*, where a previously published work is duplicated in its original appearance in a new printing. Consider this method if you have a previously published book in your family that is long out of print, one to which you have rights or one in the public domain. Facsimiles from the nineteenth century can be appealing in their old-fashioned appearance while still modern enough for easy reading. There are also *photographic editions*, which reproduce handwritten copy as it looked. This would be impractical if you hope to publish, but you can photocopy your family documents for private binding, assuming the photocopies are legible. *Clear text editing* means transcribing and reproducing the entire original document as it appeared, with minimal editing or comment, leaving annotation to extensive endnotes. Clear text editing was the norm for literary editions, although some are using expanded transcription more these days.

Expanded transcription is the type most suited to your family documentary editing projects. It is what most historical documentary editors use. It is "expanded" in the sense that you can decide how much or how little to use editorial methods in presenting the documents on their pages. You may be so conservative as to attempt to make your transcriptions look like the originals, with few footnotes or annotations. Or, you may adjust the appearance of the transcribed document to modern standards, and compose text as connective tissue from one document to the next. The rules include the following:

- State and explain your editorial decisions clearly from the beginning, in print, probably in the introduction.
- Where possible, make sure those decisions follow some established precedents in documentary editing.
- Follow the stated decisions consistently throughout.
- Explain any variations from your stated procedures.

Tip

If you're transcribing pages with writing on both sides and ink has come through and made for difficult reading, try this: Photocopy the document with the contrast set one step lower. The photocopy won't show the writing from the other side.

DIFFERENT VERSIONS TO TRANSCRIBE

Handwritten documents, especially older ones, are some of the most difficult to transcribe and the most likely to be in our families. In the seventeenth century, writing included abbreviations and symbols foreign to us now. Americans did not have standardized practices for spelling, grammar, punctuation, and penmanship until dictionaries and schoolbooks spread the words in the mid–nineteenth century. There are excellent books to help you in the Bibliography. One of the techniques Kip Sperry emphasizes for deciphering old handwriting is comparison. If a strangely formed letter leaves you with a nonsensical word, compare it with letters that match in other parts of the document. If, for example, you cannot tell whether a vowel is an *i, a, e,* or *o,* compare it with words in the same document that you know contain these letters.

My two favorite tips for reading old handwriting are to read fast, thinking of context, and to read aloud, listening for context. In family history classes, when students struggle through their first readings of wills and deeds, they stop, stumped, by an unfamiliar letter, word, or phrase. Often it overwhelms them so much that they become too incapacitated to make sense of perfectly clear sentences around the cryptic one. If, on the other hand, one urges them to keep reading, substituting "blank" or "something, something" for illegible words, they start to see the meaning of a sentence, and then the word comes to them. Context is a wonderful clarifier. If you remain stumped, set the difficult passage aside even longer. Fresh eyes see more clearly.

Tip

Two other skills that have helped me are also more possible for other people to use than they realize. One is literary writing style. As we try to improve our own literary styles, and read more and better literature, we become used to norms of expression and turns of phrase. When I studied "German for Reading Knowledge" as part of my history graduate degree program, I excelled in translation, not because I excel in German but because I am good at English. Other students would translate German phrases *literally*, word for word, which made for awkward English. I might do the same in my first effort but then would revise by thinking, "How would they really say that, more elegantly, in English?" Thus, the instructor complimented my translations as achieving a happy medium between literary and literal. We can use this awareness in our transcriptions. When the sentence doesn't make sense, ask yourself, "How would they really say that in English?" and see if you can then make out more of the words. Do not rewrite the sentence, of course. You are not translating German (at least not many of you are).

Tip

A good tip for deciphering difficult handwriting is to trace it. Place tracing paper over a copy of the document (not the original). As you slowly trace each letter, what does it seem to be?

The second skill is applying historical context, cultural literacy, or even common sense. You don't have to be a historian to do this. New family history students would stumble over a list of slave names in a will. A handwritten *J* looked like an *I* to them, and an *S* looked like a *B.* Students also mistakenly assumed that the slaves would have African-sounding names. So, they read aloud their own exotic creations: "Eye-OOO-buh" for Juba, "Eye-AWL-lee" for Jolly, and "BOO-key" for Sukey. The students would also read literally: "Virginia" as a slave name to them was "Virgin" because they did not recognize the last symbol. "Moses" was "Mofes" to them because of the long *s.* Trying not to giggle, we instructors (Sturdevant and Carmack) would explain Sperry's point about comparison of letters, but sometimes even finding matching letters didn't help. Meanwhile, my knowledge of slave-naming patterns told me the correct names automatically; they were ones the slave owners would use. Such historical knowledge does not necessarily come from vast, graduate-school training. It can come from research in scholarly books and journal articles, reading old novels, and watching old movies.

For practice and interest, see the sample handwritten letter in Figure 9-1 on page 112. I chose an easy one that you could read aloud or practice before seeing my transcription. **If you want to try transcribing eighteenth-century writing, go to Harvard University's Martha Ballard site at <www.dohistory.org> where they**

Internet Source

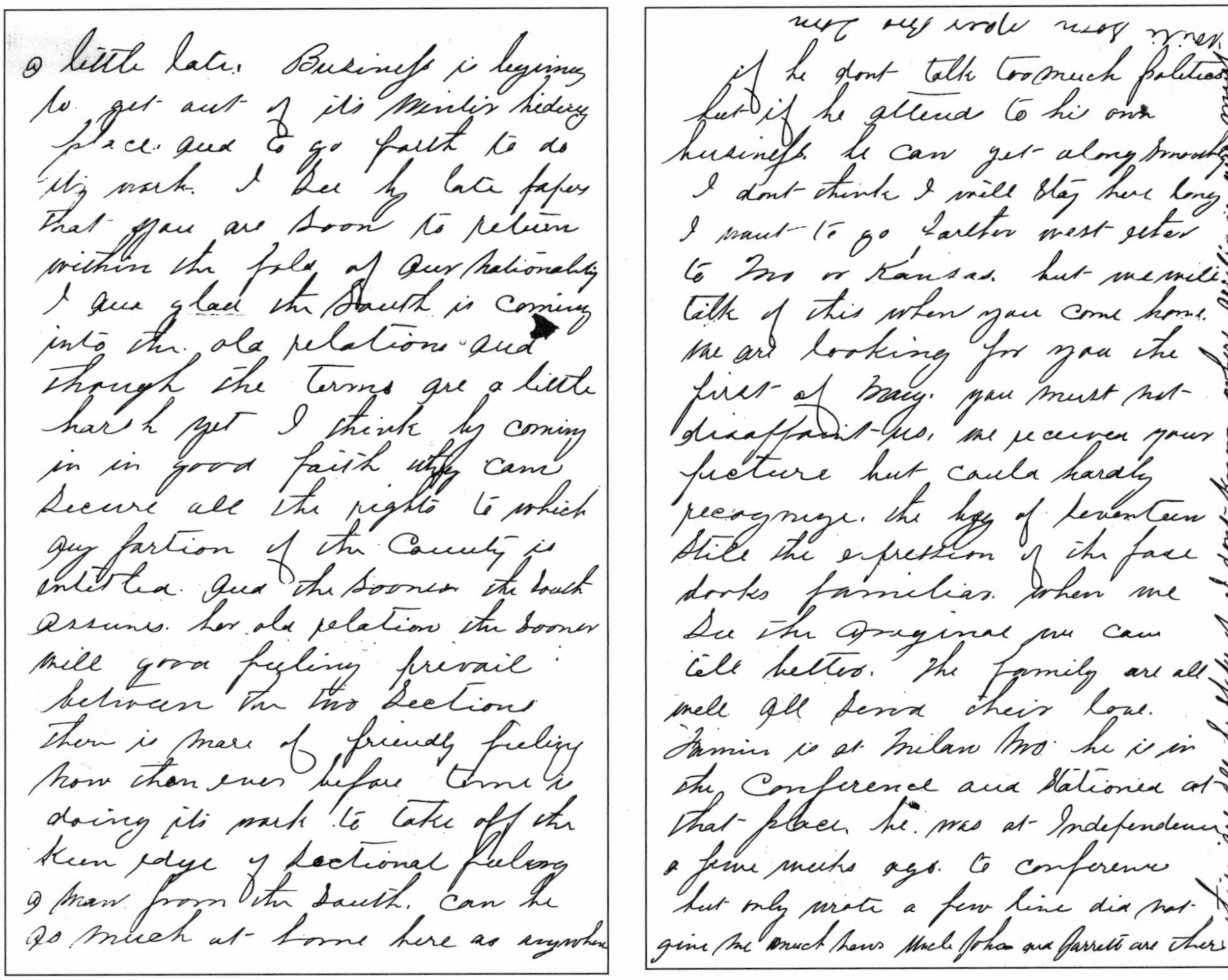

Figure 9-1 See the transcriptions below. Thomas Clemens Dickey to Otho D. Dickey, 21 March 1867. Dickey Family Papers, in author's possession.

provide opportunities to transcribe Ballard's diary line by line. Keep in mind that seventeenth- and eighteenth-century writers used some different forms for certain letters. For example, there was the long *s*, which usually appeared in the beginning and middle of a word or as the first in a double *ss*. We often mistake it for an *f* or *p*. You can see a sample of it in the word "Business" at the top of the letter in Figure 9-1. Then, there was a capital *F* represented by *ff*.

Here is my transcription of the handwritten document, Figure 9-1, above. I have retained original spelling, punctuation, and capitalization, except that I converted the long *s*, and added some terminal punctuation, opening capitalization, and paragraphing for readability.

a little late. Business is begining to get out of it's wintir hiding place and to go forth to do it's work. I see by late papers that you are Soon to return within the fold of Our Nationality. I am glad the South is coming into the old relation and though the terms are a little harsh yet I think by coming in in good faith they can Secure all the rights to which any portion of the Country is entitled. And the Sooner the South assumes her old relation the sooner will good feeling prevail between the two Sections. There is more of friendly feeling now than ever before. Time is doing its work to take off the keen edge of Sectional feeling. A man from the South can be as much at home here as anywhere if he dont talk too much politics but if he attend to his own business he can get along Smoothly.

I dont think I will Stay here long. I want to go Farther west eit[h]er to Mo or Kansas. But we will talk of this when you come home. We are looking for you the first of May. You must not disappoint us. We received your picture but could hardly recognize the boy of Seventeen. Still the expression of the face looks familiar. When we See the original we can tell better. The family are all well. All Send their love. Fannie is at Milan Mo. He is in the Conference and Stationed at that place. He was at Independence a few weeks ago to conference but only wrote a few line. Did not give me much news. Uncle John and Jarrett are there [trails off into margin and upside down at top of page] these are all he spoke of. I dont know where Arrilla is. You must write soon.

Your Bro Tom

With difficult handwriting or unidentified papers, consider the document's entire context. **Use the old "who, what, when, where, why, and how" that still helps my students.** Write it on a sheet of paper.

Notes

- Who, or what type of person, wrote this? Who was the intended reader?
- What was the purpose of the document? What type of document is it?
- When was it written? Look for clues to historical events.
- Where was it written, and where was it destined to go?
- Why did the author write it?
- How did the author go about conveying his thoughts?

If old ink is fading, making parts of the documents illegible, you may wish to take the documents to a conservator (see page 60). Ultraviolet light, chemical treatments, infrared photography, or certain camera filters can bring out faded writing without damaging a document. For me, however, such methods are a case of "Don't try this at home."

Typed or printed documents are less of a problem to read than old handwriting. If they predate modern computers and printers, however, they may not be trouble free. **Don't assume, for example, that you can safely scan them just because an electronic scanner and associated software can recognize some of the type.** There will be many old-style marks in old typeset documents. You'll spend more time and frustration trying to match a scanned copy to an original than simply transcribing as you read and study the document. If you put together ten different printed documents for a project—say, newspaper clippings from different times and papers, typed letters, telegrams, and excerpts from published articles and books—you would have the products of at least ten different machines and people, each with different symbols, arrangements, and usage.

Warning

Even recent computer material can be raw. My father wrote most of his memoir on a cheap computer and dot matrix printer. He had no spell checker or grammar checker, and he was a man who could have used both. His spelling,

ANSWERS ABOUT FIGURE 9-1 (PAGE 112)

Who, or what type of person wrote it? Who was the intended reader?

This is the latter portion of the letter quoted on page 112. Thomas Clemens Dickey wrote it to Otho D. Dickey.

What was the purpose of the document? What type of document is it?

It is a personal letter with local and family news.

When was it written, and how do you know?

Its historical references make clear that Tom Dickey wrote it soon after the Civil War. If one did not have those clues, however, the long *s* might suggest it is older than that. It looks later nineteenth century, though, because the writing instrument was obviously an ink pen, with accidental blots, and the hand is quite modern. The references to winter passing and expecting Otho to return in May place the letter in spring. We know from the first page that it was dated 21 March 1867.

Where was it written, and where was it destined to go?

We know from the heading on the first page that it was written from Clinton, Illinois, to Shreveport, Louisiana. If we didn't have that information, we could say the writer was in the Midwest, somewhere east of Missouri and Kansas. The recipient was somewhere in the South.

Why did the author write it?

Tom obviously wanted to urge his brother to come home to Illinois and stay in touch.

How did the author go about conveying his thoughts?

He used urgings, reassurances that it was safe and desirable, played upon familial guilt, and tantalized with the idea of moving West. He also mentioned Fannie.

When Tom referred to Fannie and then said "he," I know from other letters that apparently Fannie, Otho's future wife, was traveling with a Mr. Myers, an itinerant minister. Thus, the "conferences" were religious.

grammar, and pronunciations were a lifelong embarrassment to him and truly belied his fine mind, vast reading, and cultural literacy. His handwriting was admittedly atrocious, so thank goodness he adapted to computers in time to write his memoir. (Indeed, he even became a popular volunteer at a neighborhood computer center.) The technical problems were much more pronounced in his writings of the 1990s than they were in the 1980s, perhaps as senile dementia gradually developed. See the two examples of his writing, one from 1987 (Figure 9-2 on page 115) and one from 1995 (Figure 9-3 on page 116).

```
                    "My First Love", (Wr,02)   Pg 1



        I was twenty two years old when SulaMae came into my life.  She

was my first real love!  She was beautiful.  She was a flirt.  She was

saucy.  She was mine.  She was a Model A Ford!


        There is a magic about a boy's first car that is never repeated.

To earn, to pay, to buy your very own car is a momentous thing.  Its

your choice, your decision, and its all yours.


        The thrill when I first saw MY CAR.  It was Convertable with a

rumble seat.  Light green with yellow wire wheels and yellow trim: it

stood out in those days when the color of most cars was black.  And

wonder of wonders it had a radio.  Not many cars of its year had a

radio.  I had heard of the seller through a friend of my mother.  She

was a teacher who wanted something better, but to me it was just

right. Love at first sight.  I knew the price, $150 dollars, I had the

money with me.  Love is impatient!  I paid, I drove off proudly in my

NEW CAR.


        Some cars are masculine some are feminine.  My car was a

feminine.  I named the car after a character that I liked in a play

that I had seen.  Her name was SulaMae, she was from the south, from a

common sort of family.  Not a bad girl, a bit of a tease, but she had

style.  She would toss her head, flick her skirt, sashay across the

stage and in clear voice say her piece.  She was proud and cocky and

she knew it.  My car and SulaMae both had style.


        I would like to describe what my car was like.  The driving



j.scott,4/28/87
```

Figure 9-2 Even transcribing a family member's typescript can hold its special challenges. Compare this excerpt from James A. Scott's memoirs with the transcription on page 117. "My First Love" by James A. Scott, 1987. Scott Family Papers, in author's possession.

Perhaps the saddest difference was not the increase of technical errors so much as it was a decrease in creative writing.

So, I have decisions to make when I transcribe and edit this older computer printing. Fortunately, I knew him and his stories so well, that I know what he meant and what he wanted. He asked me many times to someday edit the memoir. For him, he specified that editing meant cleaning up his spelling, grammar, punctuation, and sometimes word choice. He wanted it to be a good book. See my transcriptions, with heavier than usual corrections, on page 117. Not

Figure 9-3 Compare this excerpt from James A. Scott's memoirs with the transcription on page 118. "G.I. Jim" by James A. Scott, 1995. Scott Family Papers, in author's possession.

```
GI Jim: 3

              GI Jim  (5/31/95)

        WW 11 took a big chunk out of my life.  Not only
the war years but the years proceeding it.  My war life was
cut into three parts. one before. one during. and one after.
I was in the thirties. an avid reader of time magazine .
plus I read one of two papers a day.  I was a big fan of
F.D.R. and although I was not old enough to vote (you had to
be 21 in those days).  I remember lisening to Rosevelt,
listening to him in his inaugural speech.  The theme was.
"we have nothing to fear but fear itself."  I also followed
closely the international scene.  "The Gathering Storm", in
Europe was a constant reminder. to me. that peace was a
fragil thing.  There were those Americans who were very
strict isolationest. and thought that if we ignored what was
going on in the rest of world. it would go away and not
effect our country or our lives.  Then there those (like me)
who believed that every thing that happend over there would
have an effect on what would happen over here. sooner of
later.  I followed all that was happening. world wide
and it worried me.  Would there be another war?  Could the
League of Nations keep the world at peace?  Many of us
hoped so.


        In my twenties it was a time in my life when I
should have it focused on my chosen career. advertising.  I
should have been woking my way op the ladder of my
profession.  Instead I was influenced by the world situation
and in 1939. when the war started I thought it just a mater
of time before we would be in the war.
```

having put all of the stories and versions in order yet, however, I am not sure whether I might edit the later, poorer written ones even more heavily, to give him the better, more natural style of his clear-headed days. One could make a case, though, for allowing the reader to see the decline, if that did not spoil the flow. Or, because he revised and rewrote his own stories many times, I may be able to pick and choose from his versions. What would you do?

Previous transcriptions are not usually suitable to be the text from which you would transcribe unless the originals are gone. Nevertheless, even if you disregard a previous transcription as text for your transcribing, examine and evaluate all previous transcriptions, comparing them to the original. The earlier transcribers may have made decisions, discerned order, or located information for annotation that you can use. If original documents, or parts of any, are gone, then you can transcribe from the work of earlier transcriptions, stating so in your annotation. This is apparently the case with Otho Dickey's Civil War reminiscence. I do not mourn the loss of the original much because, still worse, we could easily have no copy at all.

With Kate Dickey Harper's memoir, the many changes made by a well-meaning relative in her transcription are interesting. Some are simple mistakes in editorial judgment. Some reflect flawed efforts to put the episodes in order or to correct grammar. Most revealing are the omissions. One, for example, is Kate's recollection that Aunt Belle Taylor salvaged castoffs from her husband's junk business to make clothes for her children. Our transcribing cousin cut that out. She must have thought that was too unseemly, but it is great family social history.

TRANSCRIPTION FROM JAMES SCOTT'S MEMOIR

"My First Love"

I was twenty-two years old when SulaMae came into my life. She was my first real love. She was beautiful. She was a flirt. She was saucy. She was mine. She was a Model A Ford! There is a magic about a boy's first car that is never repeated. To earn, to pay, to buy your very own car is a momentous thing. It's your choice, your decision, and it's all yours.

The thrill when I first saw MY CAR. It was a convertible with a rumble seat. Light green with yellow wire wheels and yellow trim: it stood out in those days when the color of most cars was black. And wonder of wonders it had a radio. Not many cars of its year had a radio. I had heard of the seller through a friend of my mother. She was a teacher who wanted something better, but to me it was just right. Love at first sight. I knew the price, 150 dollars. I had the money with me. Love is impatient! I paid. I drove off proudly in my NEW CAR.

Some cars are masculine, some are feminine. My car was feminine. I named the car after a character that I liked in a play that I had seen. Her name was SulaMae, she was from the South, from a common sort of family. Not a bad girl, a bit of a tease, but she had style. She would toss her head, flick her skirt, sashay across the stage, and in clear voice say her piece. She was proud and cocky and she knew it. My car and SulaMae both had style.

—edited by Katherine Scott Sturdevant (original dated 1987)

Photocopies may also be your only means of seeing some documents. Many letters used in large documentary editing projects are transcribed from photocopies when the originals are irretrievable or scattered in the possession of others. **It's also useful to make good photocopies of the originals on acid-free paper for accessible safekeeping.** You might transcribe from a photocopy to avoid handling the original, unless something is less legible and needs checking. I have also used photocopying as a way to see an enlarged, darkened, or lightened version of some difficult text.

Tip

Drafts and revisions deserve careful study. Most documentary editors would transcribe the final, public, or sent draft. In the case of letters, for example, the great man or woman may have made several copies while drafting or through a secretary. The editor will usually transcribe the recipient's copy, the one actually sent, if it's available. Where the author himself was drafting and revising, as in the case of James Scott's memoir, the editor might take the final or best version, which would have pleased the author. If the text is a subject of intense study, such as Anne Frank's diary, the editors might print every version. Look especially through various versions of your documents for important changes. Where the changes reveal something new or interesting, you may use them in annotation.

TRANSCRIPTION FROM JAMES SCOTT'S MEMOIR

G.I. Jim

WWII took a big chunk out of my life; not only the war years but the years preceding it. My wartime life was cut into three parts: one before, one during, and one after. In the Thirties, I was an avid reader of *Time Magazine*, plus I read one or two newspapers a day. I was a big fan of FDR, and although I was not old enough to vote (you had to be 21 in those days), I remember listening to Roosevelt's inaugural speech. The theme was, we have nothing to fear "but fear itself." I also followed the international scene closely. "The Gathering Storm" in Europe was a constant reminder to me that peace was a fragile thing. There were those Americans who were very strict isolationists. They thought that, if we ignored what was going on in the rest of the world, it would go away and not affect our country or our lives. Then there were those (like me) who believed that everything that happened over there would have an effect on what would happen over here, sooner or later. I followed all that was happening, world wide, and it worried me. Would there be another war? Could the League of Nations keep the world at peace? Many of us hoped so.

My twenties was a time in my life when I should have been focused on my chosen career, advertising. I should have been working my way up the ladder of my profession. Instead I was influenced by the world situation. In 1939, when the war started, I thought it was just a matter of time before we would be in the war.

—edited by Katherine Scott Sturdevant (original dated 1995)

Business records and graphic representations, such as an account book or maps and drawings, deserve a facsimile or representational presentation. In other words, if you transcribe an account book, attempt to imitate with modern type the columnar format, headings, and positions of entries from the original. If you're transcribing a document in which the author drew a picture or sketched a map, imitate that in your transcription as closely as possible, or include a photograph or photocopy of the original graphic item. Figure 9-4 on page 119 is a good example of how a document could appear as an illustration, as well as moving your story along.

Foreign language or technical language documents deserve the attention of someone familiar with that language. Ideally, you as editor would know how to translate or correctly represent their language. If you don't, you may wish to consult with people who can, rather than attempt it alone. In most large communities you could find a college with departments of foreign language, engineering, physics, etc. where a professor might assist with translation. Many cities today have foreign language or cultural centers where translators might be available. Translators are also available online. Your money would be well spent for a reputable translation if you plan to publish a family document. If

NOTICE TO MEN CALLED FOR INDUCTION INTO THE MILITARY
SERVICE

This memorandum is intended primarily for men not employed at time of Induction into the Service.

Pursuant to the provisions of the Selective Service Act, the
first steps are now being taken to aid in securing employment, upon
satisfactory completion of the period of military training, for those
not employed at the time of entry into the Service.

The acceptance or rejection of the services here placed at your
disposal are entirely optional on your part. You are under no compulsion to utilize these services in any manner; but they are placed
at your disposal, and by making use of them now, you can materially
aid yourself in securing employment upon the satisfactory completion
of your period of military training.

Through the cooperation of the United States Employment Service
with the offices of the Employment Services of your State, it is possible for you, if you have been notified to report for Induction, and
are so located that you can reach an office of your State Employment
Service, to have a special interview with a representative of the
State Employment Service in regard to your employment after completing
your year of training. This interview may be had before you report at
your Induction Center.

At this interview, you will be able to explain to the State Employment Service representative, your experience in detail; any special aptitudes that you may possess; and you may discuss your preferences as to the type of occupation you wish to take up upon the term-
ination of your military training.

All members of the armed forces registering with the State Employment Services, will be treated as a special group in whose place-
ments other agencies also will render aid.

Any special training you receive during your career in the Army,
and any valuable qualifications or aptitudes which you may be found to
possess, will be added to your original record with the State Employment Service. Thus, you will utilize the value of these factors in
securing employment.

The nearest employment offices are located at **2461 Shattuck**
and the office hours are between **9-12am** and **1-4pm** and on Saturdays,
between **9:00** and **12:30** .

The expense of your travel to the above offices for your interview or for subsequent interviews, must be borne by yourself.

DSS Form 116

Figure 9-4 Later in his
memoirs, Scott wrote
about his attempts to volunteer or be drafted. This induction letter adds details
and interest to "G.I. Jim."
"Notice to Men," circa
1942. Scott Family Papers,
in author's possession.

the foreign language document is old, you may need a translator with special knowledge of the language's usage during that historical period.

Remember the care instructions about original documents, and don't assume you can trust others to handle them. Before translation, it would make sense for you to transcribe the document yourself. One does not need to be fluent in a language to simply transcribe it. Work closely with your translator, who needs to understand the standards of documentary editing and the purpose of your project. Once you have a good translation, you can commence the documentary editing. Official, professional, large-scale documentary editing projects tend to use literal translations. You may smooth some of the phrasing or word choices from literal to literary if your translator left them awkward in English, however. A literal translation might be "To the market went I with my money to purchase a little bread"; you might edit this to "I went to the market to buy some bread." When in doubt, check the original against the appropriate dictionary. Once the document is translated, you can also perform all of the operations of research and annotation on it as though it came to you in English. Note everything done, of course, in the introduction and annotation.

Conflation means combining the words from multiple source texts to form a single, transcribed document text. For example, if page two from an original letter is missing, but you have copies of it, you might combine the original page one and the copy of page two. It's not likely that you would conflate documents in your family collection, unless multiple copies or sets exist and something has happened to one or more. For example, if Kate Dickey Harper's memoir became damaged in a flood so that some of it was illegible, I could reconstruct parts from the well-meaning cousin's transcription, parts from photocopies, parts from my own draft transcriptions, and even parts quoted in this book. As usual, note in the text any such abnormalities.

\di'fin\ *vb*

Definitions

Oral History

TRANSCRIBING ORAL HISTORY

Your recorded oral history interview is a document in a broader sense. When you transcribe it, you can print a traditional paper document. The classic, literal oral history transcript usually appears in script form, essentially "he said/she said." Good transcribers make it exact, literal, even verbatim, so there may be more verbiage, more utterances, and more uninteresting passages in your oral history transcript than you need for family history projects. After saving the pure transcript for posterity, there are ways to extract from it or to edit the interviewee's words into paragraphs that read like a memoir. So, an oral history transcript or an edited oral history might be an excellent document to juxtapose with your collection's letters, diaries, and memoirs that tell a family story.

Oral History Transcribing Guidelines

- It takes about six to twelve hours to transcribe one hour of oral history interview. The average might be eight to ten hours. Variables include experience, whether you did the interview yourself, familiarity with the subject, quality of the recording, and amount you edit as you go.

- The header on the first transcript page should include interviewee, interviewer, place, date, and transcriber. Give the interview a topical name, such as "World War II Reminiscences," if it has a definite theme.
- The transcript should be double-spaced, with wide margins and numbered pages. It may have numbers for every line down the left margin for indexing purposes.
- Type exactly what you hear, as you hear it. When you catch yourself typing different words, such as what you might *expect* to hear, stop and backtrack to match tape and type. Transcribe verbatim.
- Include unnecessary utterances—um, er, uh, like, you know—in your first, literal transcript. Edit them out later unless they serve some purpose.
- Listen for natural endings of sentences and paragraphs. These will be legitimate editorial changes to make, such as adding punctuation, even though many speakers barely take breaths.
- Transcribe the words as pronounced, within reason. If the interviewee has an accent, attempt to re-create the most obvious changes this causes to words. Thus, you would leave off a *g* and use an apostrophe if the speaker said "fixin' " or "goin,' " but you would not normally attempt phonetic spelling to imitate colloquial speech patterns.
- Include the utterances of the interviewer, as well. Later, when editing, if they are the usual encouraging "uh-huh" sounds, you may edit them out while retaining substantive questions and comments.
- Indicate important, relevant, or revealing side sounds, gestures, and characterizations in parentheses, such as (laughter), (pointing to the photograph), or (whispering).
- Use brackets any time you insert your own words in among the interviewee's.
- Use ellipses (three periods) to indicate pauses, trailing off without completion of a sentence, or gaps.
- Use an em dash (—) to indicate someone interrupting himself.
- For most copyediting technicalities, remember that by transcribing oral history interviews, you get to decide stylistic matters in the first place. The "original document" is the tape, not a written version by the author. The logical source for determining capitalization, punctuation, and other style issues is *The Chicago Manual of Style*.
- Proofread the transcript carefully while listening to the tape again. Double and orally proofread (see my upcoming discussion of proofreading in general). Have someone else "audit" (proofread while replaying) the tape for corrections.
- Allow the interviewee to review a transcript and to request changes, as part of a typical release form. In these negotiations, try to avoid transcript revision, and try to have free use of the material for your project.
- When all of these standard oral history practices are complete, determine how you want to edit the transcript, for what purpose, in your documentary editing project.
- When you go to use some or all of a transcribed interview in a documentary editing project, do not permanently alter the final transcript. Keep it

For More Info

For advice on all aspects of oral history interviewing, see chapter five of *Bringing Your Family History to Life Through Social History*. For the classic, see *Transcribing and Editing Oral History* by Willa K. Baum.

Supplies

> ## ELECTRONIC TRANSCRIBERS
>
> To ease the burden of transcribing oral history interviews, get an electronic transcriber. No, it does not do the transcribing for you. It is a desktop-sized tape recorder/player with a foot pedal, earphones, and an adjustable, automatic rewind. The foot pedal enables you to control it while typing. Each time you stop, the machine will rewind enough to help you check your work and pick up where you left off. The stopping you do when transcribing can stretch and break a tape. This machine causes much less wear and tear. You can adjust the speed, tone, and volume. We bought Panasonic transcribers for about two hundred dollars each. Separate machines are available for standard or microcassette tapes, although you should use standard tapes. Remember to break out the protective tabs on the original (to avoid erasure), and copy your tapes for security before transcribing. Use the copy for transcribing.

separate, on both paper and disk. Start with a fresh computer copy of it to edit, summarize, or extract. Think of the final transcript as an original document like the handwritten diary or letter.

There are many ways you might use oral history transcripts with your other documents in your projects. I mentioned earlier the idea of juxtaposing Wendell Sturdevant's transcribed POW diary with the transcript of his oral interview about the same period, but emphasizing different experiences. If you were preparing a collection of family documents about a particular time period, event, or branch of the family, you could include portions of oral history interviews that relate. Note Sharon Carmack's outline of chapters on page 99. An interview formed the basis for at least one chapter in that book.

Idea Generator

Presenting Oral History with Other Documents

- Present a family diary juxtaposed with an oral history transcript from or about the same person or set of events.
- Complete a fragmentary memoir by presenting transcribed oral history that tells the rest of the story.
- Intersperse the recipes of a family collection with excerpted oral history accounts of the foodways—traditions and customs of cooking, serving, and eating—told as stories in family interviews.
- Excerpt oral history explanations as annotation—footnotes or interspersed text—within a collection of letters.
- Interview the surviving author of an account book or someone who recalls the meaning of the entries, and position the explanations opposite a transcription of the entries.
- Use quoted passages from oral history in the epilogues attached to documents to explain whatever became of the document's author or how others viewed the author.
- Juxtapose an early-day family account of a place opposite a later, oral

history account of the same place as it has changed.

- Integrate paragraphs of narrative from a written account with missing portions as told in oral history, keeping clear which is which, to flesh out the narrative.
- Use transcribed oral history as the source for provenance of a document, such as introducing a scrapbook by reproducing the descendant's oral account of how the artifact survived and changed hands in the family.

Many of the minor, stylistic editorial decisions will be the same as any other document. Some points are more sensitive with oral transcripts than with written family documents, because the speaker and those of whom he speaks are more liable to be alive than the authors of our old family diaries and letters. Thus, as you go to publish any parts of an oral history interview, consider several ethical and editorial issues.

ETHICAL, EDITORIAL QUESTIONS

- Do you have full permission to use the interview in this manner?
- Would anything in the interview offend anyone named or described? Is it worth it? Is there a sound way to disguise that person's identity to avoid hurt? Should you censor the passage entirely?
- Should you annotate any names, references, or mysteries in the interview? See chapter eleven.
- Are there places where the interviewee exhibited prejudices, narrated inaccurate versions, or stated opinions as fact, where you need to annotate? Will the annotation offend the interviewee?

IS IT WORTH IT?

Transcribing your family documents for use and for publication is like creating a work of art and craftsmanship. It can be rewarding to put what your ancestors and relatives drafted into a form that a larger world can appreciate. Transcribing is already a gratifying task for a detail person and a history lover, but when you have a family stake in the documents, it can be more exciting. Many methods and discoveries can make it fun. Most of all, you will know your ancestor-authors better than ever from transcribing their writing. **You may think you have read the documents carefully and sensitively, but nothing matches the intricate analysis you automatically do when you transcribe and proofread.** Transcription, at least into a draft, is necessary before you can begin annotating the document with additional information and explanation. That takes research, another supposedly tedious task that might engross you so much that you won't want to quit.

Timesaver

If you have many tapes and little desire or time to transcribe, consider hiring a transcribing service. They are expensive but could be well worth it. Look online or in telephone directories under transcribing or court reporting. Remember that anyone other than the interviewer may introduce errors from ignorance of the subject.

Notes

TEN

How to Edit and Proofread

I mean search it, study it. And, of course, read it aloud. I may be wrong, still it is my conviction that one cannot get out of finely wrought literature all that is in it by reading it mutely.

—Mark Twain, "William Dean Howells," *from* What Is Man? and Other Essays *(New York: Harper and Brothers, 1917)*

\di'fin\ *vb*

Definitions

You will need to make some changes in the text that you transcribe, and you will need to proofread your work. **Emendation is making editorial changes to a documentary text to clarify, correct, or "improve" it, usually for critical, scholarly use, but also for readability, research ease, economical printing, and appearance.** Emendation usually doesn't include the lengthier additions and explanatory notes, or annotations; it involves small, technical matters, such as punctuation, spelling, headings, and matters of copyediting. Emendation is different from copyediting, however, because you're doing it to a transcription of an original, historical document that is otherwise supposed to be authentic to that original. You could not, as a copyeditor, apply your "house style" to the Declaration of Independence, Harriet Beecher Stowe's *Uncle Tom's Cabin*, or U.S. Grant's *Personal Memoirs*. Well, I suppose you could, but you probably should not send it to a scholarly publisher as a documentary edition. When you emend the text of a document, you are doing something that you are really not supposed to do. So, you must do it minimally and consistently, and you must explain yourself.

Documentary editors refer to emendation as either *silent* or *overt*. Silent emendation means changes to the transcribed text that you do not mark as changes. For example, if you decided to start every sentence with a capital letter or spell out every word that the original author abbreviated, you would state that in your introduction. But if you then just did it, without marking each occasion as a change, that's silent emendation. Overt emendation is visible every time. If you used [*sic*] to indicate the author's errors or inserted anything in brackets, that's overt emendation.

OPENINGS, CLOSINGS, AND FORMATS

Most of the written documents we're discussing have heads or openings of some kind. A diary entry will often begin with a date and a "Dear Diary." Heads in letters usually contain salutations, dates, and often addresses or place names for both the writers and recipients. Letters also have closing remarks and signatures. Daybooks usually list expenses under successive dates and follow columnar formats. Memoirs may have chapters or subsections with titles. All of these tend to follow somewhat consistent formats or layouts, or should. That word: should. There's where the documentary editor may emend. The editor might do any of the following, explaining each in an introduction, and varying whether silent or overt where appropriate. The editor would normally model the standard, consistent form on whatever the original author did most often.

- Place all headings and salutations in all pieces of correspondence at the same point on each page. Fill in a missing salutation, date, or place name in brackets when known. Indicate a guess with a question mark or "circa," [28 January ?, ca. 1947].
- Follow the same method for diary entries as shown above.
- Place all closing remarks and signatures of letters in the same position at the bottom of each letter. Fill in missing information in brackets when known.
- Line up entries in daybooks, account books, diaries, and other regular records in the same format from day to day.
- In a memoir, position pre-existing chapter or subsection titles at the same points on pages. A greater editorial liberty would be to invent titles where there were none or divide subsections differently than the author had done, say, to make their lengths more consistent. Such major changes should be overt, in brackets or footnoted.
- Consistently indent paragraphs the same amount of space. A greater liberty would be to create paragraphing where none existed, although this is common. Choose moments in the text where existing paragraphs are too long and topic or themes clearly shift. There create a new paragraph for readability.

OTHER EMENDATIONS

The documentary editor might silently emend some technicalities where the practice is standard, accepted, and helps the reader.

Technique

- Consistently capitalize the first letters of sentences and the first letters of proper names.
- Add terminal punctuation (periods, question marks, etc.) at the obvious but unmarked ends of sentences.
- Spell out abbreviations, or leave them as the author had them. Be consistent.
- Represent contractions with the correct apostrophe rather than spelling out the word formally.
- Convert superscript (such as 17th) and subscript to regular text lines consistently.

- Represent lined-out passages on the edited page: She was a ~~friend~~ stranger.
- It was traditional for seventeenth- and eighteenth-century writers to capitalize every noun or to write letters as though they were erratically capitalizing almost any word. Some editors would retain these capitals and some would not, by silent emendation.
- The "thorn" was an eighteenth-century form of abbreviation. It consisted of a y symbolizing the sound of "th" in Old English. In early American writing, you might see the thorn, looking like a y, followed by superscript letters that represent the rest of the word after "th." Because it is archaic and easily confuses readers, many editors replace it silently.

  ye becomes "the"
  y^t becomes "that"
  y^m becomes "them"
  y^n becomes "then"

- Similarly, the tilde is a symbol we still have on our keyboards (~), but we no longer use it the colonial English way. We use it in Spanish to indicate a nasal sound like "ny," as in cañon. In Old English you might see it over letters as a symbol that the word has been abbreviated and should be extended by doubling those letters. Editors often replace the tilde with whatever letters authors meant it to symbolize. The tilde often looks like a hyphen above the letter rather than the squiggly line.

MARGINALIA

Definitions

Marginalia is a term for the comments people write in the margins and around the edges of a document. Usually, we think of marginalia as appearing in the margins of printed books or rough drafts. If you find marginal comments on the documents you're transcribing, determine a consistent way to transcribe them. If the comment is a continuation of the author's own writing from the body of the documents trailing into the margins, I would write in brackets, between the standard material and where the marginalia begins, that this portion was in the margins. See how I did this in Tom Dickey's letter on page 112. If the marginalia were scattered elsewhere, separate from the body of the text, or written by someone else, I would keep it separate. You could put it at the end of the transcribed document with brackets indicating where you found it and what you know about it. For example: [The following comments appear in the left margin of the letter. Perhaps they are the reactions of the recipient?]

SPELLING

Important

Although editors obviously don't mind adjusting many technicalities in transcriptions, they often balk at correcting spelling. Historically, spelling is a treasured part of the body and character of the times. Inconsistent spelling portrays the flavor of original documents. **As long as meaning is clear, spelling does not need correction.** Many documentary editors feel that correcting all of the spelling in documents would be too intrusive, making a document too pristine or modernized. They also resist correcting spelling because to do so might come from one's compulsion to correct, rather than from anything necessary for presenting historical documents. We "picky" people sometimes like to prove that we can restrain our pickiness. Follow these guidelines when dealing with misspellings:

- If your transcription retains misspellings from the original, consider whether they will confuse the reader. Leave misspellings unmarked if the intended words are still obvious. If a particular misspelling could confuse readers, footnote or bracket an explanation.
- Copyeditors retaining misspellings will insert [*sic*] after the misspelled word to make sure we all know the editor knew it was an error. Documentary editors are less liable to use [*sic*]. If the documentary editor explains that the transcription retains misspellings, and annotates any confusing ones, then [*sic*] would be an interruption in the transcribed text that serves no purpose.
- Another way to annotate a confusing misspelling is to follow the misspelled word with a correct spelling in brackets, such as "promise [premise]." Don't interrupt this way often, though. If you think it's necessary to correct that many misspellings, then you may as well do it throughout the document, with silent emendation.

Warning

Beware of, and please do not be, the well-intended documentary editor who must correct spelling in family documents even when it was intentional misspelling. Kate Dickey Harper, for example, was a good speller. There are hardly any misspellings in her memoir. So one might guess that she misspelled or misspoke intentionally in this passage from her memoir.

> She would put her two little fat hands over her eyes, leaving cracks between her fingers so she could watch how "they" were taking it, and then she would say "I cy now, I cy <u>now</u>," but she never did. I used to think: "Oh, why don't she go ahead and cry and get it over with!"

The well-meaning cousin who transcribed it would correct the "cy," even though it was obviously Kate's way of representing how the little girl sounded. This transcriber converted "why don't" to "why doesn't," as though it was embarrassing to have Kate speak or write with bad grammar. I believe Kate was representing how she would really have thought and spoken when she was a child herself. She never makes that kind of "mistake" again.

Then, again, there was my father's memoir. I know, from his lips, that he wanted his spelling corrected. Correcting the spelling and copyediting the memoir were steps he wanted me to take when he dreamed that some day he would submit his book for publication. Before he had spell-check on his computer, and after he developed senile dementia, his drafts were rough. In his case, I will correct his spelling for him and explain that in the introduction.

SECRET CODES

Many diaries, letters, and other documents contain coding. Translating your ancestors' codes can be one of the more fascinating and gratifying historical exercises in documentary editing. It can unlock their secrets, their patterns of

Important

Internet Source

living, and even how they thought. Sometimes the codes reveal mundane matters, yet still the stuff of social history. Sometimes they teach us what a government thought was important to keep secret or what one adolescent girl thought of as her "state secrets." Codes can reveal depth of affection and depth of fear. **When you've translated codes in a family document, build that explanation into your introduction or annotation.** If the codes you transcribe hid particular messages at scattered points in the transcription, reproduce the encoded material as it appears, then translate or explain it in either brackets or footnotes.

Different editors can mean different things when they refer to codes. Some call it "coding" when the author had a unique system of recording information. Coding or codes, in the case of Martha Ballard's diary, refers to the diarist's own system of dating, abbreviating, writing marginalia, structuring her daily pages, and making notes to herself. Her codes may have been secret in the sense that only she knew or cared how she organized her diary, but they do not intentionally hide private matters. Historian Laurel Thatcher Ulrich painstakingly charted the many patterns of Martha's diary entries to gain a detailed picture of her daily life as a midwife as well as an understanding of her methods as a diarist. You can use Martha as an example of how you might decode your family documents. See <www.dohistory.org/diary/exercises/decoding.html>. Did someone in your family keep a diary, account book, or other record where there are individualized systems like codes? Analyzing these and explaining them to readers can be an interesting part of documentary editing.

Documentary editor Mary-Jo Kline refers to the codes of great diplomatic leaders such as John Jay. In his European treaty negotiations, John Jay would handle some of his activities almost as a kind of espionage. So, his secret codes were truly secret. (See Kline, 118–120.) Most of us would not have so prominent a diplomat in our family history, or at least we would not be editing his papers. We could easily have coded, war-related correspondence, however. Think of World War I or II letters. You may find some that were censored with big, black lines or cutout spaces—sometimes too many to recover or guess the meaning. If you have a soldier's letters that show no sign of censorship, other than perhaps a censor's stamp, consider the possibility that there is well-hidden code no one would notice in them.

My father told me that he devised ways to do this during his overseas service in World War II, although I do not know yet whether any written evidence of this survives. Both his parents and his wife loved things British, so he knew they would be pleased to know he was shipped to Britain and that they would understand British place references. At times, the men were not allowed to state in their letters home where they were stationed or where they were going. So my father was clever. When he arrived in Scotland, he wrote home to his Scottish-Canadian parents what a pleasure it was to follow a marching pipe band down the street and watch the famous kilts swing in rhythm. He would also deliberately choose souvenir gifts to send home with his letters so that my mother would automatically associate them with the correct places. He sent a piece of Nottingham lace and a set of demitasse spoons in Sheffield Silver. These coded messages will figure in his memoir. If you discern such codes in your family documents and artifacts then, like me, you can use them for annotation or family narrative with the documents.

Popular slang language may amount to a kind of coding as well. **Slang dictionaries can help you translate.** A World War I soldier might write that his "number was up." That phrase initially meant he was chosen for service in the first lottery draft, but later it came to mean it was his time to die. He might refer to playing "African golf," which, stereotype though it regrettably was, meant he was "shooting craps." Perhaps he would write about going AWOL, which we understand, but his Civil War ancestor may have written about taking "French leave" instead. If any of your ancestors wrote about the "French disease," that was syphilis. Decoding slang in family documents can be a good lesson in social history and can make great fodder for annotation.

Printed Source

Mary-Jo Kline also notes that telegrams were messages transmitted in Morse code. Remember that meanings could have changed between sender and recipient because of the translations in and out of Morse code. (See Kline, 120–122.) As you read family telegrams, also consider that there is a clipped style to their language that could have had unintended effects. People, even schoolchildren, knew Morse code, too. You may find a sample of Morse code in your family documents. I mentioned earlier purchasing the artifacts of the "Parker" family in an antique store. One of the autograph books has a message from someone in Morse code. If you found this while transcribing the autograph book, you would want to translate the code for your own interest and for your readers if you publish. There are Morse code charts on the Internet. From one message I identified which family member owned this autograph book, because the message is addressed dot/dash-dash/dash-dash/dot-dash [./--/--/.-/]: to Emma. Similarly, you might find family documents where someone used shorthand. You can translate that from the old manual, *Gregg's Shorthand Reading Book*, or you can still find many secretaries who recall how to use it.

Children borrowed military slang as code words, too. If your World War I soldier wrote about "cooties," he meant the all-too-familiar body lice men were experiencing, perhaps for the first time. As 1960s children, we used "cooties" to mean something absolutely repulsive and contaminating about another person, although we did not know that it meant lice. Indeed, we even played with a large, plastic toy insect called a cootie and still did not make the connection. The victims of this term could be the poor, pathetic outcasts of the school (sometimes me). On the other hand, the repulsive, contaminating quality that many children had was simply that they were boys (from a girl's perspective) or that they were girls (from a boy's perspective). My students, either young ones or ones that have small children, assure me that kids still say "Eew. You've got cooties." Thus, another code broken.

PRIVATE AND PERSONAL

As a social historian and a woman, in a discussion of coded documents, I think immediately of the codes women use in their diaries and letters to record and discuss private matters. Perhaps the most common code a woman might have marked in her diary would be for her menstrual cycles. She would keep track

\di'fin\ *vb*

Definitions

INK BLOTTERS

Ink blotters were semisoft cards, usually about four by nine inches, that served multiple purposes. Stores and businesses printed advertising—often made clever and appealing—on them and gave them away. The porous backside served as a blotter. A pen writer would press it across freshly written letters or documents to collect the excess ink so it would not smear. The advertising on these ink blotters reveals subjects of popular interest. See also Figures 12-4 and 12-5.

---

every month, sometimes for a reproductive or health reason, but sometimes just instinctively or habitually. For some reason women feel awkward calling the event what it is, perhaps vestiges of how culturally taboo a subject it has been. If you see regular, monthly markings in a woman's documents, consider this explanation.

Advertisements such as ink blotters or a leftover medicine box's label could serve as illustrations for our projects. On taboo or delicate subjects, they might also carry revealing codes. See the ink blotter advertisement in Figure 10-1 below. In this case, the code is in technical, medical, or pharmaceutical terms that an average person—or perhaps a child—might not grasp. Code seemed necessary and usual when discussing "ergoapiol," a concoction of ergot made from rye and extracts of dill and parsley. It was a well-known abortifacient. Doctors, pharmacists, midwives, and many women knew how to use it for many years. One of Ernest Hemingway's women characters, Helen Gordon in *To Have and Have Not* (1937), said angrily to her husband: "Love is just another dirty lie. Love is ergoapiol pills . . . because you were afraid to have a baby. Love is quinine . . . catheters . . . douches . . . [Love] smells like Lysol." A literary editor of Hemingway's story would need to annotate these referenced methods of birth control, as would a family documentary editor if such coded clues or mysterious references appeared in a diary or letter.

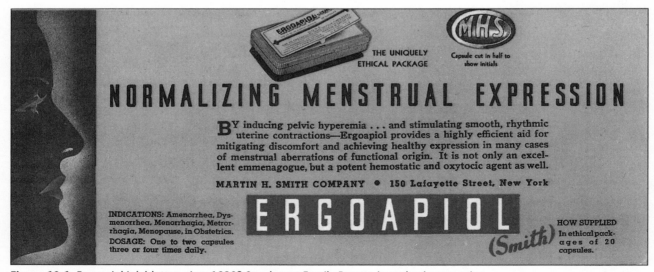

Figure 10-1 Ergoapiol ink blotter, circa 1930? Sturdevant Family Papers, in author's possession.

Women and girls have also used many code words to discuss having a menstrual period. There is a fascinating, award-winning social history Web site called the Museum of Menstruation and Women's Health at <www.mum.org/>. If you find any strange terminology in women's documents that might refer to menstrual cycles, check the twenty-page dictionary of "Words for Menstruation" at this site. Some classic examples that are more historical include the following:

Aunt Flo is visiting	monthly visitor
the Curse	my friend
the gift	on the rag (refers to homemade
having fleas (the euphemism during	sanitary napkins)
Lizzie Borden's day—she said she	the red flag is up
was menstruating when her parents	red-letter day
were murdered)	sick today
monthlies	time of the month

So, if you see these codes in family documents, you'll know what they meant. When we 1970s girls were struck by the "curse," we needed to discuss it, too, in our conversations, notes, and letters. Like so many females before us must have done, we felt the existing code words were inadequate because anyone, or at least any other female, would know what we were saying. We wanted to trust only each other as close friends. So, we invented a code for taboo subjects. The code involved assigning to each subject the name of some aspect of cameras:

I have my camera = period started
I need a camera case = sanitary napkin
Taking pictures = having sex
Developing film = being pregnant

Interestingly, none of us was sexually active or sexually knowledgeable at all, but being teenage girls, we had to have a code word for it anyway. We also used other camera parts and terms in the code, but I cannot recall how, which is probably just as well.

Similarly, we needed to have a code for having a crush on a boy so we could refer to that frequent state without nonfriends being able to translate. It started with our qualified term for a "crush." We thought we were too mature to have a "crush" or be "in love," so our casual, qualified term was to be "slightly infatuated" with a boy. Thus, our code became "S.I." We would say "I'm S.I." or "She's S.I." I'll never forget the hysterical moment when we sat on our Lowell High School side of the gymnasium bleachers opposite our opponents, Saint Ignatius High School, during a basketball game. Each side took turns calling out our school chants. We were stunned to have a packed, diverse mob of people, as aggressively as they could, thunder at us across the gym, "We're S. I.!" I saved boxes of our letters and notes from those days. Perhaps someday someone will edit them for social history purposes and use this book for both advice and as the key to decode our secret words.

Real lovers will use codes for reasons similar to teenage would-be lovers. Some subjects may have seemed so taboo that the pleasure of discussing them had to be coded. Genealogist Sharon Carmack found what she believes to be an example in a set of letters. An engaged couple, after spending a romantic weekend together, was separated by military service. Their letters became increasingly affectionate. She wrote to him: "Well, dearie, don't spend too many evenings with the girls this week. I don't want you to be all tired out when I see you Sat. I'm thinking of you, oh so often and maybe I'm not thinking sweet things. Good-night dear—How's the 'indie' tonight, sweetie?" Sharon and her colleagues compared all of the mentions of this "indie," trying to figure out what it was. No one really knows, but we have guesses. It's a good example of how a couple might develop a code name for something private. Sharon let it stand in her transcription without annotation or speculation.

Not every use of sexual coding is so lighthearted. Historian Edmund Morgan broke the coded language of the great Puritan clergyman Michael Wigglesworth. In *The Diary of Michael Wigglesworth, 1653–1657: The Conscience of a Puritan*, Morgan discovered that the minister's well-known internal struggle with sin was not with just sin in general. He had coded his references to his greatest torment: He was deeply, sexually attracted to his male students, even after his marriage. Comments by other great church leaders of his day make clear that Wigglesworth had to code these references or risk public ruination. The Reverend Cotton Mather read Wigglesworth's personal papers posthumously with stated admiration. Morgan's decoding of Wigglesworth is a good example of how the codes of a diary can make a significant difference to our understanding of our forefathers.

PROOFREADING

Important

Proofreading is vitally important in all writing and publishing but perhaps even more so in documentary editing. When we are claiming the reliability of our transcribed documents, we can hardly have many mistakes show up. Proofreading also carries a different emphasis for documentary editors than for editors in general. In documentary editing, the main proofreading practice is double, oral proofreading. Two people sit together, one holding copies of the original documents and the other holding the transcription. Usually the person holding the original will read aloud, although they might take turns or reverse roles at the end and start over. The person holding the transcription will stop the reader at every point where the two versions diverge, checking whether that divergence is an error or the result of an editorial decision. At each stop, the editor is also rethinking those decisions. Documentary editors call this method verifying the text.

Look back at Mark Twain's admonishment at the beginning of this chapter. Reading aloud is my favorite kind of proofreading for two reasons beyond Twain's wise observation: It catches the most errors, and it can be fun. You're less liable to tire, let your eyes wander, and miss something than if you're reading alone. Two pairs of eyes are better than one. Both people are using different skills in combination than one does when simply reading, causing better attention and memory usage. The fun? Well, every time I have done it or heard of other people doing it, editors have appreciated each other's senses of humor. One can't help but acknowledge funny moments. Some of them are intentionally funny parts of the documents; some are accidental mistakes or the happenstance of two words being close together that sound funny read aloud. Occasional giggling and, when tired and punch-drunk after many hours, even momentary hysteria have been perks of textual verification. Like the great Danish comedian Victor Borge, one has to pronounce even the punctuation when proofreading aloud, creating another odd effect. Try it and you will see. Stating the punctuation is awkward and unfamiliar. Sometimes it, too, becomes a double entendre or pun. Here are just a few of the conventions for oral proofreading:

SYMBOL	ORAL NAME THAT YOU SAY
!	Exclamation point
"	Open quote
"	Close quote
(	Open paren
)	Close paren
.	Period
/	Forward slash

Oral proofreading causes less wear and tear on the eyes, although you may need breaks and beverages (preferably nonalcoholic) for the voice. You could repeat the step at different stages of production with reversed roles or a different individual. **I assure you that each time you proofread you will catch more errors.** If you don't have colleagues to help you do this, a good fallback is to read the original aloud into a tape recorder and then listen while checking the transcript. Remember, you can use your transcribing machine for the playback while proofreading, so you can pause easily.

Reminder

You will also need to do one-person silent proofreading at various stages of the project. It is especially useful when you need to read for one feature at a time in the text—you can't do that orally very well. Proofreading silently can be tedious and difficult. Here are some tips to make it better, from personal experience.

TIPS FOR SOLITARY, VISUAL PROOFREADING

- Proofread after any stage of production that may have introduced new errors.
- Proofread separately for different features of the text that you might otherwise ignore.
- Proofread one round, through the whole text, for the following:
    footnote placement
    consecutive footnote/endnote numbering
    headers, footers, titles, and subtitles and their font patterns
    that page references are correct
    that figure numbers and captions match illustrations
    that index citations match correct pages
    that Table of Contents page numbers match chapter beginnings

Tip

  that there aren't "widows" and "orphans," often defined as a partial line at the top of a page or a single word on a line by itself at the end of a paragraph (widow) and the first line of a paragraph on the last line of a page (orphan)

  that special documentary features are consistent, such as letterheads and signatures, diary entries, and account book columns

  special vocabulary and spelling consistencies

  consistent capitalization and punctuation

  consistent patterns of paragraphing and indentation

  consistent emendation

  consistent annotation wherever needed

  eyeball every occasion of unusual font

  double-check proper names

  double-check any numbers or arithmetic for accuracy

  make sure that promised steps and lists match promises

- When marking copy, especially for experienced editors and publishing houses, use standard proofreaders' marks from *The Chicago Manual of Style* (14th ed., pp. 112–113).
- Use computer-generated methods of proofreading, then follow them up with your own. Spell-checks, grammar-checks, and word searches will not catch all errors, but they might catch some you missed.
- Proofread on a flat surface with a ruler or straightedge under each line as you read it.
- Keep a list of worrisome errors that you find so you can watch for them in future.
- Use plenty of sticky notes to flag the editors' attention.
- Proofread when you are alert. Give yourself breaks. Eat and drink as needed.
- Listen to music or television in the background if that doesn't distract you.
- Take some proofreading along for situations where you may sit at a table for extended periods waiting for something or someone. Proofreading in public places—where no one interrupts you—can keep you attentive.
- Allow time to pass between proofreading efforts on the same material so you approach it with fresh eyes.
- Read other, entirely different literature in between proofreading efforts.

ELEVEN

Annotating Your Documents

The humble editor is thus presented with some problems. How much of this needs to be identified and explained? For whom should it be glossed? How thoroughly should it be annotated? Does one engage in literary interpretation, pointing out how references and allusions fit and function in the stories, or does one give only the facts? Deciding what and for whom and how much to annotate causes some serious head scratching.

—*James L. W. West III, general editor of the Cambridge Edition of the Works of F. Scott Fitzgerald, in "Annotating Mr. Fitzgerald,"* Documentary Editing *22, no. 3 (September 2000): 54.*

A re you doing some serious head scratching? Are there blank spaces within and in between your documents? Do you find gaps of time or events? Are there mysterious references to people, places, events, and attitudes that may have been part of general public knowledge at the time but are lost on you now? Did your ancestors make private, inside remarks that only they could follow? When you put the multiple documents together in the order you want, do they skip periods of time without explanation, or is it clear that some documents are missing and you may never find them? As you read and analyze your ancestors' writings, knowing them as you do or as you will, do you recognize hidden or deeper meanings in their words that ordinary readers might not see? If any or all of these factors occur in your documents—and some of them do occur in most documents—there are ways documentary editors "fix" them that you can imitate. **Annotation is "the information added by editors to improve readers' understanding of historical documents"** (Stevens and Burg, 157).

\di'fin\ *vb*

Definitions

135

IS IT COMMON KNOWLEDGE?

Notes

One litmus test for whether you need to annotate something is whether it is common knowledge. To use this test, though, you need to define common knowledge for your particular book or subject. **If something is outside the realm of American common knowledge, you might want to annotate it.** But, more appropriately, determine your audience and decide whether the item in question is outside the common knowledge of that particular audience. Take, for example, this observation by Clarence E. Carter:

> But if it is deemed desirable to identify persons whose names are mentioned, such identifications should be confined to those of lesser prominence. It would not, for example, be at all seemly to identify George Washington or Robert E. Lee. But it would be pertinent to say who George Smith was if he happened to be important enough to have been, say, the governor of a State.—*Historical Editing*, 34–35.

Carter was right, even though we must acknowledge that not every potential reader in the country would know George Washington or Robert E. Lee. It's shocking, I know, but sometimes college students beginning my classes don't know such things. Sometimes they don't even know what the two opposing sides were in either the Revolutionary War or the Civil War, when the wars occurred, or who won. One way to deal with this ignorance is to recognize that readers might have *heard* of that mentioned person, but they might not know how he related to the annotated point in your document. So, you could annotate the person in reference to how the author of your document mentioned the name.

For example, if the document mentioned Washington or Lee at a particular point in the man's career or in reference to some particular event or topic, your footnote could be about that time, event, or topic. If the document, perhaps a Civil War letter, stated, "I heard that General Lee was in the vicinity," your footnote might explain, from research, "General Robert E. Lee was leading his Confederate forces toward Gettysburg, two hundred miles away, at that moment." You have given important information for following the events, and you have incidentally identified General Lee in case some readers didn't know who he was.

It can be difficult to remind ourselves, as documentary editors, to watch for items needing annotation. If the piece of information has always been familiar to us, we might not even imagine that someone else wouldn't know it. So, before we can even decide whether or how to annotate something that might be beyond common knowledge, we need to spot the candidates. As you read your transcribed documents, look for the following items and evaluate whether each needs any annotation.

WHAT MIGHT NEED ANNOTATION

- proper names of any kind
- names for objects, customs, or beliefs that may be archaic
- newsworthy events (local or national) of the past

- unclear references to actions taken
- personal family information
- slang catch phrases that are no longer in vogue (see World War I–Era Slang below)
- coded items and old code words

We're Not Getting Older, They're Getting Younger

To determine whether a piece of information in a document needs further identification, I often use the "eighteen-year-old-student litmus test." I ask myself "Would my eighteen-year-old students know what that meant?" By and large, my youngest college students average around eighteen to twenty years old, although I have many students in their twenties through forties and my "record ages" have been a fifteen-year-old and an eighty-six-year-old. When I mention something that's dated enough for my eighteen-year-old students to look puzzled or ask questions, I learn the limits of their current cultural literacy. When the reverse happens and they mention something that I don't know, say, a popular music star of theirs, I learn my limits. (I try to look it up on the Web before I confess ignorance.)

The more time passes, the younger my college students seem to become. In the 1960s to 1970s, folks called this the generation gap. I didn't expect to be on the "old" end of it so soon. Add to our age differences the fact that I'm a historian, and there are even more past "things" that I know that are foreign to my eighteen-year-olds. Furthermore, my parents were forty years older than me and their parents were born in the 1880s; my cultural literacy spans more than a century. Meanwhile, my eighteen-year-old students usually know the

Idea Generator

WORLD WAR I–ERA SLANG

World War I personal letters and diaries are often full of slang and popular cultural references. It was one of the first American wars when popular war-related music was in mass production and distribution. Folks usually bought sheet music to "get" a new song, rather than buying recordings. The wartime song lyrics picked up the slang of the war and vice versa. Thus, one World War I sailor wrote:

Dear folks,

Tonight we are thinking, "Where Do We Go from Here?" We were told today that we would surely leave tomorrow . . . Tell those who ask, that I've "gone over" to do my share, and that I'll come and see them when I get back.

—Roland Fowler, 9 September 1918,
quoted with permission from Marcia Mensing

"Where Do We Go From Here" and "Over There" were two popular World War I songs. "Going over," which is part of the refrain in "Over There," was popular terminology for troops entering war service by sailing to Europe.

preceding ten to fifteen years of youthful cultural literacy and a little bit of what their parents have told them. Their parents, by the way, seem to be about thirty-five to forty-five years old, which makes it less likely all the time that their fathers served in Vietnam or their grandfathers in World War II. Indeed, I already have students whose fathers served in the Gulf War.

Thus, the eighteen-year-old's cultural literacy makes a good litmus test. As you run across a word, thing, or concept in your documents that is no longer commonplace, ask yourself: Would an eighteen-year-old know what that meant? Better yet, ask an eighteen-year-old, if you have one handy. This test can help you determine whether you need to find a way to annotate that item in your transcribed document. These Millennials, as analysts are calling people born since 1982, often admire the "greatest generations" of earlier times, however, and care about society. They may well be among the readers of our documentary editing projects.

ANNOTATION GUIDELINES

Annotation can take many forms. Which ones you use in particular situations can vary. Consider which is best, imagining yourself as the reader. Does the reader need to see that piece of information right away? If so, perhaps you should bracket it into the transcription or place a footnote at the bottom of the page. Does the reader only need the piece of information if he is curious to do further research? Then, perhaps you need an endnote or could even place the information in your bibliography. As always, your rules should be fourfold: Stay true to the original documents, be consistent in editorial policy, clearly explain your choices, and offer what best serves the reader.

Notes

Methods of Annotation
- footnotes or endnotes
- bracketed information within the text
- headnotes (introductory paragraphs) above documents
- headings, such as subtitles for documents (in brackets)
- interspersed narrative, distinguished from the original
- changing fonts, types, indention, or italics to distinguish editing from originals
- introduction to the volume
- epilogue at the end
- additional material in charts, tables, and graphs
- illustrations (photographs, maps, and drawings)
- appendixes such as casts of characters, glossaries, and bibliographies
- a list of editorial abbreviations or symbols
- historical/biographical time lines and chronologies
- footnotes that cross-reference each other to avoid repetition ("see also")

Contents of Annotation
- provenance, the documents' history
- nature, condition, and whereabouts of the original documents

- editorial policy and specific changes
- definitions of terms
- identification and explanation of references and abbreviations
- connective tissue between documents
- related historical information to establish context
- biographical information about people mentioned
- later fate of the people involved
- visual images of things described
- resources for further research and related reading

Personal Family Annotation

One significant difference between us annotating our own family documents and the work of professional documentary editors is that we may have personal observations and knowledge to add. Some footnotes excerpted from Marcia Mensing's first editing of her father's World War I letters serve as examples:

[1]He always referred to his camera as a "Kodak."

[1]Using the term "Papa" in the greeting came as a surprise to me; I had always heard my grandfather referred to as "Pop."

[1]This expression of sentiment came as a surprise to me; I realized I never heard him verbalize these words. ["I love you."]

[1]"Ida" had been married to my grandmother's brother, Alfred Carter, a civil engineer in New York City. He was a family favorite and was greatly mourned when he died in 1912.

[1]His complexion was relatively fair and very much inclined to freckles, so it showed the effects of the sun quite easily.

[1]He kept the peacoat for many years, and I remember wearing it when I was about twelve years old.

These insights will occur to you throughout your work with the documents. You will have special firsthand knowledge of behavior, nicknames, feelings, appearances, and the provenance of artifacts. Some of your information is valuable to record, and this may be the only way you get it done. Your contributions may explain some of the mysteries and may enrich the readers' experiences. Avoid interrupting the narrative flow or the professional level of your work with strange switches of tone, tense, and voice. But don't feel restricted from using personal family annotation when it serves useful purposes.

DO NOT OVERDO IT!

If you're very enthusiastic and trying hard to be professional about all of this, then stop every so often and ask yourself if you're doing too much. Is your editing intruding on the text? Should you reduce the annotations, shorten them, or move them to less obtrusive places? Has your ego gotten the better of you? Did you place that annotation in that particular spot because the reader needs it to follow the author's flow, or did you put it there to show off your own knowledge or excitement? **Mary-Jo Kline calls overannotation the editor's "neme-**

Quotes

ONE METHOD OF ANNOTATION

Example of Documentary Editing by Integrated Text and Footnotes

From Sherry L. Smith, *Sagebrush Soldier: Private William Earl Smith's View of the Sioux War of 1876*. Norman: University of Oklahoma Press, 1989, 78–79.

> Almost within a handshake of his people, the heroic Cheyenne and his sturdy pony, freighted with so precious a burden, bore testimony to the precision of our marksmen, and fell pierced with many wounds. They had been comrades in battle and in campaign; and in death they were not divided. "Greater love than this hath no man that he lay down his life for his friend."[12]

A small, grassy plateau separated soldiers from Cheyennes. When Private Smith awoke from his nap, he too raced his horse across this flat:

> I don't [k]now how long I lay there but when I woke wright on my right side lay a fellow on his back ded with his mouth open. You bet I started to git away from hear. But found I could hardley move. . . .

[Sturdevant note: The first quote is from Lieutenant Bourke, as the editor indicated at its beginning, and the second is from Smith. The scene-setting sentence is the editor, Sherry Smith.]

[12]Ibid., 33–34. See also Wheeler, *The Frontier Trail*, 174. Cheyenne sources do not include testimony about this event. . . .

---

sis" and "disease" (219). Avoiding it may be the best reason to show your documentary editing project to selected friends and colleagues, alerting them to your concerns. Each of your efforts is so precious to you that you might need someone more objective to say, "You really don't need half of these footnotes. . . ."

KEEPING TRACK

As you read and transcribe your documents, keep track all along of what you may wish to annotate and why. Mark where it is located in the document, and also note what made it seem worthy of annotation. Keeping track of annotations planned and annotations made will help prevent oversights, redundancies, and the "disease" of overannotation.

COLUMNAR ANNOTATION

You might have a family document that you wish to transcribe into a format that represents how the original looks, even though that is an odd format for traditional annotation. Then, if you follow standards consistently, the annotation can adapt to suit the document. One could annotate an account book in a columnar format. Look at pages 142 and 143 for some entries that John Harper wrote, with some

EXAMPLE OF ANNOTATION BY FOOTNOTES

From Caleb Coker, ed., *The News From Brownsville: Helen Chapman's Letters From the Texas Military Frontier, 1848–1852.* Austin: Texas State Historical Association, 1992, 73, 129.

[Sturdevant note: These are two separate excerpts with one footnote each from different parts of the same book.]

> Tell all my friends that I have seen the elephant, not in his improved condition after traversing two or three thousand miles of civilization but fresh from the camp.[28]

---

[28] "To have seen the Elephant" was a common expression of the times, meaning to undergo a disappointment of high expectations. See Robert W. Johannsen, *To the Halls of the Montezumas: The Mexican War in the American Imagination* (New York: Oxford University Press, 1985), 87–90.

> We ride every evening at five o'clock, until dark either on horseback or in a carriage. This is my life for the last three months; no reading, no writing, none but common and daily cares. I take no medicine and none seems necessary. I use an injection pipe.[2]

---

[2] An injection pipe was a device used for enemas.

annotations from me. Note that, at this point, the annotations are more personal family notes and analysis of what I see rather than additional research.

ALBUMS: EDITED SCRAPBOOK CLIPPINGS

Scrapbooks hold some of the documents that we use for family history information. Some of these documents can almost become a family history narrative by themselves, especially with annotation. Remember the "Parker" family whose memorabilia I purchased in the antique store? I am providing a case study, an effort to string together a documentary narrative using edited and annotated obituaries found in one Parker family scrapbook. These are exact transcriptions except for changing some of the names (and most recent information) for anonymity, adding some punctuation for clarity, and bracketing some minor, helpful annotations. In the interest of saving space, I've stopped the paragraphs short (with ellipses), eliminating some flowery verbiage, lists of visitors, and burial information. Such information, however, would be valuable in genealogical research.

This can be an energizing exercise in family history deduction. Read one document after the other (starting on page 144), and see how the whole family line comes into view. Also, try to deduce how this family's memorabilia came to a Colorado Springs antiques store. Imagine this is your family. What common historical threads might you annotate with footnotes or added text?

EXAMPLE OF COLUMNAR ANNOTATION

Year and Entries		Editor's Annotations
		By K. Sturdevant, from personal knowledge, 2001.

1922
Income, Work in O.D. mine 354.55

Thus he was still working for mines, this case Old Dominion in Globe, AZ.

1923
Works of Ian McLaren [a list follows]

As a Scotsman, he liked these homey stories by a Scots author. The editions were small and prettily leather bound. I received from his granddaughter Kathleen Puckett some of these books and a collection of Robert Burns's poems. I have similar books from my father's Scottish family, too.

1926
Donations

Presbyterian Church Globe	15.00	John Harper was Presbyterian
Salvation Army	5.00	at first. These entries appeared
Moody Bible Institute	12.00	at a time when these amounts
Williamsburg Jewish Missions	5.00	would have been a challenge
Stonybrook Boys School	5.00	to donate. His recorded dona-
American Bible Society	5.00	tions stopped after 1931.
New York Bible Society	5.00	Through work and mine stock
First Christian Church	10.00	he seemed to do fine. Note he
Law Enforcement League	12.00	thought that someone should convert the Jews!

1927
Donations

Williamsburg Jewish Missions	5.00	At some point John became
Stonybrook Boys School	10.00	fundamentalist Baptist. Could
American Bible Society	5.00	this have been the year and
E.J. Bulgin Evangelistic Party	25.00	the reason? Research is neces-
First Baptist Church	30.00	sary on this "party."
Moody Bible Institute	12.00	
Salvation Army	5.00	
New York Bible Society	5.00	

Continued

1928

Donations

Williamsburg Jewish Missions	10.00	This year was the high point
American Bible Society	10.00	of listed donations. Note that
New York Bible Society	5.00	he was funding missions to
Scripture Gift Mission	5.00	Russia.
Christian Fundamentals	10.00	
Stonybrook Boys School	10.00	
Moody Bible Institute	12.00	
Denver Bible Institute	5.00	
Russia Evangelization Society	5.00	
1st Baptist Church Globe	39.00	

1934

I owe Archie on eye operation $100.00.

Taxes advanced on house in Saskatoon 53.38

Amounts received from work under the F.E.R.A.

May	7.50
June	14.00
July	14.00
Aug	12.00
Sept	12.00
Oct	12.00
Nov	12.00

Archie was his son, my grandfather, in California. Who helped whom? He still owned a house in Canada about fifteen years after Archie left! He took New Deal employment when his other income dried up. He was also older and sicker.

ANALYZING FOR ANNOTATION

When you transcribe documents, one of the first steps toward annotating them is to examine what is present in them. What is obvious? What do you learn from them? So, for example, what can we learn from the set of seven scrapbook obituaries? First, these seven obituaries in chronological order make plain a direct lineage. Even though the descendants sold the scrapbook in the antique store, thinking it was part of "remote" family memorabilia, my students and I could have drawn some genealogical charts for them from just these obituaries. The scrapbook contents trace the Parkers back to their Irish immigrant ancestors, thus achieving the dream of many genealogists: to cross the ocean with their research. Realizing that all newspaper information needs genealogical verification in other sources, the basic line is clear. See the chart on page 149.

What social history lessons or clues could we learn from these obituaries that might lead to research and annotation?

Notes

CASE STUDY # 1

OBITUARY

Edward Parker was born in Ireland in August, 1800, and died at the home of his son, Matthew Parker, May 28th, 1893. He was married to Sarah David-son in 1825. To them were born nine children. Two of them died in infancy, all the rest live to mourn their father's death.

In 1832 Mr. Parker and family came to live in America, landing at Montreal, Canada, where they lived about one year. He then moved to Niagara County, N.Y. and settled on a farm where he lived for 40 years. His children having grown up and settled in the west, he and his wife concluded to spend their declining years near them. So in 1873 they came west and settled in Leland [Illinois]. His wife died in 1885. Since that time he has made his home among his children.

Mr. Parker, being persuaded of the truths of Christianity . . . died with a well grounded hope of heaven. His funeral sermon was preached at the home of Matthew Parker. . . .

Card of Thanks
We and our families wish to express our sincere thanks to all our friends who so kindly lent us their aid and sympathy during our late bereavement.

Matthew Parker.	Geo. Parker.
Ed. Parker.	Richard Parker.

CASE STUDY # 2

DEATH CALLS ANOTHER OLD RESIDENT
*Matthew Parker, who came to Victor Township
in 1856, Passes Away Tuesday Morning*

Matthew Parker was born in County Armagh, Ireland, Feb. 25, 1827, and died April 16, 1912, at the age of 85 years, 1 month, and 21 days. In 1832 when five years of age he came with his parents, Edward and Sarah (Davidson) Parker, to Montreal, Canada, reaching that city at a time when the cholera was raging. After a residence of one year in the Dominion [of Canada], they moved to Niagara county, New York.

In the fall of 1856 the deceased came to Illinois settling in Victor township, DeKalb county, where he purchased a farm and spent the greater part of his life. May 13, 1860 he was united in marriage to Eliza Parker and had he lived a few weeks longer would have celebrated their 52nd wedding anniversary.

Of the four children born to Mr. and Mrs. Parker three survive, [M]ettie and Lizzie of Sandwich and Mrs. Charles Bonney of Remington, Ind., and one grandchild, who with the wife are left to mourn the loss of a kind father and a loving husband.

Of a family consisting of six brothers and one sister, two brothers and the sister survive, John, of Ransomville, New York, George, of Sandwich, and Mrs. C.T. Archer, of Spencer, Iowa.

Mr. Parker, along with his family, united with the Congregational Church, of Sandwich in 1901, and he was a regular attendant as long as his health would permit.

He became a member of Leland [Masonic] Lodge, A.F. & A.M., Aug. 19, 1868, and after moving transferred his membership to Meteor Lodge . . .

CASE STUDY # 3

A GOOD WOMAN CALLED

Eliza Parker was born in County Armagh, Ireland, September 3, 1826, and died July 26, 1915, aged 88 years, 10 months, and 23 days.

She came to America with her parents in 1846 and settled in Niagara county, New York.

She was married to Matthew Parker on May 13, 1860, and came to Illinois the same year, settling on the farm north of Leland, where they lived for forty years, moving to Sandwich in 1901. She was the mother of four daughters, one of whom preceded her to the better world in infancy.

Her husband preceded her in death April 16, 1912.

She leaves to mourn their loss three daughters, Metta and Lizzie of Sandwich and Mrs. C. A. Bonney of Remington, Ind., and one granddaughter, all of whom were with her during her last sickness. She also leaves one brother and one sister and a host of other relatives and friends.

While of a retiring disposition, her thoughts and influence were always for the right, and it can truly be said she was a thoughtful loving mother and a good Christian woman. She joined the M[ethodist] E[piscopal] church when she was a girl and remained a member of that church until moving to Sandwich when she with her family united with the Congregational church. . . .

CASE STUDY # 4

FUNERAL RITES HELD FOR MISS METTA PARKER
She Had Made Her Home Here For Thirty-Nine Years

Metta Parker, second daughter of the late Matthew and Eliza Parker, was born in Victor township, September 23, 1864, and passed away at the Woodward memorial hospital on July 10, 1940.

Her early life was spent at the farm in Victor and in Leland, receiving her education in the rural school and in the Leland public school. She received piano instruction from local teachers and later studied in Aurora and at Northwestern University in Evanston. As a result of this training she took her place in the musical activities of the community both as a teacher and as a performer.

In 1901, with her parents, she moved to Sandwich where she has since lived. She took an active part in Lotus chapter Eastern Star, for many years serving as treasurer. With her family she transferred her membership to the local Congregational church.

Though of a retiring disposition, she was loved and respected by all who knew her. She leaves to mourn her loss, two sisters, Lizzie with whom she lived, Mrs. Charles Bonney of Remington, Indiana; one niece Mrs. Gerald Bunyan of Colorado Springs, Colorado, and many cousins and friends.

The funeral . . .

CASE STUDY # 5

CHARLES BONNEY DIES FOLLOWING BRIEF ILLNESS
Funeral Services Were Held on Wednesday With Burial at Leland

[handwritten on clipping:] Mar. 8-1942

Charles Bonney, 74, a resident of this community for the past year and a half died at 9:30 o'clock Sunday evening at the home of his sister-in-law, Miss Lizzie Parker.

He was born near Cass, Illinois, on September 4, 1867, and when a lad accompanied his parents to Remington, Indiana, where he had made his home until coming to Sandwich. In October, 1908, he was united in marriage to Miss Emma Parker. One daughter, Elizabeth, was born to them.

He engaged in the grain business at Remington and was active in the affairs of the community, serving as township commissioner and as member of the school board. He was a member of the Masonic Lodge.

Mr. Bonney was taken ill two weeks ago with a heart attack following a stroke of paralysis.

He is survived by his widow, one daughter, Mrs. Gerald Bunyan of Colorado Springs, Colorado, and one sister, Caroline Bonney of Remington, Indiana.

Funeral services . . .

CASE STUDY # 6

Thursday, April 19, 1950 [handwritten correction to the 18th]
COMMUNITY SHOCKED BY SUDDEN DEATH OF MISS LIZZIE PARKER

Suffered Stroke on Friday Evening; Dies During the Night
CHARTER MEMBER LELAND O.E.S.

The community was shocked Saturday morning to learn of the passing of Lizzie Parker. Her death came suddenly as the result of a stroke suffered the night before.

Lizzie Parker, daughter of Mr. and Mrs. Matthew Parker, was born on a farm in Victor township, March 25, 1867, and died at the hospital, April 8, 1950, having been preceded in death by her parents and two sisters.

Lizzie received her early education in the Parker school, graduating from Leland high school in 1889. The next ten years were spent teaching in rural schools and the Leland and Rollo public schools. In 1900 the family moved to Sandwich.

Miss Parker was a charter member of the Leland Chapter of Eastern Star. Last October Lotus Chapter honored her at their golden anniversary celebration as a Past Matron and with a fifty year membership certificate. She enjoyed an active part in the work and fellowship of the Congregational church.

A life of service and devotion is a testimonial to her understanding of the Christian principles of faith, love, purity, justice and truth. Because of a personality which endeared her to all, she will be greatly missed by friends and neighbors and especially her sister, Mrs. Charles Bonney with whom she made her home and her niece's family, Mr. and Mrs. Gerald Bunyan, [and their daughters] Elizabeth and Ellen.

CASE STUDY # 7

[From the Colorado Springs, Colorado, Gazette-Telegraph, 1994, clipped by one of the my students and mailed to me, after a class project studying the scrapbook obituaries]

ELIZABETH BONNEY BUNYAN, 84, a Colorado Springs homemaker, died . . . at a local nursing home.

A memorial service will be held. . . .

Mrs. Bunyan was born . . . 1909 in Remington, Ind., to Charles and Emma (Parker) Bonney. She was married . . . 1938, in Colorado Springs to Gerald Bunyan who is deceased.

She is survived by two daughters, Elizabeth and Ellen, [both married], and four grandchildren.

Mrs. Bunyan received a master's degree in music from Northwestern University. She was [an active volunteer in community organizations dedicated to women's education, hospitals, and her church.] She had lived in Colorado Springs since 1938. . . .

- Multiple families of Irish immigrants came through Canada in the 1830s and settled in western New York.
- The same families moved west to Illinois to continue farming.
- Their patterns were to form small rural towns that grew into larger towns.
- They educated their children first in rural schools, perhaps on their own land (the Parker school), and then in town public schools and high schools.
- They were active in the Masonic Lodge and the Eastern Star.
- Child mortality was a sad fact of their lives. They remembered their lost children.
- Although Irish immigrants were often Catholics, these immigrants joined Methodist Episcopal and Congregational churches.
- Some daughters remained spinsters, although women's education was important. Even if they had "retiring dispositions," these women were teachers with music degrees from Northwestern University. They performed programs for the community.
- The style of obituaries changed.
- Individuals in the 1800s lived through illness and death at home. By the mid-1900s, we see the first hospitals and by 1994, a nursing home.

Many other documentary sources were included with the Parker family papers that I purchased. I mentioned them before generically, but now I will identify them more specifically for you.

A Classic Small Collection of Family Papers

Photographs of Metta, Lizzie, and Emma at different ages and activities. One example is Figure 11-1 on page 150.

Photographs that apparently include the little girl who died.

Photographs identified as various Parker uncles, aunts, and cousins.

Photographs that include tintypes, cabinet cards, and cartes de visite—the dealers removed these from their original velvet albums. I didn't buy the now-empty albums because of expense.

The scrapbook, which began as Metta's but became Emma's, containing:

relatives' obituaries transcribed here and many others from the 1880s–1940s.

family history clippings about weddings, reunions, club and school events.

scrap and advertising ephemera.

clippings about local Illinois pioneers.

school and public recital programs listing Parkers.

A collection of autograph albums belonging to Parkers with many family signatures:

Metta's album, 1882–1907

Lizzie's album, presented to her by her father Matthew in 1888

Emma's first album, presented to her by her father Matthew in circa 1880

Emma's second album, presented to her by her father Matthew in 1888

Charles Bonney's album, 1880s–1890s

An account book/recipe book from 1849 belonging to Matthew Parker.

Miscellaneous ephemera such as health and children's books, calling cards, recipes.

An antique brass school bell with a black wooden handle.

An old trunk that had held the collection (I couldn't afford it).

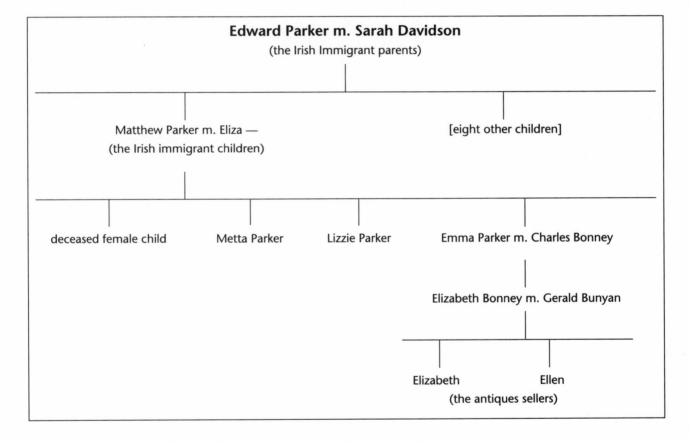

These family artifacts can enrich the stories that the obituaries tell. If they were yours, what could you, or should you, do with the scrapbook obituaries to make them a more complete family history? You could research history books and articles and develop social history material for annotation on the observations I just listed.

- The patterns of Irish immigrants coming through Canada in the 1830s— where there was easier immigration in order to attract lumbermen—and settling in western New York, where there was farming.
- The patterns of families moving west to Illinois to continue farming.
- The founding and development of small rural towns that grew into larger towns.
- Pioneer education practices, first in rural schools and then in town public schools.

Figure 11-1 The "Parker" sisters with cousins and friends. This cabinet card photograph illustrates the social lives of these young ladies who kept autograph books and scrapbooks. Metta is on the far lower right, Lizzie is on the far lower left, and Emma is the tall one in the upper center. "Parker" Family Papers, in author's possession.

- The experience of rural school teaching for young Midwestern women.
- The social importance of the Masonic Lodge and the Eastern Star in the Midwest.
- The strong background connection between being an Orangeman in County Armagh, circa 1790s–1820s, and being a Mason.
- The impacts of diseases, death, and mourning, especially for children.
- The religious issues, being (1) that Northern Irish were Protestants, but (2) it would have been the New York frontier of the Second Great Awakening period that introduced them to Methodist Episcopal and Congregational churches.
- Women's history, as it reveals more about spinsterhood, women's education, and attitude about women, all well documented for the Parkers' period.
- The changing attitudes toward care of the elderly, illness, and death.

Think, too, what a rich picture of community life you would gain by analyzing all of the Parker papers. Obviously missing are letters. I believe they existed when the items I bought landed in the antique store, but the consignors and store owners probably thought that the other collection items were more marketable. Perhaps the letters still exist in the family. Further, still, a Parker family historian would do well to research local history through the historical societies. Obviously, the Parker family's history is tied to Leland, Sandwich, and other towns. We can do so much with a collection of family documents.

TWELVE

Illustrating Your Documents

A picture is worth a thousand words.

—*hackneyed but irreplaceable Chinese proverb*

I llustrating your transcribed document(s) with pictures of the people, places, artifacts, events, and the documents themselves can enliven the text, explain the otherwise inexplicable, preserve the historical record, and make your book or article more marketable. Our visual society demands them in order to learn. Good illustrations can include photographs, sketches, maps, and photographic copies of paintings, artifacts, and the original documents. A carefully chosen and reproduced illustration truly may be worth a thousand of the words in your documents.

Serious, scholarly documentary editors strive to include only those illustrations essential and directly relevant to the text, or none at all. Few illustrations, if any, appear in classic documentary volumes. The main way scholarly editors feel forced to use illustrations is when the authors of original documents drew in the margins or when documents included graphics such as scientific experiments. Even when a whole collection is full of original pictures created by the documents' author, documentary editors have been reluctant to re-create them. We need a happy medium: conservative use of the most appropriate illustrations.

WHEN TO ILLUSTRATE

Ask yourself some questions to determine whether you need an illustration and to eliminate those you do not need.

- Could you best explain a term, example, or description within the text by means of an illustration?
- Is there a technical portion of the text that cries out for an illustration, such as discussion of a migration route that needs a map?

Technique

> ### ILLUSTRATION PLACEMENT AND PAPER QUALITY
>
> If you are planning illustrations for a family documentary book, consider the best placement and paper quality. You might want to scatter the illustrations where they best fit with the test, as we have done. Or you might use separate pages of coated paper (usually offered in multiples of sixteen). Coated stock requires separation from the text but improves quality.

- Is there a good portrait of the document or collection author(s)?
- If you have many photographs to choose from, do you have any that show people in the precise situations, doing the precise tasks, or wearing the precise clothing that the documents describe?
- Within the text, are there other interesting, even famous, people of whom you might obtain photographs?
- If you don't have a portrait of an important character in the documents—especially the author(s) of them—can you represent that person with alternative pictures, such as of the person's tombstone, heirlooms, etc.?
- Are there locations, buildings, interiors, landscapes, or other scenes in the text of your documents for which you can obtain photographs that give readers a sense of these places?
- So that readers may see the document(s) in their original form, can you provide a photograph of the outward appearance, such as the cover of the diary?
- Can you photograph or photocopy a portion of the original text that you've transcribed so readers can see the character of handwriting, old typing, or printing?
- Is there an important, mysterious point in the text, such as illegible handwriting, where you could reproduce the original so readers could join you in attempts to decipher it?
- Does the text mention an artifact or object that is worthy of illustration, either because readers might not be familiar with how it looks or because the artifact survives as a family heirloom worthy of documentation?
- If this is a substantial family history documentary collection, is there a reason to incorporate multigenerational photographs?
- Are there rare or remarkable photographs, relevant enough to the documents, that you should publish because otherwise they may become lost to society?

Important

THE MANDATED PHOTOGRAPH

Sometimes your documents will mandate for you particular photographs that are "musts" to illustrate the text. I will call these "mandated photographs," because the ancestor-authors of your documents are mandating that you use these, even if you use no others. If you have them, use them; if you don't, find them. If you can't use them, address why and see what you might substitute. For example, in Tom

Figure 12-1 Otho D. Dickey, circa 1867. This may have been the photograph he sent to brother Thomas Clemens Dickey, which made him look so different compared to before the war. Dickey Family Papers, in author's possession.

Dickey's letter on page 112, he stated, "We received your picture but could hardly recognize the boy of seventeen. Still the expression of the face looks familiar. When we see the original we can tell better." Figure 12-1 above is the photograph of Otho Dickey believed to be the one in question, or the closest that survives. By this time he would have been about twenty-three years old, and he does, indeed, look older. At the very least, this is a picture of Otho between the time of his military service and his transition to married father. It represents the man of that period. In a documentary edition of Tom's letters, the picture must appear next to Tom's comment. Tom mandated that for me.

Even when the author of a document doesn't specifically call for a particular photograph, the document may mandate one. For example, James Scott's story "My First Love" (page 117), about SulaMae, the greenish yellow Ford, calls out for a picture of the car, preferably with Scott proudly posing beside it. If I didn't have one, I could also seek a comparable vehicle from a photographic book about vintage cars. Such an illustration would have the advantage of being in glorious color. I can testify, however, that SulaMae's color stood out even in black-and-white snapshots. So far I have found only partial images of it and am still rummaging for a better shot.

PORTRAITS AND PEOPLE

When you need to illustrate a person, consider the direct function the photograph might serve. Readers will want to know what the ancestor-author(s) of the documents looked like. Even if your publisher won't allow internal photographs, you should place your diarist or letter writers on the cover. We want to read their faces and look into their eyes. Beyond portraits, consider photographs of the characters in your documents, including the authors, taken at ages, places, and activities relevant to the documents' subject matter. Have you ever seen obituaries for older people with childhood pictures beside them? One wonders why they bothered to print the picture; newspaper readers who would recall the deceased senior citizen wouldn't recognize the person at four or ten years old. Childhood pictures of people belong at points where the documents include their childhoods.

Idea Generator

If possible, also include portraits that show maturing and aging of your ancestor-authors over time. Especially if the documents cross a person's life span, it is appropriate to show readers what your ancestors looked like at different stages. If you can, include photographs of relevant family members that show resemblances from one person to the next. This can be intriguing for the reader. If you have many photographs, though, be selective and choose good reproducible images. Avoid overkill with illustrations, as with annotation.

Do your documents refer familiarly or frequently to a famous person? If so, that individual might be another logical portrait to include, especially if some readers wouldn't automatically recognize the famous person by name only. James Scott's memoir presents such a case. His best friend in high school, about whom he wrote much in his memoir, was John Dehner Forkum, called "Dehner." Under the name John Dehner, he became a familiar and respected character actor on radio, on television, and in films. We visited him when I was eight on our one trip to Hollywood. He introduced me to "Shirley Temples" (a non-alcoholic children's drink) and to his horses, which he rode in programs such as *Gunsmoke*, *Bonanza*, *Maverick*, and *The Wild Wild West*. Imagine how impressed I was! I would illustrate his portion of my father's memoir with a recognizable picture of him.

My mother had a famous acquaintance that would also call for a photograph if I were editing her documents. Raymond Burr (*Perry Mason* and *Ironside*) grew up in her hometown and attended her church, where his mother played the organ. She shared family stories about Raymond, especially as she remembered him in his boyhood. He stands tall and large at the back of my mother's school picture. Because we have that class photograph, I might investigate obtaining a later-in-life one of his familiar stature to juxtapose with it. However, before publishing photographs of other people, especially famous personages, make sure you have permission from them or their estates, since their images may still be commodities.

FURTHER ANNOTATION AND ILLUSTRATION

Consider the case study on page 155 for other documentary editing concerns, too. What might I annotate or explain somewhere with these documents? Obviously, I would need a source on the Boer War to explain several references. The war itself spanned about the same time period as the Spanish-American War and Philippine Insurrection, 1898 to 1902, in which Kate's brothers were volun-

MUST-INCLUDE PHOTOGRAPHS

Kate Dickey Harper wrote an opportunity for a mandated photograph in her memoir. She had already described growing up with Paul Rouse, son of her parents' friends.

> . . . about the time the Boer War broke out in Africa, Paul visited us for 24 or 36 hours. He was on his way to Africa to report the Boer War . . . Paul was handsome as a picture and sweet as any boy that ever lived . . . He gave me, on that visit, the brooch which I am wearing in the picture Pop calls "his girl." It was simple, but sweet, and I loved it. I wept many tears when I lost it at a movie in Saskatoon.

Placed with Kate's memoir was a news clipping from the *Kansas City Journal* dated 15 November 1899. The clipping related the story of a news photographer, Paul Rouse, who had just left for the Boer War in South Africa with a war correspondent named Knight. Passing through Boulder, Colorado, by train, Rouse had stopped, the clipping related, to visit "the prettiest little brown-haired girl." Knight told the story of how Rouse sent successive messages explaining delays, so instead of reuniting in Denver, the two men met in Kansas City several days later. The article concluded:

> . . . if any British dum-dum bullets reach the region of Rouse's heart while he is in the Boer camp taking snapshots of Oom Paul, they will rebound from force of contact with the gold locket which contains the picture of a pretty mountain maid.

So, we have a fine romantic, historical account from two sources to edit together. Since it's Kate's memoir that I'm editing, I would especially want the photograph that her husband ("Pop") called "my girl." It is the mandated photograph in Figure 12-2 on page 156. It's important because she describes it, it illustrates the lost brooch that figures in the story, and most important, it shows readers Kate as she was when she attracted both of the young men in her memoir. I am fortunate in that Kate's daughter showed me which photograph it was. Were I rummaging through Kate's family photographs, though, I could also have picked it out easily. It's the only formal portrait of her at the right age, prominently displaying the brooch, or any brooch.

teers. Dumdum bullets had soft or hollow noses so that they expanded when they hit their targets. Dumdums were considered unnecessarily cruel and even banned in some parts of Britain in 1899. Oom Paul was the popular name of Paul Kruger, the Dutch Transvaal statesman who resisted British conquest of South Africa.

Unless it was apparent earlier in the documents, I would need to identify "Pop," Saskatoon, who "we" was in Boulder, and so forth. Because Paul Rouse was an important and interesting character in the memoir, and Kate describes him as "handsome as a picture," I would attempt to include more about him

Figure 12-2 Kate Dickey, circa 1898. This is the picture that her husband would later call "my girl" and that shows the brooch from Paul Rouse. It would be a mandated photograph for that part of her memoirs. Dickey Family Papers, in author's possession.

and an appropriate picture of him. Kate wrote that he fell out of touch and seemed to disappear. Researching him will be a challenge.

Is there anything else crying out for illustration in these passages? Well, one could show pictures of the Boer War, but they would be peripheral to the memoir. If, on the other hand, they were photographs identified as Paul Rouse's handiwork, there might be a stronger point to including them. One could show "Pop," Boulder, Saskatoon, Kate as a "little brown-haired girl," or the gold locket Kate supposedly gave Paul. The gold locket, if there was one, is lost to Kate's family. It might have been poetic license on the newspaper's part. It wouldn't have held the same picture of Kate as "my girl," because that was obviously taken in a studio after Paul gave her the brooch.

The other illustration I would seek for these passages would be a picture of Paul. Any reader would want to see this young man who was "handsome as a picture." Unfortunately, the only identified photograph of Paul Rouse in Kate's family collection was a cartes de visite taken when he was still in knickers, perhaps age six. The childhood picture would be appropriate to illustrate earlier memoir sections about growing up with Paul, but it would seem silly placed here.

Idea Generator

CREATIVE ILLUSTRATIONS

Consider illustrating your documents with pictures beyond the obvious portraits. What needs an illustration?

Figure 12-3 Gibson's Camp near Globe, Arizona, circa 1906, from a cyanotype. "A picture is worth a thousand words" to illustrate what Kate Dickey thought was a godforsaken place. Harper Family Papers, in author's possession.

Places

In a complete edition of *The Diary of Anne Frank*, for example, we would benefit from exterior and interior pictures of the secret annex in Amsterdam where the Franks' friends hid them from the Nazis. See <www.angelfire.com/journal2/afdiary/annexe.htm> for both a photograph and floor plans, adapted from page 213 of *The Critical Edition*. Even with less dramatic narrative to illustrate, you can probably obtain photographs or drawings of interiors or exteriors as illustrations. Oral history interviews are great opportunities to enlist relatives in drawing floor plans of, say, Great-Grandma's house or the layout of the farm.

Does the ancestor-author describe a place or events that occurred in a unique place? Kate Dickey Harper wrote of their first home in Arizona, circa 1906, "Gibson's Camp was not so nice when I got there." Without describing how it looked, she told stories about the rustic sleeping and cooking conditions, the spiders and snakes, the heat, and the beautiful sunsets. Figure 12-3 above is an enlarged picture of Gibson's Camp from a cyanotype (blue-toned photograph) probably taken by Archie Harper or his brother. Sometimes a picture really is worth a thousand words. See also Figures 13-2 and 13-3 on page 167.

Events and Situations

On page 5, I gave the Sneden Collection as an example of a documentary editing project. Sneden was an artist, and the point of the collection is partly his excellent representations of Civil War scenes. Obviously, the exhibit or volume based on Sneden's art and papers features, and is sometimes dominated by, the illustrations. See <www.sneden.com/about.discovering.html>. If your ancestor-author created artistic renderings that match content in the documents, these would be wonderful illustrations.

My father tried to be an artist, with less success than Sneden. Nevertheless, he left several paintings of his favorite San Francisco scenes. He would be

Figure 12-4 Ink blotter commemorating the 1927 cross-Atlantic flight of Charles Lindbergh. Sturdevant Family Papers, with permission of Rick W. and Wendell F. Sturdevant, in author's possession.

pleased to know that I want to use one or more of these paintings for cover or internal illustrations in his memoir. He also was a good scenic photographer, thus providing more possible illustrations. It was common for people to snap pictures of him at work, too, and he kept wartime photographs from most places he was stationed. Check your home and family sources for these kinds of illustrations.

Perhaps a famous event or national trend was meaningful to your relatives. In some cases, folks kept or even later collected memorabilia from that event that you could use for illustrations. For example, many people admired Charles Lindbergh for his Atlantic solo flight in 1927. "Lucky Lindy" was the childhood hero of many boys and inspired some to become pilots. Figure 12-4 above is another ink blotter, illustrating the popular interest in anything about Lindy. The smaller ink blotter in Figure 12-5 on page 159 is revealing about wartime concerns in Waverly, Iowa, of the 1940s, and thus an amusing illustration for family history documents from that period.

As you conduct research through historical societies and archives, you may find more ideal illustrations of events, places, and situations. Kate Withers Leonard wrote a four-page "Early Remembrances of Sherman County, Kansas" that mentions many scenes and events that occurred from 1885 to about 1902. If I were editing and annotating it for publication, I could choose from many family photographs of Kate and her entrepreneurial husband Thomas, their homes, and their activities. But the nature of the remembrances dictates my choice. I would choose Figure 4-4 (page 35), courtesy of Marion C. Parker and the Sherman County Historical Society. First, it shows Kate Leonard typing; her little memoir is a typescript that I imagine she did there on that machine. Second, it shows her husband at work as well. Third, it is the interior of the "Leonard Brick," a historically preserved building that retains some of the same features and that stands as a local monument to Leonard's role in early Goodland, Kansas. Finally, it is a great photograph for analysis of busi-

Figure 12-5 Waverly Lumber Company ink blotter, circa 1944. Sturdevant Family Papers, with permission of Rick W. and Wendell F. Sturdevant, in author's possession.

ness and regional symbols. Try it with a magnifying glass. Do the same with Figure 4-5, which was the Leonards' parlor in Goodland. Using these photographs would accentuate the Leonards' later success, so the "Remembrances" would also need some early, more rustic pictures of Goodland—which the local society has.

DOCUMENTS AND ARTIFACTS AS ILLUSTRATIONS

Remember that photocopies and photographs of objects can be good illustrations, when relevant. See the telegram in Figure 6-1 and the V-mail in Figure 6-3 on pages 67 and 69. Is there something special about the letterhead your ancestor used? Perhaps it was Civil War army letterhead or revealed your ancestor's business logo or fraternal emblems? By all means, show your readers a picture of the original diary or scrapbook before it disintegrates or disappears. Kate Harper's brooch is another example. If I had that artifact, and no picture of Kate wearing it, I could photograph it to illustrate the Paul Rouse story.

Reminder

ILLUSTRATIONS QUIZ

If a publisher takes on your documentary editing project, you will probably have to focus your selection of illustrations on a few of the best or most useful. Here is a brief quiz to practice your selection skills.

Reread the example. Then, of the choices given, what would be the best illustration to accompany the section of the document presented?

- On page 24, Carol Sturdevant wrote about running home, frightened by a bull. What would you most want to provide an illustration of?
  a. Carol at that approximate age
  b. the "home place" as it was then
  c. a picture of a bull
  d. the lyrics to "Jesus Loves Me"
- On page 72 is the story of Rick in the woodshed. If you were going to illustrate that, what would you include?
  a. a picture of the woodshed
  b. a picture of an orange cat
  c. a picture of Rick
  d. a picture of the ledger book damaged by ants
- On page 98, Wendell Sturdevant's POW diary revealed he was starving. What would you use to illustrate that document?
  a. a photograph of Wendell in dress uniform
  b. a photograph of the original diary
  c. a photograph of Wendell's dream meal
  d. a photograph of a dead horse's head
- On page 169, Roland Fowler writes about a race fight during his World War I service. What would you use to illustrate his collection of letters?
  a. a photograph of Roland in his navy uniform
  b. a photograph of a race riot
  c. a photograph of African Americans standing on a bus
  d. a copy of what Roland's original letters look like

I think the best answers are *a, d, b,* and *a.* Much depends on the function the illustration must serve. Think about function as you illustrate your documents.

THIRTEEN

Researching Annotation and Illustrations

Researchers and professional writers need accurate statistics, authoritative quotations, historical background, scholarly conjecture, biographical tidbits, arcane facts, and detailed explanations of every process, theory, concept, methodology, and function imaginable.

—*Ellen Metter,* Facts in a Flash: A Research Guide for Writers, *3*

I t will be necessary to research details in and illustrations for your documents all through your project. With every proper name, event, place, person, custom, or object mentioned in your documents, consider the following questions:

1. Is there a way I need to research and expand upon that information?
2. And, less often, is there a way I can illustrate my documents by finding a picture of that item?

RESEARCH FOR ANNOTATION

Although documentary editing guidebooks imply that you should research to get information for your annotations, rarely do they tell you *when* to do this and *how* to do this. Historians and historical editors assume everyone knows or can figure out how to do good historical research. Probably the main reason for this assumption is that research skills develop over a long time, on a trial-and-error basis, through someone or something thrusting you into a research project. Historians assume everyone has to earn their own on-the-job training, learning by experience. Nevertheless, you have to start somewhere, and it helps to know where to start. **A few guides, such as Richard Marius's *A Short Guide to Writing About History*, provide clues to historical research.** Chapter seven in *Bringing Your Family History to Life Through Social History* introduces genealogists to scholarly historical research, especially in college libraries, for writing family narrative.

Printed Source

You will need to identify many people in your documents who were not famous. You will be thinking as a social historian, wanting to clarify and expand upon the interesting aspects of popular culture mentioned in your documents. You will want your documents to hang together like narrative, not cause readers to stop and stumble over mysterious references.

Specific Historical Information vs. General Historical Background

To annotate your documents you will do at least two types of historical research. There will be the detailed work of locating specific tidbits of information for traditional annotation by footnotes. If you decide to do the more substantive, contextual annotation, such as interspersed connective tissue, which I recommend, then you will also do general historical research to understand, summarize, and analyze trends and attitudes of the past. In family history, this most likely will involve social history.

Researching People, Events, and Trends

Sources

When you want to identify historical references in your documents so you can develop annotation for them, start with books that are extended time lines, chronologies, encyclopedias, and directories. **Here are a few examples of that type of resource:**

Faragher, John Mack, ed. *The Encyclopedia of Colonial and Revolutionary America*. New York: De Capo Press, 1996.

Gaustad, Edwin Scott and Philip L. Barlow, eds. *New Historical Atlas of Religion in America*. New York: Oxford University Press, 2001.

Morris, Jeffrey B. and Richard B. Morris, eds. *Encyclopedia of American History*. 7th ed. New York: HarperCollins, 1996.

Sturtevant, William C. *The Handbook of the North American Indians*. 20 vols. Washington, D.C.: Smithsonian Institution, 1970s–1980s.

Thernstrom, Stephan, ed. *Harvard Encyclopedia of American Ethnic Groups*. Cambridge: Harvard University Press, 1980.

Urdang, Laurence, ed. *Timetables of American History*. New York: Touchstone Books, 1996.

Wilson, Charles Reagan and William Ferris, eds. *Encyclopedia of Southern Culture*. Chapel Hill: University of North Carolina Press, 1989.

For More Info

See *Bringing Your Family History to Life Through Social History* (166–195) about using college libraries, and see its bibliography for more recommended sources.

None of these books are enough to form the basis for a family history narrative, but they are all excellent starting places for documentary annotation. They may be enough, though, for smaller informational notes. Then, if you need more information about a particular item, research it in scholarly monographs (single-topic books) about the subject under which it falls. There are social history sources today—especially in college libraries—on almost any group of people, time period, and place in American history.

For example, a family historian had the diaries, letters, interviews, recollections, and memorabilia of his Jewish immigrant grandparents and their children, from their European experiences through their lives in New York City. As he put these together into a project, he would find both small and large

THE HISTORICAL RESEARCH PROCESS ADAPTED TO FAMILY HISTORY DOCUMENTS

For documentary editions:

1. Select a topic for historical research, one of the mysteries of your documents that you must solve for the project to go forward.

2. Determine which sources and source repositories might be best suited to answering your question. Start from your easiest, most accessible sources (such as Web searches or directories of information), and move on from there.

3. Formulate a hypothesis, a possible answer to your research question, and test it as you do more research. You might reformulate your hypothesis many times.

4. Evaluate your sources as you go. Adjust your hypothesis based partly on the relative reliability of your sources. Keep track of all conflicting information. If the answer seems common to all the sources, works within your documents, and comes from highly reliable sources, stop research on that issue.

5. Expect and cope with dead ends, brick walls, and unanticipated new wrinkles.

6. Collect, record, and organize the research results to a high scholarly and professional standard, so the results will be more convenient to use and more acceptable to your colleagues or audience. See methods in *Bringing Your Family History to Life Through Social History*.

7. Analyze the research results to determine how they answer your question. If they're inadequate, either continue research in additional sources or change the question.

8. Incorporate your conclusions into your transcribed family history documents. Use professional methods of annotation, and cite your sources properly.

9. Keep going and do not hesitate to start over. Most historical research involves juggling all of the previous steps, in reference to several topics, simultaneously and repeatedly.

matters that needed background explanation. If he wanted to learn what ingredients women like his grandmother used in an ethnic dish, he could go to a specialized cookbook. If he wanted to know the meaning of a certain word or event, he could use a dictionary or time line. If, however, he wanted to study and be able to portray the whole experience of people like his ancestors, he could go to social histories. From these resources he could verify the commonness of what his relatives described, flesh out descriptive details and explanations that they left out, and realize clues for more research. Here are some of the sources I suggested to him as an example of what one can find about almost any large group in American social history:

Sources

Berrol, Selma Cantor. *Growing Up American: Immigrant Children in America, Then and Now*. New York: Twayne Publishers, 1995.

Frommer, Myrna Katz and Harvey Frommer, comps. *Growing Up Jewish in America: An Oral History*. New York: Harcourt Brace and Company, 1995.

Harzig, Christiane, ed. *Peasant Maids, City Women: From the European Countryside to Urban America*. Ithaca: Cornell University Press, 1997.

Nasaw, David. *Children of the City: At Work and At Play*. New York: Oxford University Press, 1985.

Stave, Bruce M., et al. *From the Old Country: An Oral History of European Migration to America*. New York: Twayne Publishers, 1994.

The Jewish People in America Series. 5 vols. Baltimore: Johns Hopkins University Press, 1992.

1. Faber, Eli. *A Time for Planting: The First Migration, 1654–1820*.
2. Diner, Hasia. *A Time for Gathering: The Second Migration, 1820–1880*.
3. Sorin, Gerald. *A Time for Building: The Third Migration, 1880–1920*.
4. Feingold, Henry L. *A Time for Searching: Entering the Mainstream, 1920–1945*.
5. Shapiro, Edward S. *A Time for Healing: American Jewry Since World War II*.

RESEARCHING ARTIFACTS AND CUSTOMS

Idea Generator

You can also research any artifacts or popular customs mentioned in your documents. In some cases that may lead you to identify a described object and its function from printed sources. In other cases you may still own the item or have access to pictures of it or of one like it. Social history resources in libraries can help you with almost any such topics.

FINDING ILLUSTRATIONS

To obtain a good selection of illustrations, first organize your own and gather what you can from your family. Make sure you have permissions from the owners if you intend to publish the illustrations. If you need pictures, maps, or other illustrations from places that figure in your documents, contact archives, libraries, museums, and historical societies in the locations where the family lived. Use the AASLH directory to find contact information and which agencies have photograph archives. Some photograph archives now put their images on Web sites.

Remember to look in books, too, as you conduct your historical research. The books should offer credits for their photographs so you can track them down. If they don't, contact the publishers to ask for photograph sources. Old

POPULAR "GOOD OL' DAYS" AND "VANISHING AMERICANA" BOOKS

Nostalgia waves have caused publishing trends. Decades ago, numerous books came out on "good old days" and collecting Americana themes. Today there are still more, although they may appear different. All are helpful to family historians and all are heavily oriented toward material culture—"vanishing Americana"—letting artifacts inspire and illustrate stories. The older books tended to be cheaply produced, with black-and-white woodcuts, sketches, and cartoons. Libraries discard them as too dated, but book dealers price them highly for the value of the illustrations. The newer nostalgia books tend to be glossy, coffee-table affairs with plenty of photographs, some color, and sometimes an outrageous cover. Look for and use both the old and the new. Question the scholarship behind them, checking their sources before you rely on a piece of information in your family history. These books may, however, be the handiest guides to the artifacts and customs of the very times and places you seek. They are a legitimate starting place, and perhaps using them will prime you to seek and use the scholarly sources.

"Pop" Culture in Your Family History

We all have popular material culture in our families and lives . . . Examine your nuclear family's popular material culture. See how many artifacts you can list. There are many, many non-academic books about pop culture these days, what with "oldies but goodies" referring to anything more than a few years old. One example is *Jane and Michael Stern's Encyclopedia of Pop Culture*. The Sterns identify a list of pop culture artifacts that I am sure contains something familiar to you. Here are just a few:

answering machines	hula hoops
Avon products	lunch boxes
Baby on Board signs	microwave ovens
baseball caps	miniskirts
Cabbage Patch dolls	pantyhose
CB radio	Pet Rocks
Cheese Whiz	Pez
Cuisinart	pickup trucks
deodorant	refrigerator magnets
disposable diapers	remote control
fanny packs	Tang
Frisbee	toilet bowl cleaner

Adapted from *Bringing Your Family History to Life Through Social History* (39, 58–59).

magazines and ephemera offer excellent period illustrations, but be aware of copyright issues.

Keep in mind that you want to illustrate places, people, and customs. So, whether you're searching your own family photographs or some in an archive or book,

Reminder

Figure 13-1 The Peter Scott family in Canada, circa 1885, including Peter, Mary, Duncan, James, and Janet (in order of age). James, the wee boy holding his father's hand, was my grandfather. Ethnic family photographs are superb illustrations for family documents. Scott Family Papers, in author's possession.

choose ones that illustrate place, work, or ethnicity, ideally as your family lived them. For example, Figure 13-1 above is a family portrait that illustrates Scottish (Canadian) customs, particularly dressing children. This is the Scott family about whom I might write, but if I didn't have a picture of them and found this in an archive, I might use it even if the family was unrelated, because it reveals families of that background, time, and place. Figure 13-2 on page 167 offers classic scenery that adds setting to your family project, along with style clues (cars and clothing) as to the year. Figure 13-3 on page 167 is a good example of how an interior photograph can situate and date someone's position in a workplace. It can even offer details of what such a place might contain.

A LESS ATTRACTIVE SIDE OF OUR ANCESTORS

Warning

There is a delicate area of family documentary editing that research can help put in context. **You may find a semantic skeleton in the closet.** People of the past spoke (wrote) their minds freely, the way we would want them to, especially in their private writings. This sometimes means that the otherwise delightful letters, diaries, or memoirs that we want to share with the world contain embarrassing, offensive remarks when our ancestor-authors were candidly prejudiced, bigoted, uncouth, sexist, racist, or just plain ignorant.

Many of the documents we edit in our families date from the Civil War through World War II. For most Americans, this was more a period of class and cultural friction than it was a period of enlightenment about diversity. Racist language or ethnic and religious slurs seem inevitable, especially when the diarist or correspondent abruptly visited different places with unfamiliar cultural mixes, as a serviceman would do. So, we need to prepare ourselves and determine how to prepare our readers to handle past prejudices. Understanding the context of people's times requires research, too.

Figure 13-2 Leonard "Len" Harper and his second wife, Holly, circa 1937, on the Golden Gate Bridge. This is a good example of illustrating a recognizable place, plus time period, with clothing and automobile styles. Yes, this is Leonard of the baby book. Scott/Harper Family Papers, in author's possession.

Figure 13-3 James A. Scott Jr. working for his father who was manager of the Owl Drug Store on Market Street in San Francisco, circa 1935. This is a good social history photograph for its setting and props. Note also his cigarette. Scott Family Papers, in author's possession.

I still have trouble with Archie Bunkerisms. When I find bigoted statements in documents, they leap off the page and seem to prey on my mind, nagging me to wholly disapprove of the person who wrote them. This reaction, though, is ahistorical. The objectivity for which historians strive requires that we understand people in the context of their times and places. Think of former President Harry Truman. His autobiographical oral history interviews with Merle Miller became a book called *Plain Speaking*. Truman, being a white man of common background from Missouri, still hadn't lost his habit of using "the n word." Yet he had risen above his roots to risk fighting the Ku Klux Klan, to be the president who finally desegregated the military services, and to support more improvements in civil rights than even his liberal predecessor had. It would have been unethical for Merle Miller to censor Truman's using "the n word." He would have presented an inaccurate historical record. We need to be objective and accurate when editing our family documents, too.

I have especially noticed the words "nigger" and "pickaninny" in a series of wartime documents—my family's and others. One example occurred in some letters being edited for publication. The well-to-do, East Coast white man wrote "nigger" to describe some jazz musicians before World War I. The publisher of the documentary editing volume in question seriously considered doing away with the section so as not to offend readers or embarrass the family. Then, the publisher wanted to edit the passages to substitute other words or blank them out with ellipses. Although one can get away with editorial censorship in such a selected edition, the editor then takes away from public access a historically important feature of the documents.

Reminder

Good people used bad words, or we have since decided that they were bad words. Frank Sturdevant would not use "the n word" in his documents. But he did use "pickaninnies" toward another group. He was arriving in New Mexico during the border conflicts with Mexican revolutionary Pancho Villa in 1917, and he described numbers of "pickaninnies" running alongside the train as it entered the Southwest desert country. We think he was referring to children of Mexican or Indian descent. Research makes plain that his word choice was common among men from the Midwest. Thus, Frank documented for us some attitudes of men in his circumstances.

Kate Harper reacted negatively to the native peoples she saw when she unhappily arrived in El Paso, Texas, circa 1906. She complained that "Indians came prowling around, grunting. Also dirty, furtive looking Mexicans." She "was so scared that I was almost ill." Thus, her descriptions, even without epithets, project unfortunate stereotypes. The same Kate, however, wrote that she had tried all of her life to "cure myself of that silly fear" of African Americans that she had developed in childhood. Kate wrote, "the longer I live the more I know that as for *me*, I *must not* indulge in any degree of race hatred. God made us all—and I have no reason to boast because I happened to be born white." Research tells me that her prejudices were common.

Kate's brother Harry Dickey wrote letters home from the Spanish-American War. He used "the n word," but he used it about Filipinos. As the native population rebelled against the Americans, who appeared to be conquering them rather than just freeing them from Spanish rule, American troops fought Filipino insurrectionists rather than the Spanish. So, Harry wrote in one letter, "We're going to thrash them Niggers." Historical research informed me that this was a common response of the American volunteers. If I were editing Harry's letters, then, I would want to convey that context to my readers through annotation.

Family historian Marcia Mensing faces this issue with her father's World War I letters. Wartime might infuse your documents with hateful terminology toward enemies, such as the Germans, Japanese, Koreans, or Vietnamese, but it also inspired new tension among American racial and ethnic groups. As a sailor from Omaha, Nebraska, stationed in eastern cities, Marcia's father, Roland Fowler, wrote passages such as the following to his mother and family back home:

Case Study

> We treat a soldier and a marine as an equal here. They are grateful for the favor or compliment which ever it is. They showed it the other evening by helping the sailors lick the civilian niggers down on one of the main corners of the town's main street. About 500 people were engaged in it. Sorry but I wasn't near, didn't even know about it till next A.M. I'd like to have seen it.
>
> That is a common occurrence here. Only good thing about town. A nigger won't sit down in the car if a sailor is standing. Oh! Yes they remember what they are taught. (9 September 1918)

What can Marcia do with passages that would offend some of us so much we might reject Roland, or his letters, in disgust? In her preliminary efforts to annotate, she wrote a brief introduction with a disclaimer:

> These letters are in remarkably good condition, enabling me to record them exactly as originally written. Several passages contain what we now consider "politically incorrect" terms; in order to remain true to his writing, I have not changed his words.
>
> —*Quoted with permission from the unpublished World War I letters of Roland Fowler, Marcia Mensing, editor*

So racist or offensive terminology creates cases in which we documentary editors may have to explain why we did *not* edit something out. One misunderstanding we want to avoid is having readers think that, because we make no annotative comment about an offensive clause, we don't recognize or care that it might offend. Marcia's approach of announcing the problem in the beginning is responsible and would prepare those who read introductions for the shock of finding the taboo statements later. Her next step could be historical research into the period's social attitudes to provide the appropriate context for her annotation.

Important

I recommend two additional steps in documentary editing projects. Each occasion that such offensive language or reporting of events occurs, footnote or somehow annotate with contextual explanation. That would take care of the reader who reacts strongly to the passage, never having read the introduction. To compose the annotation, research the norms and events of the time. For example, with the passage from Roland's September 9 letter, one could write the following:

The World War I era brought many middle-American white men and urban or southern African-American men into contact for the first time. The war was a key cause of the "Great Migration" north of hundreds of thousands of African Americans seeking employment and housing. Resentments and tensions mounted. The group fights Roland described were part of the 1918–1919 race riots. These occurred in many eastern cities when white and black soldiers returned home to overcrowded, segregated communities. Such postwar riots also spread to Roland's hometown, Omaha.

This is historical context. It teaches, and it is interesting. Notice how it pulls the reader away from condemning Roland to the point of rejection, yet it makes clear that he represented a serious problem in history. This effect points out the best lesson of substantive historical annotation: We and our ancestors are usually part of group behavior. On the one hand, that means we shouldn't completely condemn the individual as evil incarnate for being typical of his ilk. On the other hand, we need to be reminded of the challenging truth: Each person who participates, perpetuates, or tolerates bigotry and hatred is part of the problem. In family documentary editing, researching narrative annotation can help you address, rather than cover, a multitude of sins.

FOURTEEN

To Keep or to Donate?

Layer upon layer, past times preserve themselves in the city until life itself
is finally threatened with suffocation; then, in sheer defense, modern man
invents the museum.

—*Lewis Mumford in* The Culture of Cities, *New York: Harcourt, 1938*

W as Lewis Mumford describing your life or your home, today or in the future? Just as you reach a point when it's time for a trip to Goodwill or Salvation Army with your bags of used clothing, you may reach a point when you need the boxes of family documents to go somewhere else. Part of the purpose in convincing people that their family documents and artifacts are valuable is to get them to save them, even if that means passing responsibility for them on to someone else.

If you've been reading this book through, then you should have some idea of what you want to do with your family papers. There are many options.

DOCUMENTARY PROJECTS
- edit for commercial or scholarly publication
- edit for self-publication
- prepare single documents or small groups for briefer publications
- use documents as resources in family history narrative
- use documents as resources in genealogical narrative
- donate originals to a repository
- share documents within family

What you do with your heirloom papers is up to you, especially if you're the sole owner or have the cooperation of all other claimants. If you do have historically valuable, personally meaningful documents, though, there are responsibilities tied to them. You are responsible to the ancestor-authors, who in many cases treasured these documents, entrusting them to posterity and the possibility of someone like you completing their projects. You are responsible to history, because your original documents, perhaps enhanced by your work as a transcriber and documentary editor, are treasure troves for historical research. You could be responsible to your surviving family and its heirs, to whom the family papers could also be precious but who might never see or know of them if you don't do the right things now with them. You are responsible to yourself, too. These heirloom artifacts mean something to you, and you would regret any loss or damage that might befall them. **You might also regret it if you didn't complete the projects you could do so well: presenting your family papers in their best light.**

Reminder

DONATING FAMILY PAPERS

Donation is an alternative. It's important to reiterate, though, that there is no better alternative for your *original* papers. Surely there are variables of time and place, but, eventually, all of us with historically significant original family documents should donate them to the appropriate repositories. We may hang on to them as we study and analyze, organize and transcribe, edit and annotate, and enjoy "the real thing." Yet, somewhere amongst the list of tasks comes a time where we really don't need the original documents anymore. We can work with copies and transcriptions. At some point each of us should acknowledge that we would never do as good a job of conserving original documents in the right environment as a good repository can do.

Idea Generator

More and more archives, libraries, and museums are reaching out to families with encouragement to donate. They recognize that we are the source and subjects of social history. Now, too, they have the convenience of the Web to address us all. One site after another invites donations but also offers conservation advice for those taking care of their own documents. One friendly but standard announcement I reproduce here is from the New England Historic Genealogical Society (NEHGS). It indicates several points to watch when choosing a proper resting place for your documents. Does the organization genuinely care about your documents? Does it have a topical collecting policy that your documents suit? Does it have a professional staff using high standards for organizing, preserving, cataloging, and making available your documents?

Almost all of the archival sites with information about donations recommend the SAA publication mentioned in the NEHGS announcement on page 173. You can read it in its entirety online. This guide, like all of the other substantial donation pages, makes certain basic observations for you about donating your documents. Here are some points of consensus to ponder.

Tip

DONATING TIPS
- The listed family documents that would be suitable for donation resemble what we might have and edit. That is because it is standard and typical for a family with documents to have some or all of these: diaries, letters, photographs,

HOW TO DONATE YOUR FAMILY PAPERS—AND WHY

If you have ever experienced the thrill of discovering your family's papers or artifacts in a repository, then you know firsthand the value of these collections. You may have even offered up a huge "Thank you!" to whoever saw the need to donate the manuscripts in the first place.

If you are the keeper of family documents you believe could be of interest to historians, genealogists, and other scholars, you may wish to donate them to an institution where they will be properly archived and available for others to use.

While much of the New England Historic Genealogical Society's collections focus on the New England region, NEHGS actively seeks any and all donations of genealogical manuscripts and historical records for the benefit of genealogical research.

NEHGS employs professional archivists, librarians, and genealogists with the expertise to care for your documents and promote their use. Not only does NEHGS store collections within a properly controlled environment; it also cares about the importance of these vital links to our nation's past. In fact, NEHGS was founded in 1845 for the purpose of collecting and preserving genealogical and historical materials. This continues to be an essential part of its mission today.

The Society of American Archivists provides an excellent Web site with general information about collections and donations. Visit <www.archivists.org> and click on the link to the site map and index. Look specifically for the SAA publication "A Guide to Donating Your Personal or Family Papers to a Repository" at <www.archivists.org/catalog/donating-familyrecs.html>.

To learn more about donating your materials to NEHGS, please contact the manuscript department at 101 Newbury St., Boston, MA 02116, call (617) 536-5740 (ext. 232), or e-mail tsalls@nehgs.org.

By donating your documents, you are providing records to other researchers, which can link families and contribute to a better understanding of history. It is a generous gift and worthy of consideration. At NEHGS, we want to make it an easy and rewarding decision for you.

Reprinted by permission of the New England Historic Genealogical Society. "How to Donate Your Family Papers—and Why," *New England Ancestors* 2 (Winter 2001): 16. For more information about *New England Ancestors* magazine and the New England Historic Genealogical Society, please visit <www.newenglandancestors.org>.

scrapbooks, ephemera, and memorabilia. These are also the most useful to history.

- Repositories today usually use professional standards, trained archivists and conservators, and archival supplies and environments. Ask whether they do. Normally they can provide a safer home for our documents than any of us can.

• As they make our documents available to researchers, including us, repositories usually don't allow the materials to leave the sites. Generally, researchers have to request to see documents, staffs closely monitor them, and there are restrictions as to whether the researcher can photocopy, photograph, or even handle originals. Many special collections departments have separate rooms for viewing documents, where a visitor cannot carry bags in and out or write with anything more than a pencil.

• If you're unsure of the most appropriate repositories in your area, start with your state historical society (see AASLH directory), or e-mail the Society of American Archivists at info@archivists.org.

• Some repositories specialize more than others do. Military repositories abound. See, for example, the Wright Museum, which is collecting World War II home front memorabilia, at <www.wrightmuseum.org/Artifacts.htm>. The new U.S. Army Women's Museum in Ft. Lee, Virginia, is collecting now. See <www.awm.lee.army.mil/>.

• State historical societies usually collect state history collections. Many other repositories have geographical specializations as well. Special Collections at the University of Arizona at <http://dizzy.library.arizona.edu/branches/spc/homepage/Donations1.htm> collects Arizona subjects. The Western Historical Manuscript Collection at the University of Missouri collects the obvious regional topic. The Center for American History at the University of Texas at <www.cah.utexas.edu/about/donors.html> collects widely in Texas, regional, and media history.

• Colleges often collect the personal papers of their alumni. See, for example, Mount Holyoke College at <www.mtholyoke.edu/offices/library/arch/msdonor.htm>, Syracuse University at <http://sumweb.syr.edu/archives/papers/alumpapr/alumguid.htm>, Oregon State University at <www.orst.edu/dept/archives/archive/arch132.html>, or Duke University at <http://odyssey.lib.duke.edu/specoll/donating.html>.

• A current trend in collecting is in the documents and memorabilia of World War II. This special attention should last several more decades, as the World War II generation disappears. You will find college archives specializing in their World War II alumni, state historical society collections specializing in World War II service men and women from their states, and many oral history programs. This interest has also spread backward into World War I, where a few veterans still survive, and forward into the Korean War period and beyond.

• Most repositories will be interested in the records of organizations over a span of years, again, depending on the themes of their collections.

• Many archivists would rather you not organize, sort, or discard your materials before you contact them. They will assist you and do the cataloging themselves.

• Most repositories would like you to contact them and discuss donating a collection before bringing it to them, especially a large one.

• A repository may accept anywhere from a single item to a large collection if they deem it relevant and worthy of preservation.

• Archivists and special collections librarians will often work with a family over a long period of time, sometimes years, to help identify and preserve additional documents as you uncover, locate, or decide to part with them.

• If your documents don't suit the themes of a particular repository, you can request their help finding the appropriate homes for the documents. Many archivists have good networks of communication across the country and internationally.

• Most archives will ask you to transfer to them ownership of and copyright to the collection. This is one reason to consider seriously what to do with the originals while you still have any publishing projects in mind. You can request to retain copyright for a period of time. Then, researchers have to seek your permission to publish anything from your documents. The inconvenience of that for them, and for you, is a good reason to transfer copyright. Make sure the copyright is yours to transfer. It first belongs to the writers of the documents and their heirs. (See pages 36–39.)

• Repositories will ask you to sign a deed of gift to keep the agreement clear and legal. Most public archives cannot spend their resources to maintain your collection for you, so they want to "own" it for public access to justify their investment of resources. Again, the repository may seek evidence from you that you truly own and have the rights to donate the collection.

• You can request the ability to later amend the deed of gift.

• Both parties should sign the deed of gift and any amendments.

• Archivists prefer that you allow unrestricted access to your donated collection, but if there is reason to keep something private you may arrange such specifications for a period of time, say twenty-five years, through negotiations with the archival managers. Therefore, don't censor your own documents; discuss with archivists and librarians about limiting access to delicate materials.

• If your documents are recent enough that privacy laws may apply, discuss with the archivists whether there is private information about anyone they need, by law, to protect. Such documents might include medical, school, tax, or legal records.

• As they process the collection, the repository staff will make decisions about whether to discard some items as valueless. You can state to them in advance what you want them to do with discards, including that they might return them to you.

• You may wish to determine a monetary value of your collection so you can take a charitable tax donation. Seek tax experts or attorneys for advice. You may need a professional appraiser. The Internal Revenue Service requires an independent appraisal if you value the donation above a certain amount. The archives cannot provide this service but may keep a list of appraisers. For tax purposes, make sure you get receipts.

• If possible, you may also wish to offer a monetary donation to the repository to help support the care of the collection.

• Discuss with the representatives of the repository what they will call the collection. Remember your title: The _____ Family Papers. Archivists and librarians will want a title that makes the content most clear to researchers.

• If an item has more sentimental value than research use or if you don't

See Also

See Appendix B for a sample Deed of Gift Agreement. You might use it as a model or to remind you of questions to ask the repository. See page 216.

feel emotionally ready to part with it, keep it in the family. You can preserve its contents for posterity by filing or donating copies elsewhere.

If you donate your documents to a research repository, you make them available to students, historical researchers, and genealogists. Your papers might provide evidence and quotations for doctoral dissertations, books and articles, films, and school projects. Documentary editors might work with your family diaries and letters. This way your family papers may, indeed, become published. They might also inspire a student or researcher in a way that only "the real thing" could do.

DONATING DOCUMENTS YOU CREATED

You may also ask archivists about their interest in accepting modern documents from your lifetime and your immediate family. Try not to overestimate the value of what you have. For example, a friend of mine donated all of the boxes of income tax receipts she and her husband had saved over the years. I understood her instinctive desire to do something with them after she obediently followed the tax-expert advice to keep them for seven years or more. She thought these records would make a great resource some day for researching the everyday life of a family. There is some logic to that, but I knew firsthand that the librarians were just humoring her by taking the boxes. Imagine if they accepted such donations from very many families—they would run out of storage space even faster!

So, develop your own collection for donation along the same lines as your historical collection. Personal writings—diaries, letters, and memoirs—would be desirable even if not yet old. Original certificates, photographs, school records, or memorabilia would suit a collection. Scrapbooks and even organized clipping files could be good. If you set out to donate your own materials, document them well first. Identify photographs and date clippings, and label things by using archival methods and supplies. Also, identify the creators of artistic works such as needlecraft, paintings, or stories in the collection. Some archives would take such family papers even from the 1990s or 2000s. Just keep in mind the collections of family papers we have discussed as models for what to create and collect.

SELLING YOUR FAMILY

I hope you won't sell your family. The money you would receive at an antique store would not exceed the value you could deduct for a charitable donation to an archive. Once sold, your documents might fall into good hands, but they would most likely be lost to all of the other researchers who could use them. Your documents and memorabilia would most likely become separated from one another. It was highly unusual for someone like me to walk in and buy so many different items from the same Parker family. The storekeepers had already separated the photographs from their album pages, and I don't know whether any letters survived with the other items. I came to the store a day or two after the heirlooms arrived, the storekeepers knew me as a teacher who bought items

Idea Generator

DONATING RARE BOOKS

If your family memorabilia includes old, possibly rare books, consider donating these to a library or archives as well. A story in *The Tennessean* (15 July 2001) told of a retired professor who, at age eighty-eight, decided to donate his collection of 1,500 editions to the University of Kentucky Library. The gentleman regretted somewhat parting with his "babies," but the library will make tremendous use and take good care of them. When I worked at the State Historical Society of Iowa, for another example, it had a remarkable collection of antique primers, readers, and schoolbooks. Isolated, individual, personal books in your family papers may stay with the papers, but if you have some other old books, ask your archivist about donating them to a library collection.

---

as teaching aids, and, being a consignment store, they have a good system of marking items with numbers that represent the owners. Thus, it was still possible to reconstruct the batch of items so I could determine some of the family history, and the storekeepers are unusually supportive of what I do. Your family papers would more likely become scattered and lose their significance in stores.

You can see online that some diaries, journals, account books, and albums are for sale. At the used-book site Abebooks.com, <http://dogbert.abebooks.com>, I have seen a 1920s high school girl's autograph album for $35; an 1877 Boston grocer's account book for $100; a collection of fifteen 1890s diaries from a Long Island farmer for $250; a scrapbook/photo album from the family of the British Ambassador to Russia, circa 1898–1904 for $1,360; and an Indiana Civil War record book listed for $8,000. In my opinion, these fascinating documents belong in public repositories where researchers could use them. The prices, even if extravagantly hopeful sellers set them, are helpful, though. They remind us that someone may see value in our heirloom documents. They may reflect the size of a deduction you could take. Yet think of the difference when you keep things together. If you watch *Antiques Roadshow* on PBS, you know how much more valuable a group of items can be, where one item, such as a letter or a photograph, documents the story behind the others. Remember, too, that if you want to conduct a documentary editing project outside of your family, you could "adopt" a diary or album from an archive or purchase one, making it available to the rest of us through publication.

Internet Source

FIFTEEN

Publishing Your Documentary Book

Y ou have several advantages in trying to publish a documentary volume over those authors seeking a publisher for their original works, especially fiction. A fiction writer, at least an unknown one, has to complete the manuscript, have a good agent, and compete with everyone else who thinks he can write the Great American Novel. A nonfiction writer, however, usually draws up a detailed book proposal and submits that directly (or through an agent) to the publisher. The publisher then might help finance the writing with an advance. The writer doesn't necessarily have to dedicate time and effort without hope for publication and may even have a contract.

A documentary volume might also attract a publisher more readily than something you compose yourself. If your project would be making available (especially for the first time) a historical diary, letters collection, or memoir, some publishers will be interested. You do need guidance to write a good proposal and research to determine the best places to submit. **There are several how-to guides about writing and submitting nonfiction book proposals in the Bibliography.** Key elements in such book proposals include demonstrating the market and need for the book. You can use the examples, resources, guidebooks, and knowledge of documentary editing I have offered here to place your volume in context of the field and its markets. Use the Elements of Social History chart (*Bringing Your Family History to Life Through Social History*, 18–19) to help determine the larger themes of your documents. Include with the documents the apparatus outlined here, presented professionally, and the proposal will be stronger.

Idea Generator

See Also

To be acceptable as a legitimate publication, your volume, proposal, and cover letters need to be professional. Use, and state that you are using, documentary editing guidebooks such as *Editing Historical Documents*, *A Guide to Documentary Editing*, and this book. Research the field in which your volume fits, such as Civil War diaries and letters, so you can analyze for the publishers how it fits and why it is worthwhile.

Consider carefully which publishers might be most interested in your project and which ones might do it the most good. There is no harm in aiming high, commercially or in terms of prestige, even if you have to lower your sights later. If the diary, memoir, letters, or other documents truly have a broad appeal, relating to a popular topic, a larger commercial press might be interested. If the documents have research value to historians or literary experts, a scholarly press might publish them. For example, many university presses are today reprinting diaries, journals, memoirs, and letters that someone edited for them decades ago. It is unusual for old, scholarly historical books (monographs) to see reprint or new editions many decades later, but original documents do.

Your volume might seem insignificant standing alone but can be important as a case study. Does your project reflect the history of a region or community as well as a time period? It probably does. Many state and university presses publish regional literature, especially firsthand, documentary accounts. A southern, western, midwestern, or New England university press might take special interest if your diary or letters reveal historical material about life in their region. Or, perhaps your documents reveal women's history, war experiences, or some other currently popular area. **See Paul Parsons's *Getting Published: The Acquisition Process at University Presses* for an appendix that cites the major university presses and in what topical areas they are currently adding to their catalogs.** See the Association of American University Presses' annual directory for how to contact the presses. This organization's Web site is <http://aaupnet.org/>, and the annual directory is available through the University of Chicago Press. It includes the specialty interests of presses as well as submission guidelines. State historical societies with large presses also seek publishable documents set in their states. Remember the AASLH directory for locating all such societies. This directory cites whether the societies have book-publishing programs.

Printed Source

There are also publishers who specialize in genealogical books and in books that are of special help to genealogists and local historians. See Appendix A for a list. Picton Press might be especially worthwhile to contact. They specialize in "genealogical and historical manuscripts, whether long out of print or never published before." They have published diaries, journals, and memoirs, with a special appreciation of the social history context into which each fits. For example, the full transcription of Martha Ballard's diary is a Picton publication. Known historians, genealogists, and their periodicals comment favorably on Picton Press books. Its Web site, <www.pictonpress.com/catalog/about.htm>, offers introductory guidelines and examples of their publications that might inspire you.

There is a long tradition of self-publishing or using "vanity presses" in genealogy. See Appendix A for some of these resources as well. I strongly encourage you, however, to attempt the broader, more lucrative and prestigious publication outlets with any special, book-length document. A good historical diary, letter collection, or memoir deserves better distribution. If you want this level of publication but feel the documentary editing efforts are beyond your time or skills, rethink the donation information in chapter fourteen. You could donate your original documents, copyright and all, to a repository where professionals may edit and publish some family documents.

INTRODUCING DOCUMENTS

As you study other published documents that are comparable to yours, seriously consider the patterns that their titles follow. Your publisher will probably "play" with whatever title you choose anyway, based on knowledge of what sells, but first impressions on publishers are important, too. **Most scholarly publishers of documents use titles that are somewhat formulaic.** For example, I might try "Kate: The Memoir of a Frontier Girlhood." Or, cumbersome though it may seem, the subtitle might be "A Woman's Life on the Kansas, Colorado, and Arizona Frontiers, 1885–1915." Scholarly publishers offer subtitles that inform the readers exactly what themes might be present in a family document. By all means, avoid a standard genealogical title such as Seven Generations of the Brown Family, and keep in the title that the volume consists of original documents.

As for your introduction, try to imagine how confusing the documents would be to a newcomer reading them for the first time. When you write an introduction, then, you are explaining what the documents are about and what you have done with them to someone who could be completely ignorant about them. The latter—what you have done with them—is standard fare for documentary editing introductions. This is the place to explain your fundamental editorial decisions so that any reader can evaluate those choices and know what's original and what's not while reading the documents. The introduction at minimum should contain three basics:

- a summary of the documents, their value, and their historical context
- an explanation of the provenance of the documents, their origins, where they have been, how they changed hands, and how you got them
- clear outlining of your editorial practices, including whether you changed, added, or deleted anything in the text and how a reader might recognize those emendations

One bonus for gaining the attention of the historical and genealogical communities would be a foreword written by a known professional. Julie Jones-Eddy had historian Elizabeth Jameson write an introduction for her oral history book, *Homesteading Women*. Jameson is a known specialist in western women's history. Laurel Thatcher Ulrich of Martha Ballard's diary introduced a Picton Press publication, *The Diary of Matthew Patten of Bedford, New Hampshire, 1754–1788.* Historian David Hackett Fischer, renowned among genealogists for *Albion's Seed*, wrote the foreword for Peter Haring Judd's *The Hatch and Brood of Time.* It may be your publisher who makes such arrangements, but keep this idea in mind. The expert may be more capable of

Notes

Important

Please don't make the common, embarrassing mistake of misspelling "foreword." Perhaps people think it is "forward" because it takes us forward into the book? But I teach students to remember spelling by thinking about meaning: It is a fore word.

placing your family documents in historical context than you, or the expert's credentials may capture the faith of your potential readers.

EPILOGUING DOCUMENTS

It's also important to conclude your documentary project with an epilogue or afterword, a separate "chapter" that you can write yourself as editor. In an epilogue, you can explain what happened to people and events after the time covered in the document(s). Most diaries, letter collections, account books, baby books, scrapbooks, and other personal documents are incomplete and were kept contemporaneously. Thus, they end without "closure," as we tritely call it today. Most don't even end with the deaths of the main characters but with an unexplained change in circumstances that caused people to stop recording. Sometimes this change was dramatic, such as when Nazi SS men raided Anne Frank's secret annex, ending her diary keeping. Other documents ceased when people moved, married, had more children, came home from war, or just tired of the project.

Memoirs and reminiscences leave room for epilogues, too, although the closer they are to autobiographies the more complete they are. The memoir writer may have left the work incomplete. You can "finish" it by explaining why the memoirist never completed it and speculating on what the memoirist might have added, adding things from other sources if available. Then, you can follow the characters to their deaths and events to their fruition. For example, James Scott never organized his anecdotal memoir, and he became senile. These events, plus the poignant stories of his recalling his memoirs in his senile state, will be part of my epilogue to his memoir. It will be an important chapter of his life, of the memoir, and of human realities in caring for a senile parent.

In classical theatre, the epilogue summarized and even evaluated the body of the play. Often the epilogue pointed out the play's deficiencies and apologized for them in a mock way in an attempt to deflate criticism. You can use your epilogue this way, too. Your documents have deficiencies that you will have remedied with annotation. The deficiency of ending abruptly, before people's deaths and before closure of the story, is too much to remedy with a footnote, however. Thus, the epilogue can conclude the story, complete the characters, and explain or reemphasize your editorial policies.

Your documents might cause you to take a family history approach to the epilogue. Kirk Polking, in *Writing Family Histories and Memoirs*, suggested that an epilogue in a family history volume might be the place to announce that your volume is part of a series, to tease readers with the future volumes, and to solicit possible contributions for the next book. Peter Haring Judd's *The Hatch and Brood of Time* is a narrative family history in historical context. Judd's epilogue summed up his project's themes in a context of how researching and writing about them made him feel as though he knew them, in a fulfilling way.

Many epilogues for documentary volumes simply follow the characters, but that can require firsthand knowledge and significant research. In *The Roy Bedichek Family Letters*, editor Jane Gracy Bedichek provided a brief, two-paragraph "epilogue" from personal knowledge. The last letter in the volume was May 1959, so the editor concluded with how, on 20 May 1959, Bedichek died. The epilogue matter-of-factly summarized the death and burial of the main letter writer, Roy, who was a prominent Texas naturalist. Janet Lecompte, in *Emily: The Diary of a Hard-Worked Woman*, provided a businesslike accounting of what each of the main characters did after the diary's end. Her research took her to city directories, homestead applications, vital records, court and tax records, censuses, hospital records, and cemetery records. Lecompte concluded her epilogue with a paragraph of provenance—about how the diary became part of the library collection where she found it.

Idea Generator

Scholars have sometimes used epilogues to discuss the historical events represented in the documents. So, for example, Thomas Dublin, in his edited volume *Farm to Factory: Women's Letters, 1830–1860*, provided an afterword in which he explained the broader historical context of the letters. "The omissions in these letters suggest how important it is to supplement the picture one derives from women's correspondence with evidence drawn from other sources," Dublin wrote (190). To him, the "omissions" in the letters included historically recognizable events of the period, such as labor unrest, and the diversity of other mill workers besides these Yankee women, such as recent Irish immigrants. Sherry L. Smith included an epilogue in *Sagebrush Soldier* that not only followed through with the later life of the protagonist, but also included related events of the later Plains Indian Wars and analysis of varying documented interpretations of them.

WE LIKE SEQUELS

Although we know from movies and television that sequels are rarely as good as the originals, we also know that we provide a willing market for sequels anyway. Especially when we focus on characters we like or with whom we identify, or even just characters who have become familiar and memorable, we want to know what happened to them after the story ended. They are that real to us. They live on, we think, even though the story is over. So, for example, there are Web sites dedicated to dead television soap operas, where lingering fans keep track of and even develop new romantic plots about the characters of a story that has already ended.

Wanting further knowledge of beloved characters in a story is nothing new. In "I'll Be Back," Harvard University English Professor Marjorie Garber analyzed the book, *Part Two: Reflections on the Sequel*, edited by Paul Budra and Betty Schellenberg. Garber pointed out that many classical literary authors deliberately left characters hanging and plots unresolved. Writers ever since have tried to tie up those loose ends. Jane Austen answered questions from family and friends about whatever became of her characters by telling them what happened later, as though the stories were continuing in her mind.

Consider that readers love sequels and epilogues. **Your readers will want to know the following:**

Notes

- Whatever became of the main characters, until their deaths?
- Whether their heirs carried on the traditions revealed in the documents.

- What became of organizations, places, groups, projects, events, and trends discussed in the documents?
- When, why, and how did the document(s) end?
- What was the meaning of preparing these documents for you?
- What is the ultimate historical significance of these documents?
- The outcome of any decision, turning point, or relationship left unresolved in the documents.
- How this information was transmitted from the family to you.
- Provenance, if not already included in introduction.

INDEXING DOCUMENTS

The index to your documents is the most valuable aid you can give historians and genealogists. Think about it. Your ancestor's diary was inaccessible to them. Now you will publish it and put it on library shelves. You can't dictate how the library system will catalog it, except by what you emphasize in title and content. Perhaps it will be in the genealogy section. I hope it will also be in the history section. Because the title or subtitle carries the family surname, some genealogists might pick it up. Because you have been careful to build a place, event, or time period into the title, people researching those subjects might pick it up. Because people like to read firsthand accounts, they might pick it up. The index can determine how quickly, or how reluctantly, they put it back on the shelf. Scholars reject books without indexes immediately unless the topic requires their attention.

Using indexes this way will help you understand the behavior of the researcher. Say you are the genealogist. If you see that there are plentiful entries about that family, you start to study those entries. If they include your relatives, especially with new information, bingo! Now, say you are doing historical research. You realize that a diary can be an excellent primary resource. The title and other outward clues suggest this one might contain some useful information for your project. You open the back of the book, crossing your fingers that there will be an index. Eureka! But your topic is something generic, such as how American schools treated immigrant children. Sure, you could eyeball the book, but that could be a needle-in-the-haystack proposition. There it is, in the index:

Childhood
  schooling, 2–7

or

Education
  grammar school, 2–7

or

Prejudice
  in school, 2–7

Important

For More Info

For answers to your technical questions and for an overview of indexing, see Nancy C. Mulvany's *Indexing Books*, an in-depth extension of the *Chicago Manual of Style* chapter on indexing. For advice with documentary examples, see Michael Stevens and Steven Burg's *Editing Historical Documents*. See also Patricia Law Hatcher and John Wylie's *Indexing Family Histories*.

Pay dirt! But if the index hadn't existed or only listed proper names, the historical researcher, at least the one in a hurry, might have put your book back on the shelf.

From an author's perspective (including a documentary editor's), it's sad but true: Most researchers don't read many books from cover to cover. They cannot, in the interest of time. Indexes—good, thorough ones—save time. There will be some readers who savor every word, but they will also use the index. Indeed, you will use the index of your own book. At least I do. Why memorize the placement of topics within a book when one can always look them up in a good index?

Whom to Index

So you must determine your audience—the likely users of the index. If yours is a documentary volume of letters, a diary, a memoir, or any of the other examples, your most likely users are historians and historical researchers, genealogists, and librarians or archivists seeking particular references. Documentary editors might read your work, too, as a model or to test it against their models. Knowing your audience will make a difference with respect to what topics you index and how you list them. You don't want to use terminology in your index that only certain insiders would recognize.

There is also the question of whether you should compile your own index. You or your publisher could hire a professional, which would certainly be less work for you. Locate and hire the indexer about two months in advance. The American Society of Indexers maintains a register of indexers, your publisher may have recommendations, or there are suggestions in *Indexing Books*. Envision yourself at the bitter end of the publishing process. Will you be too tired of the editing project to be an alert indexer? Will the subject matter be so familiar that you are blind to what needs indexing? You can supply a seed list of terms you want indexed.

Consider all ramifications, however. You know the project best. What you might need more than an indexer is consultation with a historian who could identify historical topics for your index, if those aren't obvious to you. There are several reasons I have, so far, decided to do my own indexes. I know how, as part of my editorial background, and I believe I can do a better job of producing a social history index than others might do. Being the indexer means that you get to proofread the manuscript at the latest available opportunity. If you don't do your own index, your last chance to catch errors in the manuscript would be at an earlier stage.

What to Index

For genealogists, the index should include all proper names that appear in the document. This is also the most basic information to index in any book for any audience. Still more helpful, you can identify those pages where there is greater attention to the person indexed. For example, here is a hypothetical entry for the edited memoir of Kate Dickey Harper. I'm using italics to indicate where there is a picture of the subject person.

Internet Source

For additional advice and resources, see the American Society of Indexers Web site at <www.asindexing.org/>. For a model, see the *Papers of George Washington* at <www.virginia.edu/gwpapers/stylemanual/indexing.html>.

Important

Harper, Archibald Leslie (1881–1965), husband of Kate, met Kate Dickey, *23–25*; biographical note 24n; marriage of, *28–32*; law school, *28–35*; goes to Denver, CO, *36–37*; goes to Goldfield, NV, *38*; goes to Bisbee and Globe, AZ, *39–42*; father of John Leonard, *43–44*; campaigns for district attorney, *45–46*; becomes superintendent of State Industrial School, *47–49*. . . .

Thus, your index entries can offer the reader much useful information, even becoming quick biographical or genealogical summaries.

Historical researchers, too, will want to see proper names as the basis of an index. They would ask you to index historical events and topics. Some indexing guides refer to these as "general topics." Unless the ancestor-author named the events or topics outright, they can be difficult to determine if you're not a historian, and a rather eclectic one at that. Many of the important references to a historical topic will be somewhat hidden. For example, a diarist might have written, "Mary died of the flu" in 1918, but you might not realize that her death was part of the international Spanish influenza epidemic unless you did historical research. By the time you're indexing, you should have researched and gained some understanding and annotation for most of the historical topics in the text. If you feel ill-prepared to recognize all of the historical references in the text you're editing and indexing, then keep close at hand a textbook history, chronology, or book such as Morrises' *Encyclopedia of American History*.

Most useful and unusual for the sakes of both genealogists and historians would be a social history index. This index would list topics about your family that researchers could compare to their own or to society generally. Below I have listed a few of the "elements of social history." For more, see *Bringing Your Family History to Life Through Social History* (18–19). As you read your family documents for indexing (or for researching annotation), see whether the topics

Reminder

SOME ELEMENTS OF SOCIAL HISTORY

Marriage	ceremonies, relationships, gender roles, sexuality, courtship, methods of choice, infidelity and response, widowhood, inheritance, premarital relations, customs, dress, property, divorce, nontraditional partnerships
Dress	fabrics, sewing, fashions, motives, styles, fads, dress events, age and class distinctions, needlework, shopping, catalogs, accessories
Migration	mobility rates, transportation, push and pull factors, group behavior, routes, assimilation, enclaves, return migration, foodways, health, transported possessions, written accounts, work, recreation, vehicles

mentioned in the documents match the social history trends and themes listed in the chart. Then, you can index them as social history topics in your general index.

You also need to decide whether to include parts of your volume beyond the body of text, such as front and back matter or footnotes and endnotes. My example of an index entry on Archibald Harper shows the value of including notes in your indexing but indicating that it's a note you're citing. How many times have I searched an indexed page for a reference, then realized the index entry really referred to a footnote! We save our readers frustration by marking index entries for footnotes as such.

Most editors and publishers don't index forewords or afterwords but do index an introduction or epilogue if it appeared as a chapter in the body of text. It's up to you. As a rule of thumb, decide whether indexing those parts is (1) reasonable in terms of space, cost, labor, and time, and (2) how much would it help your readers?

When to Index

Don't put the proverbial cart before the horse. The index is one of the last projects you should undertake. Obviously, it would be a mistake to compile your index before you know what the page numbers might be. That knowledge comes at a later page-proof stage, unless you're producing your own informal volume. But it is wise to make decisions and perhaps even mark a copy of the manuscript in advance of completing an index. For example, you might decide what indexing terminology you will use and make notes of this as you go, such as the decisions you could make using the Elements of Social History chart.

Technique

To index for your documentary volume's several themes, purposes, and audiences, you have to make several passes through the entire text. This approach is similar to proofreading separately for heads, footnote numbering, and textual errors. If you marked the text well previously, you might reduce this later effort. But I do recommend that you index once for names and at least one other round for the less obvious themes, even though this is time-consuming.

How to Index

There are several ways to compile an index. I find that each indexer adheres to a favorite method, but that method varies from one indexer to the next. I like to use a simple Microsoft Word file on my computer, adding entries alphabetically as I discover them. *Indexing Books* calls this the "text file method." The main drawback of this method is having to run through a long list after a while. The advantages are that I can use all of the familiar Microsoft Word tools. Each subentry just requires a tab indention. Everything is familiar, easy to print at any time, and there is no middle step as there is between index cards and an electronic file. One cannot use a simple electronic indexing feature with this method, though, because the subentries or other decisions I make are different from electronic indexing. Mine is the transitional way between index cards and indexing software. I trust myself, still, more than the software.

Ever wonder why those little three-by-five cards are called "index cards"? They are the classic precomputer way to compile and index. Nancy Mulvany gives a good explanation of this method in *Indexing Books*. I've never liked index cards for this purpose or for note taking, but perhaps you will. Your only outside consideration is what form your publisher will want the index to take for electronic reproduction. The cost of having a typist work from your well-organized cards would be less than the cost of hiring an indexer. Index cards are the old-fashioned way.

If you like high-tech solutions, you can buy software that will index a list you provide and software that will retrieve from your text and make a list. *Indexing Books* has a lengthy discussion of these. Someday, I'm sure they will equal and exceed our abilities, but not yet. Some of my friends swear by them, though. I think the time it would take to familiarize myself with one of these computer programs and adjust it to my needs would be double the time it takes me to index my way. You may be different.

INDEXING QUIZ/CASE STUDY

There is always more to index in a passage than first meets the eye. **What would you find to index in this passage from Kate Dickey Harper's memoir?**

Case Study

> [In Olathe] we lived beside the railroad. I remember how many times the boys were punished because they persisted in laying crossed pins on the tracks so the train would make "scissors" of them. I remember the section men going by in their little hand car and calling to me.

On first glance, the only proper name to index is:

Olathe (KS)

If you have indexing categories about the memoir author herself, you might have:

Dickey, Kate "B."
    see *Harper, Kate Dickey*
Harper, Kate Dickey
    childhood
    railroads, trains

Who are these boys? From preceding paragraphs you would know they were Kate's older brothers. So additional entries might be:

Dickey, Frank Mahlon
    childhood games
    childhood punishments
Dickey, Harry St. Clair
    childhood games
    childhood punishments

You might have a Dickey family listing such as:

Dickey family
    homes
    see also individual family members

For general history topics you might index the following, with social history subentries:

Railroads
    childhood games
    crews
    hand cars
Trains
    see *railroads*

For social history topics, you could add:

Childhood
    games
    gender differences
    punishments

It's amazing how much there is to index in even the simplest passage from a document. But each level of indexing that you achieve makes that document so much more valuable to researchers. Note, too, that word choices become important and need to be consistent, as does your use of "see."

Tip

TECHNICAL TIPS FOR INDEXING

- Know your audience and provide the best index for its purposes.
- Index proper names, with appropriate subentries and indicators of points where individuals receive biographical treatment.
- Indicate, perhaps by italics or boldface, where you have placed illustrations of the items indexed.
- Index general history and social history topics and subtopics.
- Choose the most accurate and informative term for each indexed item, and use that term for that item consistently.
- Follow all of the policies you choose consistently.
- If a policy or term doesn't fit certain entries, adjust the term or policy until it serves all adequately.
- Index as a final stage of the publication, but prepare terms and make decisions earlier.
- Index footnote or endnote material. Index front and back matter when it pertains to the subject matter in detailed and unique ways.
- Choose the indexing method or technology that best suits your purposes or skills.
- As you list entries and subentries, if any one gains more than about seven page references, consider whether you can break it down into more entries

and subentries.

- Double list and cross list entries and subentries so researchers can find the same material by looking under their different topics of interest.
- Keep entries and subentries concise. Avoid generic words such as "concerning," "relating to," "the," etc. Nouns make the best entries.
- **Decide (or ask your editor's preference) about elision (how to list multiple, consecutive page references), and use the method consistently, i.e., 135–6, 135–36, or 135–136.**
- If you decide to list the author or "main character" in the index, determine ways to break up the many subentries with thematic or chronological subheads.
- Use "see" to mean a synonym, another term you have used entirely in its place, such as the entry I used for Kate Dickey Harper.
- Use "see also" to send readers to additional entries that are related to the first. Use "see also" in both cases for any two connected entries.
- For cross listing to assist readers, consider and list at least the most obvious synonyms, such as railroads and trains.
- If a person's name changed, such as when a woman married, cross list the variables.
- When subentries pass onto the next page, repeat the original entry. Thus, *Railroads (cont'd)*, to avoid confusion.
- Choose between two methods of alphabetizing (or ask your editor), and use your choice consistently. One is word by word and one is letter by letter.

Word-by-Word	Letter-by-Letter
New Hampshire	New Hampshire
New York	Newman, Richard
Newman, Richard	New York

- As you list page numbers after an entry or subentry, connect consecutive pages if the topic appears throughout those connected pages (147–155). Separate those pages with commas if the topic appears on each separately but not continuously (147, 149, 150).

\di'fin\ *vb*

Definitions

OTHER BACK MATTER

Readers will appreciate a variety of charts, tables, lists, and directories in a documentary editing volume. Of course, a bibliography is vital to list the sources you used and the sources that relate to the documents' content. Randall Miller, in *"Dear Master": Letters of a Slave Family*, used a bibliographic essay rather than a listed bibliography. The bibliographic essay discusses and analyzes the sources in the context of all literature on the subject. This is an acceptable substitution, is more manageable than an annotated bibliography, and provides the editor with an opportunity to place the volume in the context of other literature on the subject.

I especially recommend for the back of your book a "cast of characters," an annotated directory of names, and genealogical charts showing family relationships. The reader will lose track of the people mentioned in your documents or how they're

Idea Generator

related to one another. It would be too intrusive to jump in as the editor and remind readers who's who as they read the documents. So, appendixes that briefly identify people are helpful.

Many documentary editions include chronologies. The life and work of Thomas Edison or the creative decisions and life events of Anne Frank have justified chronologies. These may help your reader keep events straight and could include historical events, if relevant, for cross-referencing. Keeping helpfulness in mind, you may find several other types of documents, reports, or charts that are suited to appendixes. Perhaps the only worries are that they all be of acceptable quality to keep company with the main documents, that you present them professionally, and that they do not overwhelm the central documents.

SIXTEEN

What Else Can You Do?

The only thing new in the world is the history you don't know.

—*Harry Truman in Merle Miller's* Plain Speaking: An Oral Biography of Harry S. Truman, *New York: G. P. Putnam and Sons, 1974.*

W hen you have original, unpublished family documents in your possession, you have history that the rest of us don't know. There are many imaginative projects you might undertake to share your family documents. They can be more modest, quicker, or less ambitious projects than a full-length, widely published book. You could seek electronic publishing, develop a Web site, make a private family volume, publish an article, write your life stories, encourage someone else to write, or use oral history interviewing to create new family documents.

E-BOOKS, POD, AND WEB SITES

An "e-book" is an electronically produced book rather than one printed on paper. Some are electronically published on the Internet. Electronic "manuscripts" can transfer to CD-ROM, diskettes, or PDAs. A PDA, or personal digital assistant, is a gadget such as a Palm Pilot that you hold in your hand as you read books on its screen. Sometimes insiders call these "digi-books." Most e-publishers put your e-book online for free, and readers gain access for a fee and by having Adobe Acrobat Reader, which is also free. Another way to obtain an electronic book for reading is POD, or print-on-demand. You would gain a paper manuscript, but you would order your copy printed just for you rather than the publisher printing many copies in hopes of people buying them.

Electronic books are one wave of the future that family documentary editors need to investigate, but they aren't the only wave. There is some real potential in the medium, though, for short-run efforts, such as an edition of a family diary or memoir for relatives and libraries. **E-book methods of production save**

Money Saver

191

so much money that e-book publishers might be more open to your family publication than would traditional presses. The e-book publisher doesn't have large-scale overhead, warehouse costs, supply and printing costs, or the dreaded surplus of unwanted books returned by the brick-and-mortar bookstores. On the other hand, the e-book publisher does have huge market exposure, low-cost books that move fast, and the appeal of modern technology and convenience.

If you investigate electronic publishing for your family documents or your own memoir, advantages could include higher royalties, saved time, and perhaps a higher quality product, especially in its ability to link to seemingly unlimited resources and graphics on the World Wide Web. You can save time because from outlines to finished product, these methods cut many hard-copy editing steps. You might receive higher royalties than most of us authors—we get 10 to 15 percent and e-authors may get 35 to 70 percent (low end is POD, high end is e-books)—because e-publishers can afford to share more with you when they have so few costs. Some e-publishers want a fee from you, perhaps two hundred to three hundred dollars to start, especially for POD. Publishing simple e-books is often free. Some e-publishers allow you to print whatever you want, as long as you meet certain criteria such as contracting not to commit plagiarism or include pornography. Even the more discriminating e-publishers can be less so than a traditional print publisher, however, because they don't need a minimum, marketable print run to justify printing your book.

The documentary editing profession has ventured into electronic documentary texts. The best example is the Model Editions Partnership, begun in 1995. See <http://adh.sc.edu>. By making excerpts from great collections of papers available online, documentary editors increase research and public access. Each of the Model Editions Partnership projects includes Web sites that introduce the papers collections, images of the original documents, excerpts from the documents, and hyperlinks to other resources and illustrations. These separate sites could be models for some of your efforts. If you're experienced with electronic publishing and want some intense, scholarly, technical, documentary editing guidelines for it, see the "Markup Guidelines for Documentary Editions" at <http://adh.sc.edu/MepGuide.html>.

One reason documentary editors are carefully discussing the potential of electronic publishing is because modern search engines should be adaptable for high-quality indexing. Before long, editors might be able to "teach" search engines the subtleties of historical indexing. Another scholarly project to watch is the History E-Book Project, in which the American Council of Learned Societies is operating under a three-million-dollar grant from the Andrew Mellon Foundation. That project is not soliciting our manuscripts now, but it's preparing to publish (electronically) old and new scholarly editions. These excellent research materials will be available through library subscriptions. Eventually, the project could lead to scholarly presses obtaining formerly unknown documents like ours for e-publishing. See <www.historyebook.org/>.

Internet Source

Some E-Publishers to Investigate

Booklocker.com

www.booklocker.com/getpublished/published.html

Ebookstand.com
   www.ebookstand.com/authors_1.html
Electron Press
   www.electronpress.com/Epexec/frmain.asp
Fatbrain.com
   www.fatbrain.com
iUniverse.com
   www.iuniverse.com
xlibris.com
   www2.xlibris.com

Hesitate and Investigate

Most writers, publishers, and historians do not yet foresee the e-book supplanting the printed book. Bound, paper books are already portable and handheld (although a PDA could store several books at once). Electronic publishing is new, flashy, and in some cases fly-by-night. (Some e-book publishers have gone out of business just during the production of this book.) We who do historical and documentary research, writing, editing, and publishing cannot yet pinpoint which e-publishers might be the most reliable for your projects. Furthermore, we cannot recommend this route, and we cannot offer case studies or examples of happy family historians who have published documents this way.

I recommend looking for writers guides to e-publishing. See Debbie Ridpath Ohi's *Writer's Online Marketplace* for specific advice on publishers, techniques, how to apply for publication and promote, making Web sites, and the experiences of those who have ventured there. If I were entering into my first e-book contract, I would seek legal advice. Some recent court cases have clearly protected authors' copyrights in electronic formats, but one cannot be too careful in a new and fast-changing environment. Typically, an e-book publisher might purchase your rights for a few years. Be sure to protect the rights from transferring into other media without your say-so. Be aware, too, that as e-publishers become more established, they are introducing review processes and closer scrutiny of manuscripts. Quality standards can only become more demanding, as they are in any field. You might as well look for a "right" way to publish your precious family documents rather than just an "easy" way.

Questions to Ask an E-Publisher*

*The best e-publishers already answer most of these questions openly on their Web sites.

- Do I retain complete copyright to my work?
- What do you charge me up front?
- What royalties do you pay for POD? For e-books?
- Do you pay monthly?
- Do you provide each author with a Web site?
- How quickly do you turn out a POD book for an order (forty-eight hours or six weeks)?
- How much discount do you give the author for POD copies?
- How will you promote my e-book?

Reminder

- Do you have a sales-tracking system I can view?
- If I don't have a disk, can you scan my manuscript?
- Do you offer any training workshops or guidelines?
- Do you sponsor a writers' club or peer review of some kind?

WEB SITES

You may already have or be planning a family Web site. A Web site can be a way to bring about contact with other descendants of your ancestors, which can lead to treasure troves of information, documents, and heirlooms. It also can provide the satisfaction of sharing and making friends. Both privacy and copyright concerns, however, suggest we should exercise caution with serious family history information and materials. Enthusiasts casually place family information online as though there are no restrictions. Yet that is giving broad access, without permission, to sometimes private and sensitive information about others. The best advice is to be just as cautious as you would be if putting the same information in print. As for family documents, consider who owns copyright and, then also consider your plans and purposes for the documents, if you do have the rights to them.

If you have no other publishing plans for your family heirloom documents, you may wish to share them on a Web site. This is especially safe and helpful to others in the case of brief, informational or bureaucratic documents (such as an old will) rather than book-length diaries, memoirs, or letter collections. But for these text-rich pieces that could qualify for print publishing, even on a commercial scale, why not at least attempt that before disseminating them far and wide on the Internet? If you do transcribe or scan them onto a Web site, you should still follow high standards regarding copyright permissions, transcription, annotation, and emendation, as delineated here and in the documentary editing guides. There is little point to making documents available for research if the researchers cannot rely on the accuracy of the electronic versions.

Internet Source

Examples abound of documentary editing onto Web sites. **In chapter one, I mentioned genealogist Birdie Holsclaw's work with the Colorado School for the Deaf and the Blind. To see this example, go to <www.holsclaw.net/CSDBPupils/csdbproj.htm>,** where Holsclaw placed a chronological table of the students; indexes of them, their families, and their localities; a list of the records used; and a photo of students, 1887–1888. Thus, she found a way to share her discoveries with others, transcribing and organizing the information in a professional way. This kind of documentary editing is most valuable and is not the release of text-rich documents that might better suit book publishing.

Another interesting example of using a Web site is the 106th Infantry Division Home Page, whose Web master, Sgt. John Kline, is also the editor of a regiment magazine *The Cub*. See <www.mm.com/user/jpk/>. The 106th Infantry Division fought in World War II's Battle of the Bulge. I became familiar with Kline's Web site for the 106th veterans association because of my husband's research on his father's war experiences. At this site, Kline presents his own war diary, copyrighted but available to print, along with writings other veterans wish to share. The site includes news of reunions, members' life events, and relevant publications. Through Kline's information, Rick has located books and resources that support our documenting of Wendell's war experiences.

Some of the discoveries have held great personal meaning. Partly through the association, Rick located an officer whom Wendell remembered from 1944. In 1999, thanks to Rick's research through the Internet, we had an address and phone number for the officer. I telephoned him to ask him if he was, indeed, the man we were looking for and had a wonderful interview with him. We then put him in touch with Wendell. A new correspondence and friendship grew between the veterans. When Carol Sturdevant died, Rick informed Kline, who spread the word of her death among members through the association listserv. Wendell received condolences from peers who had shared his war experiences and similar losses of loved ones. One poem was so appropriate that Rick read it aloud at Carol's memorial service.

A VISUAL VOLUME

If you have a particularly visual family heirloom document, such as a text-rich scrapbook or photograph album, consider proposing an artistically representative book to a publisher. I'm sorry to say that the best example I've found of this so far is fictional. The author presents it throughout as though it were a family album passed down in her husband's family. One might never know it's fiction without reading the fine-print notes in the back. That subterfuge aside, Sallyann J. Murphey's *The Metcalfe Family Album: Six Generations of Traditions and Memories* is still an excellent model for publishing a factual, nonfiction family album.

Case Study

The Metcalfe Family Album includes firsthand accounts by members of the family from 1835 through 1996 (all fictional, remember). Clearly, the author researched the social history and typical experiences of the times to create these accounts. Other documents appear as though transcribed from family papers: recipes, household hints, children's games, home remedies, and holiday customs. Illustrations include authentic ephemera such as greeting cards, needlework, advertisements, pressed flowers and herbs, political campaign memorabilia, tickets, pictures of clothing, sketches of homes, autograph books, postcards, seed packets, theatre programs, paper souvenirs, news clippings and headlines, and scraps. For representations of family members, Murphey provided photographs (historic unrelated ones from archives or ones of unrelated, living people who posed in character for the author), portraits, and the characters' fictional names on authentic representations of funeral cards, letters, invitations, telegrams, certificates, and even a ration book. There is an introduction "written by" the album's fictitious author, Jan Andersen Metcalfe, which offers the provenance for the family collection, as though real.

In the fine-print acknowledgments in the back of the book, Murphey wrote in her own voice and made clear that friends and experts provided archival research; calligraphy; photography; drawing; computer graphics; ephemera collections; cooking, medical, and weather expertise; knowledge of Indian, Catholic, military, and foreign ways; and the answers to many technical questions. The repositories of materials and expertise included county and state historical

Figures 16-1 and 16-2 Outside and inside of a birthday card from Archibald "Papa" Harper to his granddaughter, Katherine Scott, 13 February 1958. Scott Family Papers, in author's possession.

Figure 16-3 Christmas gift tag from Archibald "Papa" Harper to his granddaughter, Katherine Scott, 1957. Scott Family Papers, in author's possession.

societies, foreign consulates, university archives, families to whom some items belonged, and a wide variety of specialized museums. Murphey interviewed and used the oral history interviews of others. In the research fashion of a journalist, she pinned down reliable experts and asked them what she needed to know.

We could look at *The Metcalfe Family Album* as a statement that no one family has so much material for a book, and so an author had to make it up for it to be this good. But reverse that point of view. Sallyann J. Murphey and her many helpers could put together such an appealing and seemingly authentic family album because the information and materials are there, in our families

Figure 16-4 Archibald "Papa" Harper holding his granddaughter, Katherine Scott, May 1955. Scott Family Papers, in author's possession.

EPHEMERA AS ILLUSTRATIONS

Among ephemera, even Christmas gift tags and greeting cards can serve as documentary illustrations. They are appealing period pieces. They portray sentiment, which is always a challenge in family history writing and documentary editing, and they even reveal family history information. Obviously, in Figures 16-1, 16-2, 16-3 (page 196), and 16-4 (above), Archibald L. Harper commemorated his granddaughter's birthday (13 February 1955) and gave her a Christmas gift when she was two to three years old. Her parents named her Katherine (after Harper's mother). Her mother called her "Kathie." Yet "Papa" insisted on calling his first granddaughter "my Katie," perhaps as a reference to his late wife, Kate.

Idea Generator

and in public collections about families and social history. **Take a model like this as a way to organize and illustrate your papers.** Note that the effort involved some of the same background research you can do for your family history. As you annotate your documents, the questions you need to answer will be similar to the ones that sent Murphey seeking technical experts. You can even do as she did with illustrations, sometimes using a picture or piece of ephemera that was not from your family but that illustrates what was typical of families like yours. Please, always write nonfiction family history and identify the true source of anything included—but don't hesitate to learn from fictional works. As with fine literature, they teach us artistic style that we can blend with our factual accuracy, without necessarily compromising either.

PUBLISHING AN ARTICLE

Remember that you may have a document or a group of documents suitable for publication in periodicals. Use the AASLH directory again, this time for historical societies that publish magazines and journals. It is common for state historical societies to publish one or both of the following types of periodicals:

1. a scholarly journal (rarely illustrated) of research articles and documents
2. a heavily illustrated magazine of more popularly written articles

If your document(s) reveals some unusually useful historical information for scholars, the first kind of journal might publish it, especially with a serious introduction, annotation, and provenance. If you have several appealing illustrations to go with it and it has general appeal, give it a lighter-toned introduction, annotation, and provenance. Read an issue of the journal or magazine to see the house style, tone, and presentation, or request their style sheet. Attempt to imitate it.

Some genealogical society magazines will also feature articles about documents or collections of papers. *New England Ancestors*, "Newsmagazine of the New England Historic Genealogical Society," for example, recently published an issue on "Exploring Manuscript Collections at the NEHGS" (winter 2001). In this case, it was articles resulting from family donations to the archives. In Virginia, one of the most prestigious scholarly historical journals, the *William and Mary Quarterly*, carries on the tradition of publishing even single, brief documents if they offer new insight into early American history to 1820. The quarterly provides guidelines for preparing documents (based on the Kline and Stevens/Burg books) at <www.oieahc.h-net.msu.edu/prep.html>. Keep in mind the possibility that there may be a suitable magazine or scholarly journal for your shorter family documents.

THE LIFE STORY PHENOMENON

Come back to the idea of creating new family documents. Perhaps you or some of your relatives should be writing memoirs today. There is a movement afoot to write life stories, or personal or family memoirs. Some of it is generated by writers such as Denis Ledoux in *Turning Family Memories Into Memoirs* and *The Photo*

Scribe. These books encourage and guide you to write in the form of family stories, or combine photographs with storytelling captions and "cameo narratives." See also <www.turningmemories.com/> for companion workshops, leader training, editing services, and memoirs. The National Endowment for the Humanities Web site, "My History is America's History," at <www.myhistory.org>, offers interactive sections where you can record family and personal stories for posterity. This is also a good place to read other people's stories and see how they did it.

Use whatever it takes to get memoirs recorded. Many people use classes, workshops, guidebooks, clubs, and mentors to keep them motivated. Perhaps most urgent is that you convince an older relative to write. In that case, especially if the relative is reluctant, modest, insecure, or truly not a good writer, your reassurances and constant enthusiasm are key to creating new documents. Remember that you could edit the relative's memoir later.

How to Get Yourself or a Relative Writing

Technique

- Stress how important this memoir will be as a historical document, a legacy to family, or even a publication for a larger audience.
- Appeal to the writer's desire to "get it all down" before it's too late.
- Write now and write often, even in fragments.
- Write story by story. This usually causes the accounts to have themes, beginnings, and conclusions.
- Don't worry about whether it is "good enough."
- Identify who's who and what's what as you go.
- Include how you felt or what you thought at the time.
- Use memory jogs such as photographs, scrapbooks, or letters.
- Start with outlines or chronologies as memory jogs.
- Consider audience to the extent of explaining things but not so as to handicap yourself. You can always revise later.

Writer's Digest offers many writing workshops, including some specializing in writing personal or family memoirs, which I've team taught. The students have been an interesting mix of middle-aged people writing personal memoirs of self-discovery after major life events, family historians writing narrative on their families or biographies of individual relatives, and memoirists who, at the end of long lives, have much to record. See <www.writersonlineworkshops.com/>. In addition to what students learn from reading assignments, instructors find ourselves repeating the same advice to one student after another.

Tips for Better Memoir Writing

Tip

- Research the social history of the times of your story so you can explain the family or individuals, even yourself, in a larger context.
- Look for and pursue the guiding themes and subthemes of the narrative.
- Establish your "voice," including whether to use first person (in your own memoir) or third person (in a biography of someone else or a family memoir).
- Write about the past in past tense.
- Show, don't tell: Describe events, characters, and scenes as they unfolded

rather than summarizing them with generalizations.

- Look outward, writing about others, events, and settings, rather than seeming preoccupied with yourself and your introspection.
- Identify esoteric or dated references that may be unfamiliar to your readers.
- Try to be objective enough as a storyteller to overcome your life's prejudices.
- Introduce the story with a "hook," a scene or statement that draws readers in.
- Always keep your audience in mind.
- Do not fictionalize or state anything you do not know as fact, unless you make clear what is speculative.

Printed Source

These kinds of tips are available in more advanced memoir-writing guides that assist you in writing publishable-quality reminiscences. **For example, Tristine Rainer's** *Your Life as Story* **and Judith Barrington's** *Writing the Memoir* **specifically orient their guidelines toward literary style.** Your memoirs can be nonfiction and still have flow, plot, setting, characterization, humor, pathos, and style. This will make them more publishable and more rewarding. See the Bibliography for additional memoir and creative nonfiction writing guides.

THE ORAL HISTORY IMPERATIVE

Oral History

If your older relatives can not or will not write their memoirs, remember the value of oral history interviewing. Indeed, don't wait for them to write memoirs. Even if you have no other documents of substantive length in your family, if you have elderly relatives who can remember and communicate, you have documents in the making. As soon as those relatives die or lose their abilities to remember or communicate, you have lost documents.

For guidelines, see chapter five in *Bringing Your Family History to Life Through Social History*. For questions phrased to fit the decades of twentieth-century lives, see William Fletcher's *Recording Your Family History*. For guidance about transcribing oral history, see pages 120–123 of this book. Just do it. Write or call folks now and ask whether they will tell stories for you. Take your equipment whenever you visit likely interviewees, and break it out. You can transcribe, edit, and prepare for publication later, but now is the time to create the original document by taping your older relatives.

FAMILY CONTINUITY AND SOCIAL CONTRIBUTION

Ultimately, why should you organize, edit, preserve, or even publish your family documents? Look back to the beginning of chapter one. Each of us who has a diary, memoir, letters, or other firsthand account in our families feels compelled to "get them out there." We feel a responsibility to our ancestors, even if they expected nothing of us. Our responsibility is more to what we thought of them or what we came to think when we discovered their documents. We want to show them in their best light, even if the ancestors are long gone and didn't really care about posthumous repute. We want to do them justice.

The documents themselves are relics, and, though it may seem overly sentimental of us, we attach feelings to the relics. Just seeing, touching, and reading "the real thing" is a family history experience for many of us. We infuse each word of each document with deeper meaning because we know more stories and personalities than the words themselves reveal. Adding our extra knowledge as annotation or integrated text makes the stories whole and connects us with our ancestor-authors in a collaborative effort.

Discovering firsthand accounts, we come to know people for the first time or to know them better. After my mother-in-law, Carol Sturdevant, died, her daughters and I were sorting through her notebooks and Bibles to find her writings and favored scriptures for use in her memorial service. Sister Susie found a homemade scrapbook by Carol, probably circa 1970. The fragile booklet's childlike simplicity was breathtaking. Always one to make do with little, ever since her Depression-era childhood, Carol had pieced the scrapbook from what she had. The cover was from a floral "Pee-Chee" folder, left over from her children's school supplies. She illustrated each stage of her life with a few photographs and with many cutouts from worn children's books and magazine advertisements.

The scrapbook was a self-conscious testimonial to Carol's "acceptance of the Lord," sort of a modest woman's *Pilgrim's Progress*. There was valuable family history, such as memories of her mother in the 1930s: "Her hard working hands to earn more money for the family. Taking in laundry, baking brown bobbies to sell. I went with her and these were long walks but happy memories." Carol used cigarette ads to illustrate her decision to quit trying to be "Lady Cool." She told of overcoming worries, of her happy marriage, and of her joy in having six children. She left a precious document, made of simple cut and paste, that still helps family know her, her life's priorities, and her final wishes.

Historical analysts of diaries and scrapbooks are finding deeper family and psychological meanings in these documents, too. In an article called "Within a Scrapbook's Pages," curator Susan Tucker noted that college women kept scrapbooks in the late nineteenth and early twentieth centuries as an acceptable transition from the domestic sphere to the broader world. Archivist Jim Hofer was pleased to receive the 1920s diary of Walter Thomas, a University of Redlands student, because it captures student life at that time. Descendant Jerry Thomas, who donated the diary, will be glad to see it displayed with honor during the university's centennial. (See the Bibliography for an article about this by Mark Henry.) Walter's diary included accounts of his remarkable efforts to make ends meet, including cleaning streetlights, in order to pay his total tuition and expenses of $500.

Biographer Judy Temple has been studying the diary and scrapbook fragments of the infamous "Baby Doe" Tabor, who went from mistress to wife to hermit-widow of mining tycoon Horace Tabor in Leadville, Colorado. Temple believes that even the scraps of sporadic writing by an unstable woman, who called them her "Dreams and Visions," can, with editorial explanation, become revealing of women and society at that time. Another series of historians has

\di'fin *vb*

Definitions

> ## HISTORICAL EMPATHY
>
> Historical empathy (a term I believe I am coining) is the ability to research and understand past lives well enough to walk a mile in their shoes, experience intellectually and emotionally what they must have experienced, and thus deeply understand their behaviors. Empathy does not mean just tolerance for (putting up with) someone or something. It does not mean sympathy or pity. It means imagining what the other person feels so accurately and deeply that you feel it yourself.
>
> —From *Bringing Your Family History to Life Through Social History*, 215

studied the diaries of Emily Hawley Gillespie and Sarah Gillespie Huftalen. The mother and daughter occasionally wrote entries for each other, as they suffered their own and their menfolks' nervous exhaustion or "crazy spells." English professor Suzanne Bunkers noted the many layers of careful analysis needed to understand diaries created under those circumstances. Again, literary analysis sometimes suits our documents best.

One family even felt that its albums were so important to family cohesion that taking apart the books meant taking apart the family. In "Division of Things Past: An Account of the Making and Unmaking of a Family Album," Madeleine Blais wrote what a mistake it was to dismantle and subdivide the albums her mother had compiled. There were six children, so they believed it was best to urge Mother to split the "big, bulging repositories," so each child could keep the parts most pertinent to herself. "More than just a file keeper," Blais wrote, "my mother was in fact an author, a shaping intelligence, and we were the characters, the players." Later, with their mother gone, the sisters realized their mistake. The second-generation albums didn't make sense, ended abruptly, and reflected the divergence of the family members. They felt it would be impossible to restore the original order. In a way, it seemed, they had added to their family split by splitting the family album.

We relate to our ancestors through their written relics and thus can empathize with them. Ultimately, this is the contribution our documents can make to society as well. Every primary document made available for public research or reading provides untold information and perspective. Historians and other analysts might find in our documents answers to specific questions or whole pictures of times, places, and lifestyles. They might even reach deep into the hearts of our ancestor-authors, learning lessons about life and relationships that are timeless.

By reading our ancestors' thoughts and experiences, people could gain new insight, walk a mile in our ancestors' shoes, and perhaps apply those lessons not only to research but to life. What we gain from our family documents, society can also gain, and then some. By bringing our ancestors' documents to light, we share our ancestors' contributions with a larger world. It is a gift to those who came before, to researchers and readers, and to ourselves. Preserving and making available your family papers could be one of the most important accomplishments of your life. It is an achievement you can share with your ancestor-authors, a partnership with people of the past, people you miss, or even people you never met. Your ancestors spoke to their times in the documents they created. Now you can give them voice for present and future generations.

Selected Glossary

Note: This glossary is an additional key to some of the terminology of the fields—documentary editing in particular—that I interpret in this book. I have tried to define these terms and other unfamiliar words with examples within the text. So please, when in doubt, go to the index to find the most definitive mentions of such terms. This glossary is in everyday language for people working on family history projects, not for professionals.

Annotation, to annotate—Annotation is the explanatory information that you add, as a documentary editor, to make original documents clear and complete for your audience. You usually do this through footnotes or endnotes, although integrated paragraphs of text can make smoother or more convenient reading. Remember to make sure, however, that the documents are true to their original form and that the distinction between them and the annotation is clear.

Archival, archivist, archival quality—Archives are where you would find most collections of original documents. An archivist specializes in collecting, organizing, and caring for those documents while making them and the information they contain accessible for researchers. Archival quality is the term commonly applied to supplies that meet standards for conservation, such as paper, folders, and albums made acid-free, buffered, or otherwise protective against deterioration.

Authoritative edition—The authoritative edition of a book or collection of documents is the ultimate, final, comprehensive edition. This normally requires the editors to have completed exhaustive research to make sure they have included or rejected every other version of those documents and every relevant piece of information that they can. We most often use the term to apply to editions of literary classics, where there have been many versions over the years through which editors have sifted to pinpoint the author's original intent.

Conservation, conservator—In this context, conservation refers to preserving original documents, books, and artifacts. The conservator is an expert on all aspects of care for museum and library collections. He or she knows how to protect rare items, rescue them from disaster, and restore them from damage.

Documentary editing, documentary edition, documentary editor—Documentary editing is the profession and practice of collecting, organizing, transcribing, annotating, emending, analyzing, and usually publishing original papers of historical or literary interest. Although the term most purely applies to preparing a published edition of documents, the typical documentary editor also serves as the collection's archivist, historian, and protector.

Emendation, to emend, silent or overt emendation—Even though we call the field documentary editing, when we deal with original documents we are reluctant to refer to the small, necessary changes made after transcription as "editing." Editing implies a heavier hand bringing documents into a "house style." It's a fine distinction, but to emend means to make the small but consistent changes needed for clarity in a transcribed document. A common example is capitalization and punctuation to make clear sentence breaks where the document's author did not. Silent emendation is when we announce the changes only in an introduction, not at every occasion. Overt emendation is when we call attention to a change every time by a device such as brackets.

Ephemera—Ephemera is a general term for printed materials that are not full-length documents, for commercially or publicly produced materials, and for three-dimensional memorabilia, all of which we find among our ancestors' documents and many documentary collections. Typical ephemera illustrated in this book include booklets, ink blotters, greeting cards, and death notices. The term implies insignificance, but today we recognize the social history documented by such materials.

Genre—A literary genre is a category or type of literary writing. We can also use the term to apply to other types of writing such as memoir and life-story writing.

Literary criticism, literary critic, critical edition—Literary criticism sounds as though it might mean writing critical reviews of new novels. That certainly falls under literary criticism. When we speak of it in connection with original manuscripts and authoritative editions of classic literature, however, we mean that the critic, the authority on that author or work, uses knowledge and research to evaluate and comment upon aspects of the work. In a critical edition, the comments appear throughout, usually by means of footnotes and endnotes.

Manuscripts collection—In libraries and archives, collections of the kinds of documents we're discussing are called manuscripts collections. This distinguishes them from published books on the library shelves, the assumption being that manuscripts are unpublished.

Marginalia—Marginalia is the term for writings and drawings that someone has marked in the margins of a book, printed page, or document. We don't usually mean simple editing or additions, such as those someone might write into the margins of his own letter. Marginalia implies separate comments added later, often to someone else's writing.

Oral history, oral history interview—Oral history is the field and practice of carefully interviewing people, usually on tape, to gain a record of their recollections. The oral history interview is one that follows professional standards and usually one that is a whole story (such as that person's whole life story or whole account of an incident) in the taped session(s).

Provenance—The provenance of a document or artifact is the record of its life, ownership, and location. With documents, provenance statements at least direct the reader where to go and whom to contact for the original document. Usually, for historically old and significant documents or artifacts, provenance also includes documentation of the item's origins, how it passed from one owner or home to the next, any "adventures" it had along the way, and how it came into its current location.

Repositories—This term means places where professional archivists, librarians, and curators care for valuable and historical collections. It's easier and more inclusive to use this term than to try to list all the possible places you can find or donate a document or an artifact.

Scholarly, scholarly sources—Scholarly research, writing, editing, publishing, or methods refer to work performed by scholars to a high, reliable, scholarly standard. We usually define a scholar as one with at least graduate degrees and successful research experience in a recognized research field, if not also a college teaching or research position and publications. Some of the methods and standards of scholarly work are, however, accessible to others, such as you working with your family heirloom documents. To determine whether a book is a scholarly source, and therefore presumably more accurate and reliable, read the author's credentials and research acknowledgments, reviews in scholarly journals, and footnotes and endnotes. These should indicate intense, original research in primary sources such as records, not just the other books on the subject.

Series—In documentary editing and archives, a series is a way to categorize and organize documents such as letters within a collection. The series is usually a chronological group within a larger collection, such as the Revolutionary War Series or Presidential Series of George Washington's papers.

Style—In editing, style refers to how writers and editors adjust the appearance, readability, and consistency of text. It may refer to a style dictated by one professional organization's manual, or it may refer to the house style of a given publisher or magazine. Style includes everything an editor may expect of or do to a manuscript, especially the technicalities of grammar, punctuation, capitalization, etc. As an editor of documents, you will want to establish a minimalist style for emendations but not a house style that changes the original document for reasons of passing preference. Nevertheless, most documentary editing style choices are based on the patterns recommended by prominent publishing style manuals.

Text, textual document—In documentary editing, text might mean any written passages but often means the original documents' words. When I refer to a textual document, I am differentiating one of your documents with a lot of worthy verbiage to transcribe, such as a letter, vs. one with scattered, sparse words, such as a diary or an account book with meager entries. A document rich in lengthy original text is probably a better candidate for a documentary editing project.

Transcribe, transcription, expanded transcription—A transcription of a document or other recording should be as exact a copy as possible. The transcriber does that, then the documentary editor (often the same individual) may decide how to emend or edit. The machine that helps play tapes for transcribing oral history is also called a transcriber or transcribing machine, even though it doesn't literally do the job for you. Expanded transcription is the type you are most likely to do with your own documents. It means you transcribe them but also make decisions of what to leave in or out, as well as emendations and annotations, all well explained and consistent.

Verifying the text—Documentary editors use this term often in place of proofreading, although verifying includes proofreading. Verifying, more importantly, means that you have proofread transcriptions against the originals, after whatever emendations and annotations, to verify that your new version accurately reproduces the original.

Reaching the Professionals

ARCHIVAL PRODUCTS SUPPLIERS

Archival Products

P.O. Box 1413, Des Moines, IA 50305-1413
Phone: (800) 526-5640   Fax: (515) 262-6013 or (888) 220-2397
E-mail: info@archival.com
Web site: www.archival.com

Conservation Materials Ltd.

1165 Marietta Way, P.O. Box 2884, Sparks, NV 89431
Phone: (702) 331-0582

Exposures

1 Memory Lane, Oshkosh, WI 54903-3615
Phone: (800) 222-4947   Fax: (888) 345-3702 or (888) 345-6693
Help: (800) 428-3631
E-mail: csr@exposuresonline.com
Web site: www.exposuresonline.com/

Gaylord Brothers

P.O. Box 4901, Syracuse, NY 13221-4901
Phone: (800) 448-6160   Fax: (800) 272-3412
Web site: www.gaylord.com/

Hollinger Corporation

P.O. Box 8360, Fredericksburg, VA 22404
Phone: (800) 634-0491
Web site: www.genealogicalstorageproducts.com/

Light Impressions Archival Supplies

P.O. Box 787, Brea, CA 92822-0787
Phone: (800) 828-6216   Fax: (800) 828-5539
E-mail: LiWebsite@limpressions.com
Web site: www.LightImpressionsDirect.com

Metal Edge, Inc.

Archival Storage Materials
6340 Bandini Blvd., Commerce, CA 90040
Phone: (800) 862-2228   Fax: (888) 822-6937
E-mail: info@metaledgeinc.com
Web site: www.metaledgeinc.com

University Products, Inc.

517 Main St., P.O. Box 101, Holyoke, MA 01041-0101
Phone: (800) 628-1912   Fax: (800) 532-9281
Questions: (800) 762-1165
E-mail: info@universityproducts.com
Web site: www.universityproducts.com

ORGANIZATIONS CITED

American Association for State and Local History (AASLH)

1717 Church St., Nashville, TN 37203-2991

Phone: (615) 320-3203   Fax: (615) 327-9013

E-mail: history@aaslh.org

Web site: www.aaslh.org

American Institute for Conservation of Historic and Artistic Works (AIC)

1717 K St., NW, Suite 310, Washington, DC 20006

Phone: (202) 452-9545   Fax: (202) 452-9328

E-mail: info@aic-faic.org

Web site: http://aic.stanford.edu/

American Society of Indexers (ASI)

10200 W. Forty-fourth Ave., Suite 304, Wheat Ridge, CO 80033

Phone: (303) 463-2887   Fax: (303) 422-8894

E-mail: info@asindexing.org

Web site: www.asindexing.org/

Association for Documentary Editing (ADE)

Secretary James P. McClure

Papers of Thomas Jefferson

Firestone Library, Princeton University, Princeton, NJ 08544

Phone: (609) 258-5687   Fax: (609) 258-1630

E-mail: mcclure@princeton.edu

Web site: http://etext.virginia.edu/ade/

Association of American University Presses (AAUP)

71 W. Twenty-third St., New York, NY 10010

Phone: (212) 989-1010   Fax: (212) 989-0275

Web site: http://aaupnet.org/

Heritage Preservation (HP)

1730 K St., NW, Suite 566, Washington, DC 20006-3836

Phone: (202) 634-1422 or (888) 388-6789   Fax: (202) 634-1435

E-mail: rhouse@heritagepreservation.org

Web site: www.heritagepreservation.org

Library of Congress

101 Independence Ave. SE, Washington, DC 20540

Phone: (202) 707-5000

E-mail: lcweb@loc.gov

Web site: www.loc.gov

Modern Language Association (MLA)

26 Broadway, Third Floor, New York, NY 10004-1789

Phone: (646) 576-5000   Fax: (646) 458-0030

Web site: www.mla.org/

National Endowment for the Humanities (NEH)

1100 Pennsylvania Ave. NW, Washington, DC 20506

Phone: (202) 606-8400

Web sites: www.neh.gov/ or www.myhistory.org

National Historical Publications and Records Commission (NHPRC)

National Archives and Records Administration

700 Pennsylvania Ave. NW, Room 111, Washington, DC 20408-0001

Phone: (202) 501-5610   Fax: (202) 501-5601

Web site: www.nara.gov/nhprc/

New England Historic Genealogical Society (NEHGS)

101 Newbury St., Boston, MA 02116-3007

Phone: (617) 536-5740

Web site: www.nehgs.org

Northeast Document Conservation Center (NDCC)

100 Brickstone Square, Andover, MA 01810-1494

Phone: (978) 470-1010   Fax: (978) 475-6021

E-mail: nedcc@nedcc.org

Web site: www.nedcc.org/

Oral History Association (OHA)

Dickinson College, P.O. Box 1773, Carlisle, PA 17013

Phone: (717) 245-1036   Fax: (717) 245-1046

E-mail: OHA@dickinson.edu

Web site: www.dickinson.edu/oha/

Smithsonian Center for Materials Research and Education (SCMRE)

Museum Support Center, 4210 Silver Hill Rd., Suitland, MD 20746

Phone: (301) 238-3700   Fax: (301) 238-3709

Web site: www.si.edu/scmre

Society of American Archivists (SAA)

527 S. Wells St., Fifth Floor, Chicago, IL 60607-3922

Phone: (312) 922-0140   Fax: (312) 347-1452

E-mail: info@archivists.org

Web site: www.archivists.org/

OTHER HISTORICAL AND GENEALOGICAL ORGANIZATIONS

The American Historical Association (AHA)

400 A St. SE, Washington, DC 20003-3899

Phone: (202) 544-2422   Fax: (202) 544-8307

E-mail: aha@theaha.org

Web site: www.theaha.org/

Association of Personal Historians (APH)

1509 S. Raitt St., Unit C

Santa Ana, CA 92704

Phone: (800) 449-7483

Web site: www.personalhistorians.org/

Association of Professional Genealogists (APG)

P.O. Box 40393, Denver, CO 80204-0393

Phone: (303) 422-9371   Fax: (303) 456-8825

E-mail: admin@apgen.org

Web site: www.apgen.org

Ephemera Society of America

P.O. Box 95, Cazenovia, NY 13035-0095

Web site: www.ephmerasociety.org/index.html

Family History Library of the Church of Jesus Christ of Latter-day Saints (FHL, LDS)

35 N. West Temple St., Salt Lake City, UT 84150-3400

Phone: (801) 240-2331   Fax: (801) 240-1584

E-mail: fhl@ldschurch.org

Web site: www.familysearch.org

Federation of Genealogical Societies (FGS)

P.O. Box 200940, Austin, TX 78720-0940

Phone: (888) FGS-1500   Fax: (888) 380-0500

E-mail: fgs-office@fgs.org

Web site: www.fgs.org/

National Genealogical Society (NGS)

4527 Seventeenth St. N., Arlington, VA 22207-2399

Phone: (703) 525-0050 or (800) 473-0060   Fax: (703) 525-0052

E-mail: ngs@ngsgenealogy.org

Web site: www.ngsgenealogy.org

National Society, Daughters of the American Revolution (DAR)

1776 D St., NW, Washington, DC 20006-5303

Phone: (202) 628-1776

E-mail: museum@dar.org

Web site: www.dar.org/natsociety/default.html

Organization of American Historians (OAH)

112 N. Bryan Ave., Bloomington, IN 47408-4199

Phone: (812) 855-7311   Fax: (812) 855-0696

E-mail: oah@oah.org

Web site: www.oah.org

Western History Association (WHA)

1080 Mesa Vista Hall, University of New Mexico, Albuquerque, NM 87131-1181

Phone: (505) 277-5234   Fax: (505) 277-6023

E-mail: wha@unm.edu

Web site: www.unm.edu/~wha/

SUGGESTED POTENTIAL PUBLISHERS

AltaMira Press (for AASLH directory)

1630 N. Main St., Suite 367, Walnut Creek, CA 94596

Phone: (925) 938-7243 or (800) 462-6420   Fax: (925) 933-9720

E-mail: explore@altamirapress.com

Web site: www.altamirapress.com

Anundsen Publishing Co.

P.O. Box 230, 108 Washington St., Decorah, IA 52101

Phone: (319) 382-4295 or (888) 382-4291   Fax: (319) 382-6532

E-mail: mail@anundsenpubl.com

Web site: www.anundsenpubl.com

Booklocker.com, Inc.
E-mail: Angela@booklocker.com
Web site: www.booklocker.com/getpublished/published.html

Ebookstand.com
P.O. Box 7670, Auburn, CA 95604
Web site: www.ebookstand.com/authors_1.html

Electron Press
E-mail: editor@electronpress.com
Web site: www.electronpress.com/Epexec/frmain.asp

Family History Publishers
845 S. Main St., Bountiful, UT 84010
Phone: (801) 295-7490
E-mail: Jayl@familyhistorypublisher.com
Web site: www.familyhistorypublisher.com

Family Tree Press at iUniverse.com
5220 S. Sixteenth, Suite 200, Lincoln, NE 68512
Phone: (800) 376-1736
E-mail: pubservices@iuniverse.com
Web sites: www.iuniverse.com or www.iuniverse.com/publish/family_tree/
family_tree.asp

Fatbrain.com
Phone: (877) 328-2724 or (201) 272-3652
E-mail: contact-us@fatbrain.com
Web site: www.fatbrain.com/

Gateway Press
1001 N. Calvert St., Baltimore, MD 21202-3897
Phone: (800) 296-6687   Fax: (410) 752-8492
E-mail: ahughes@GatewayPress.com
Web site: www.gatewaypress.com

The Gregath Publishing Co.
P.O. Box 505, Wyandotte, OK 74370
Phone: (918) 542-4148
E-mail: staff@gregathcompany.com
Web site: www.gregathcompany.com/

Newbury Street Press
101 Newbury St., Boston, MA 02116-3007
Phone: (617) 536-5740   Fax: (617) 536-7307
E-mail: nsp@nehgs.org
Web site: www.newenglandancestors.org/articles/newbury_press/

Picton Press
P.O. Box 250, Rockport, ME 04856
Phone: (207) 236-6565   Fax: (207) 236-6713
E-mail: sales@pictonpress.com
Web site: www.pictonpress.com/catalog/about.htm

Tennessee Valley Publishing
P.O. Box 52527, Knoxville, TN 37950-2577
Phone: (800) 762-7079.

E-mail: info@tvp1.com

Web site: http://tvp1.com/

William and Mary Quarterly (WMQ)

P.O. Box 8781, Williamsburg, VA 23187-8781

Phone: (757) 221-1126   Fax: (757) 221-1047

E-mail: kawahl@facstaff.wm.edu

Web site: www.oieahc.h-net.msu.edu/WMQ.html

Windmill Publications

6628 Uebelhack Rd., Mt. Vernon, IN 47620

Phone: (812) 985-9214

E-mail: information@windmillpublications.com

Web site: www.windmillpublications.com

Xlibris.com

Phone: (888) 795-4247

E-mail: info@xlibris.com

Web site: www2.xlibris.com/

APPENDIX B

Forms for Family Documentary Editors

PROJECT DEVELOPMENT FORM

Name of Project _____

Documentary Editor _____

Date Commenced/Planned Completion _____

Historical Time Period Represented by Document(s) _____

Other Documents to Include _____

_____

Themes Developed in Project _____

_____

_____

_____

Examples of Comparable Projects/Models _____

_____

Research _____

_____

_____

Attach an outline of the proposed contents of the project.

DOCUMENTARY EDITING PROJECT LOG

Name of Project	Date of Entry	Event	Result/Comment

SAMPLE DEED OF GIFT AGREEMENT

[Name of Donor] (here referred to as the Donor), sole owner of these materials, hereby transfers, gives, grants, and assigns to [Name of Archives or Repository] and its successors and assigns the materials described as follows:

[Title, List, and Description of Papers and Materials in Collection]

[The Repository] accepts the materials described above under the terms of this agreement. These materials will be housed in the [department] and cared for professionally, with archival methods and equipment, in perpetuity.

Copyright

Donor shall initial the correct statement and cross out the other.

____ Donor retains all copyrights he/she holds in the materials.

____ Donor transfers all copyrights he/she holds in the materials to [the Repository].

Disposal of Materials

Donor shall initial the correct statement and cross out the other.

____ [The Repository] will dispose of any materials that the [Repository] determines to be inappropriate for retention, by its standard procedures.

____ [The Repository] will return to the Donor any materials that it determines to be inappropriate for retention.

Processing

[The Repository] will organize, catalog, conserve, and provide access to these materials using the standards of the profession.

Access

Donor shall initial the correct statement and cross out the other.

____ The materials will be open for research in accordance with the regulations and procedures of the [Repository] for unrestricted collections.

____ Public access to the materials will be restricted in the following manner: _____

_____

_____

This agreement applies to all future transfer of materials by the Donor to [the Repository] unless there is an addendum stating otherwise for a specific individual or group materials.

_____   _____   _____   _____
(Donor's signature)   (date)   [Repository manager]   (date)

Bibliography

DOCUMENTARY EDITING

Boyd, Julian P. "Editorial Method." In *The Papers of Thomas Jefferson*. Vol. 1. Princeton: Princeton University Press, 1950, xxv–xxxviii.

Carter, Clarence E. *Historical Editing*. Washington, D.C.: National Archives, 1952.

Handlin, Oscar, et al. "The Editing and Printing of Manuscripts." In *Harvard Guide to American History*. Cambridge: Harvard University Press, 1954, 95–104.

Kline, Mary-Jo. *A Guide to Documentary Editing*. 2d ed. Baltimore: Johns Hopkins University Press, 1987, 1998.

Luey, Beth. *Editing Documents and Texts: An Annotated Bibliography*. Madison, Wisc.: Madison House, 1990.

Morgan, George G. "Tips for Transcribing/Abstracting/Extracting Documents." <www.ancestry.com/library/view/columns/george/2384.asp>, posted September 22, 2000.

Root, Robert. "A Guide to Editing and Publishing Family Manuscripts." Sponsored by Mt. Pleasant, Mich.: Clarke Historical Library, et al. <www.ch sbs.cmich.edu/Robert_Root/Guide/Intro.htm>, posted 1998.

Stevens, Michael E. and Steven B. Burg. *Editing Historical Documents: A Handbook of Practice*. Walnut Creek, Calif.: AltaMira Press, 1997.

Sturdevant, Katherine Scott. "Documentary Editing for Family Historians." *Association for Professional Genealogists Quarterly* 3: 51–57.

Tanselle, G. Thomas. *The Editing of Historical Documents*. Charlottesville: Bibliographical Society of the University of Virginia, 1977.

Trask, David F. and Robert W. Pomeroy III. *The Craft of Public History: An Annotated Select Bibliography*. Westport, Conn.: Greenwood Press, 1983.

Vogt, George L. and John Bush Jones, eds. *Literary and Historical Editing*. Lawrence: University of Kansas Libraries, 1981.

West, James L. W. III. "Annotating Mr. Fitzgerald." *Documentary Editing* 22, no. 3 (September 2000): 54.

SELECTED DOCUMENTARY EDITIONS

Barnouw, David and Gerrold van der Stroom, eds. *The Diary of Anne Frank: The Critical Edition, Prepared by the Netherlands State Institute for War Documentation*. New York: Doubleday, 1989.

Bedichek, Jane Gracy. *The Roy Bedichek Family Letters*. Denton: University of North Texas Press, 1998.

Berry, Mary Clay. *Voices From the Century Before: The Odyssey of a Nineteenth-Century Kentucky Family*. New York: Arcade Publishing, 1997.

Bland, Larry I. *The Papers of George Catlett Marshall*. Baltimore: Johns Hopkins University Press, 1981–present.

Blecki, Catherine La Courreye and Karin A. Wulf, eds. *Milcah Martha Moore's Books: A Commonplace Book From Revolutionary America*. University Park: Pennsylvania State University Press, 1997.

Bryan, Charles F. Jr. and Nelson D. Lankford, eds. *Eye of the Storm: A Civil War Odyssey*. New York: Free Press, 2000.

Butterfield, Lyman H., et al, eds. *The Adams Papers*. Cambridge: Harvard University Press, 1961–present. See <www.masshist.org/>.

Castellan, James W. and Norman H. Clark, eds. "The Memoir of Eleanor Castellan: The Years in the Pacific Northwest, 1910–1919." *Pacific Northwest Quarterly* (Winter 1999/2000) 91:1, 3–24.

Coker, Caleb, ed. *The News From Brownsville: Helen Chapman's Letters From the Texas Military Frontier, 1848–1852*. Austin: Texas State Historical Association, 1992.

DeCosta-Willis, Miriam, ed. *The Memphis Diary of Ida B. Wells: An Intimate Portrait of the Activist as a Young Woman*. Boston: Beacon Press, 1995.

Dublin, Thomas, ed. *Farm to Factory: Women's Letters, 1830–1860*. New York: Columbia University Press, 1981.

Garvin, James L., ed. *The Diary of Matthew Patten of Bedford, New Hampshire, 1754–1788*. Rockport, Maine: Picton Press, 1993.

Gibbens, Byrd, ed. *This Is a Strange Country: Letters of a Westering Family, 1880–1906*. Albuquerque: University of New Mexico Press, 1988.

Gordon, Ann D., et al, eds. *The Papers of Elizabeth Cady Stanton and Susan B. Anthony*. Columbia, S.C.: Model Editions Partnership, 1999. Electronic version. <http://mep.cla.sc.edu/sa/sa-table.html>, posted 2000.

Hirst, Robert H., ed. *The Works of Mark Twain*. Berkeley: University of California Press, 1967–present.

Holmes, Kenneth L., ed. *Covered Wagon Women: Diaries and Letters From the Western Trails, 1840–1890 and 1875–1883, 1879–1903*. 11 vols. Glendale, Calif. and Spokane, Wash.: Arthur H. Clark Co., 1983–1993. Paperback reprints. Lincoln: University of Nebraska Press, 1995–2000.

Jacobs, Jane, ed. *A Schoolteacher in Old Alaska: The Story of Hannah Breece*. New York: Random House, 1995.

Lecompte, Janet, ed. *Emily: The Diary of a Hard-Worked Woman*. Lincoln: University of Nebraska Press, 1987.

Loomis, F.A., ed. *As Long as Life: The Memoirs of a Frontier Woman Doctor, Mary Canaga Rowland, MD, 1873-1966*. Seattle: Storm Peak Press, 1995.

McCausland, Robert R. and Cynthia MacAlman McCausland, eds. *The Diary of Martha Ballard, 1785–1812*. Rockport, Maine: Picton Press, 1998. See also citation under Laurel Thatcher Ulrich.

Miller, Randall M., ed. *"Dear Master": Letters of a Slave Family*. Ithaca: Cornell University Press, 1978.

Morgan, Edmund S., ed. *The Diary of Michael Wigglesworth, 1653–1657: The Conscience of a Puritan*. New York: Harper and Row, 1965.

Murphey, Sallyann J. *The Metcalfe Family Album: Six Generations of Traditions and Memories*. [Fiction] San Francisco: Chronicle Books, 1999.

Oberg, Barbara, et al, eds. *The Papers of Thomas Jefferson*. Princeton: Princeton University Press, 1950–present. See <www.princeton.edu/~tjpapers/>. See also citation under Paul G. Sifton.

Root, Robert L. Jr. *"Time by Moments Steals Away": The 1848 Journal of Ruth Douglass*. Detroit: Wayne State University Press, 1998.

Rozier, John, ed. *The Granite Farm Letters: The Civil War Correspondence of Edgeworth and Sallie Bird*. Athens: University of Georgia Press, 1988.

Rutland, Rutland, et al, eds. *The Papers of James Madison*. Chicago: University of Chicago Press, 1962–1977, Charlottesville: University Press of Virginia, 1977–present.

Sifton, Paul G. "Thomas Jefferson Papers: Provenance and Publication History." Washington, D.C.: Manuscript Division, Library of Congress, <http://rs6.loc.gov/ammem/mtjhtml/mtjprov.html>. See also citation under Barbara Oberg.

Smith, Sherry L. *Sagebrush Soldier: Private William Earl Smith's View of the Sioux War of 1876*. Norman: University of Oklahoma Press, 1989.

Steinman, Louise. *The Souvenir: A Daughter Discovers Her Father's War*. Chapel Hill, N.C.: Algonquin Books of Chapel Hill, 2001.

Sulloway, Alvah W., ed. *Put It in Writing: A Way of Life for Three Generations of a New Hampshire Family: Books, Journals, and Letters, 1892–1996*. West Kennebunk, Maine: New Hampshire Historical Society and Phoenix Publications, 1998.

Twohig, Dorothy, ed. *Papers of George Washington*. Charlottesville: University Press of Virginia, 1976–2001. See also "Papers of George Washington Editorial Project." <www.virginia.edu/gwpapers/stylemanual/>, posted October 1998.

Ulrich, Laurel Thatcher. *A Midwife's Tale: The Life of Martha Ballard, Based on Her Diary, 1785–1812*. New York: Alfred A. Knopf, 1990. See also the citation under Robert and Cynthia McCausland and the Film Study Center at Harvard University citation under "Analyzing Heirloom Documents."

Virginia Historical Society. "The Sneden Civil War Collection." Richmond: Virginia Historical Society, <www.sneden.com/about/discovering.html>.

Woodward, C. Vann, ed. *Mary Chesnut's Civil War*. New Haven, Conn.: Yale University Press, 1981.

ARCHIVES AND CONSERVATION

American Institute for Conservation of Historic and Artistic Works. "Guidelines for Selecting a Conservator," "Tips for the Care of Water-Damaged Family Heirlooms and Other Valuables." Washington, D.C.: AIC, <http://aic.stanford.edu/>.

Bachmann, Konstanze, ed. *Conservation Concerns: A Guide for Collectors and Curators*. Washington, D.C.: Smithsonian Institution Press, 1992.

Baker, Nicholson. *Double Fold: Libraries and the Assault on Paper*. New York: Random House, 2001.

Beinecke Rare Book and Manuscript Library. "Archival Processing Manual."

New Haven, Conn.: Yale University, 1997, <www.library.yale.edu/beinecke/manuscript/process/index.html>, posted 1997.

Braun, Bev Kirschner. *Crafting Your Own Heritage Album*. Cincinnati: Betterway Books, 2000.

Carini, Peter. "Donating Collections." South Hadley, Mass.: Archives and Special Collections, Mount Holyoke College, <www.mtholyoke.edu/offices/library/arch/msdonor.htm>, posted 1997.

Center for American History. "Donors and Donations." Austin: Center for American History, University of Texas, <www.cah.utexas.edu/about/donors.html>.

Central New York Library Resources Council. "Documenting Family History." Syracuse: CNYLRC, <www.clrc.org/dhp/dhpfam.shtml>, 1997.

Clarke Historical Library Preservation. "Preserving Memories: Caring for Your Heritage." Mt. Pleasant, Mich.: Clarke Historical Library, <www.lib.cmich.edu/clarke/pres.htm>, posted August 1996.

Colorado Preservation Alliance. "Preserving Your Scrapbook of Memorabilia," "How to Flatten Folded or Rolled Paper Documents," etc. <www.archives.state.co.us/cpa/publications.htm#paper>, posted July 2001.

Cox, Richard J. "Don't Fold Up: Responding to Nicholson Baker's *Double Fold*." <www.archivists.org/news/doublefold.html>, posted April 2001.

Duffy, Laura Prescott. "Exploring Manuscript Collections at NEHGS, The Thorndike Family Papers: A Case Study." *New England Ancestors* 2, no. 1 (Winter 2001): 11–15.

Ellison, Todd. "Special Collections Archival Procedure Manual." Durango, Colo.: Center of Southwest Studies, Fort Lewis College, <www.fortlewis.edu/tools/FLCArchivalProcedureManual.htm>, posted August 2001.

Gaylord Brothers. *Gaylord Preservation Pathfinder No.1: An Introduction to Preservation*. Syracuse: Gaylord Brothers, 1998.

———. *Gaylord Preservation Pathfinder No. 2: Archival Storage of Paper*. Syracuse: Gaylord Brothers, 1998.

Glaser, Mary Todd. *Framing and Preservation of Works of Art on Paper*. Colorado Springs, Colo.: Bernard Ewell Art Appraisals, 1999.

Henry Ford Museum and Greenfield Village. "The Care and Preservation of Works of Art on Paper." <www.hfmgv.org/research/cis/paper.html>, posted 2000.

Herskovitz, Bob. "Preserving Your Personal and Family Treasures." Minneapolis: Minnesota Historical Society, <www.mnhs.org/preserve/treasures/>.

Jackson, Albert and David Day. *Antiques Care and Repair Handbook*. New York: Alfred A. Knopf, 1984.

James, Michael. "Fading Bits of History," "Dearly Departed" (9 July 2001), and "Recording History" (10 July 2001). Abcnews.com.

Kraft, Nancy, et al. "Tips on Preserving Scrapbooks," "Tips on Creating an Archival Scrapbook," Tips on Preserving Your Documents," etc. Iowa City: Iowa Conservation and Preservation Consortium and State Historical Society of Iowa, <www.uni.edu/petersog/icpcmenu.html>, posted October 1996.

Library of Congress. "Care, Handling, and Storage of Books," "Preservation

Photocopying," "Preserving Works on Paper," etc. Washington, D.C.: Library of Congress, <http://lcweb.loc.gov/preserv/care/>, posted September 2000.

Library of Virginia. "Guide to Preserving Family Historical Records." Richmond: Library of Virginia, <www.lva.lib.va.us/pubserv/archives/preserve.htm>.

Long, Jane S. and Richard W. Long. *Caring for Your Family Treasures: Heritage Preservation*. New York: Harry N. Abrams, 2000.

McColgin, Michael. "Preservation Guidelines, "Conservation," etc. Phoenix: Arizona History and Archives Division, <www.dlapr.lib.az.us/archives/conservation.htm>, posted 2000.

Mibach, Lisa. *Collections Care: What to Do When You Can't Afford to Do Anything*. Nashville: American Association for State and Local History, 1997. Technical leaflet no. 198.

Miller, Fredric M. *Arranging and Describing Archives and Manuscripts*. Chicago: Society of American Archivists, 1990.

Miller, Ilene Chandler. *Preserving Family Keepsakes: Dos and Don'ts*. Yorba Linda, Calif.: Shumway Family History Services, 1995.

New England Historic Genealogical Society. "How to Donate Your Family Papers and Why." *New England Ancestors* 2, no. 1 (Winter 2001): 16.

Niemeyer, Shirley. "Preservation of Paper Items." Lincoln: Nebraska Cooperative Extension, University of Nebraska, <www.ianr.unl.edu/pubs/homemgt/nf138.htm>, posted July 1995.

Northeast Document Conservation Center. *Encapsulation*. Andover, Mass.: 1987. NEDCC leaflet.

Ogden, Sherelyn. *Protection From Loss*. Andover, Mass.: Northeast Document Conservation Center, <www.nedcc.org/plam3/tleaf31.htm>, posted 1999.

O'Toole, James M. *Understanding Archives and Manuscripts*. Chicago: Society of American Archivists, 1990.

Paulsen, Deidre M. and Jeanne S. English. *Preserving the Precious*. Rev. ed. Salt Lake City: Restoration Source, 1989.

Rare Book, Manuscript, and Special Collections Library, "A Guide for Donating Materials." Durham, N.C.: Duke University, <http://odyssey.lib.duke.edu/specoll/donating.html>.

Ritzenthaler, Mary Lynn. *Archives and Manuscripts: Conservation: A Manual on Physical Care and Management*. Chicago: Society of American Archivists, 1983.

———. *Preserving Archives and Manuscripts*. Chicago: Society of American Archivists, 1993.

Schultz, Arthur W., ed. *Caring for Your Collections*. New York: Harry N. Abrams, 1992.

Snyder, Mike. "Why So Much in So Many Basements?" *Houston Chronicle*, 13 June 2001.

Society of American Archivists. "A Guide to Donating Your Personal or Family Papers to a Repository." <www.archivists.org/catalog/donating-familyrecs.html>, posted 1994.

———. "A Guide to Deeds of Gift." <www.archivists.org/catalog/deed_of_gift. html>, posted 1998.

———. "SAA Council's Response to Nicholson Baker's *Double Fold*." <www.a rchivists.org/statements/council-doublefold.html>, posted May 2001.

Thomas, Jill. "Retired Professor Donating Life's Collection of Epic Books." *Cookeville Herald-Citizen*, <www.tennessean.com/local/archives/01/04/065 72717.shtml?Element_ID>, posted 15 July 2001.

Tuttle, Craig A. *An Ounce of Preservation: A Guide to the Care of Papers and Photographs*. Highland City, Fla.: Rainbow Books, Inc., 1995.

Van der Reyden, Dianne. "Framing and Unframing," "Handling Paper Artifacts." Smithsonian Center for Materials Research and Education, <www .si.edu/scmre/>.

Webb, Martha Ellen. *How to Clean, Repair, Store, and Display Your Heirloom Papers and Photographs*. Omaha, Neb.: Making History, 1999.

Western Historical Manuscript Collection. "Donor's Guide." Columbia, Mo.: University of Missouri, <www.system.missouri.edu/whmc/query.htm>.

HANDWRITING

Joslyn, Roger D. "The Lowly Capital *F*." *The American Genealogist* 74 (January 1999): 31–32.

Kirkham, E. Kay. *The Handwriting of American Records for a Period of 300 Years*. Logan, Utah: Everton Publishers, 1973.

Sperry, Kip. "Guidelines for Reading Old Documents." <www.genealogy.com/ 68_sperry.html?Welcome=992873250>, posted May 2000.

———. *Reading Early American Handwriting*. Baltimore: Genealogical Publishing Company, 1998.

Stryker-Rodda, Harriet. *Understanding Colonial Handwriting*. Rev. ed. Baltimore: Genealogical Publishing Company, 1986.

Taylor, Maureen. "Getting a Hand." *Family Tree Magazine* (October 2001): 56–61.

PHOTOGRAPHS

Albright, Gary. "Storage Enclosures for Photographic Materials." Andover, Mass.: Northeast Document Conservation Center, 1989.

Bennett, Mary. "Tips on Handling and Labeling Historical Photographs," "Tips on Storing Historical Photographs," "Tips on Storing Historical Negatives," and "Tips on Displaying Historical Photographs in Albums and Frames." 4 parts. *The Palimpsest* [now *Iowa Heritage Illustrated* of the State Historical Society of Iowa] 71, nos. 1–4 (Spring, Summer, Fall, Winter 1990).

Davies, Thomas L. *Shoots: A Guide to Your Family's Photographic Heritage*. Danbury, N.H.: Addison House, 1977.

Frisch-Ripley, Karen. *Unlocking the Secrets in Old Photographs*. Salt Lake City: Ancestry Publishing, 1991.

Gear, Josephine. "The Baby's Picture: Woman as Image Maker in Small-Town America." *Feminist Studies* 13, no. 2 (Summer 1987): 419–442.

Henisch, Heinz K. and Bridget A. Henisch. *The Photographic Experience, 1839–1914: Images and Attitudes.* University Park: Pennsylvania State University Press, 1994.

Hirsch, Julia. *Family Photographs: Content, Meaning, and Effect.* New York: Oxford University Press, 1981.

Horton, Loren. "Interpreting the Image: How to Understand Historical Photographs." 4 parts. *The Palimpsest* [now *Iowa Heritage Illustrated* of the State Historical Society of Iowa] 71, nos. 1–4 (Spring, Summer, Fall, Winter 1990).

Horton, Richard W. "Photo Album Structures, 1850–1960." *Guild of Book Workers Journal* 32, no. 1 (Spring 1994): 32–43.

Light Impressions. "Tips for Proper Negative Storage." Rochester, N.Y.: Light Impressions, 1985.

Motz, Marilyn F. "Visual Autobiography: Photograph Albums of Turn-of-the-Century Midwestern Women." *American Quarterly* 41 (March 1989): 63–92.

Reilly, James M. *Care and Identification of Nineteenth-Century Photographic Prints.* Rochester, N.Y.: Eastman Kodak Company, 1986.

Ritzenthaler, Mary Lynn, et al. *Archives and Manuscripts: Administration of Photographic Collections.* Chicago: Society of American Archivists, 1984.

Taylor, Maureen. *Preserving Your Family Photographs.* Cincinnati: Betterway Books, 2001.

———. *Uncovering Your Ancestry Through Family Photographs.* Cincinnati: Betterway Books, 2000.

Time-Life Books. *Caring for Photographs: Display, Storage, Restoration.* New York: Time-Life Books, 1976.

Vanderbilt, Paul. *Evaluating Historical Photographs: A Personal Perspective.* Nashville: American Association for State and Local History, 1979. Technical leaflet no. 120.

Wajda, Shirley. "A Room With a Viewer: The Parlor Stereoscope, Comic Stereographs, and the Psychic Role of Play in Victorian America." In *Hard at Play: Leisure in America, 1840–1940,* edited by Kathryn Grover, 112–138. Amherst: University of Massachusetts Press, 1992.

Weinstein, Robert A. and Larry Booth. *Collection, Use, and Care of Historical Photographs.* Nashville: American Association for State and Local History, 1977.

ORAL HISTORY

Allen, Barbara and Lynwood Montell. *From Memory to History: Using Oral Sources in Local Historical Research.* Nashville: American Association for State and Local History, 1981.

Arnold, Eleanor, ed. *Voices of American Homemakers.* Bloomington: Indiana University Press, 1985.

Banks, Ann, ed. *First-Person America: Voices of the Great Depression.* New York: Alfred A. Knopf, 1980.

Baum, Willa K. *Transcribing and Editing Oral History*. Nashville: American Association for State and Local History, 1977, 1991.

Baylor University. "Oral History Workshop on the Web: Transcribing Style Guide." Institute for Oral History, Baylor University, <www.baylor.edu/Oral _History/Styleguide.html>, posted 1997.

Dunaway, David K. and Willa K. Baum, eds. *Oral History: An Interdisciplinary Anthology*. Nashville: American Association for State and Local History, 1984.

Epstein, Ellen Robinson and Rona Mendelsohn. *Record and Remember: Tracing Your Roots Through Oral History*. New York: Monarch, 1978.

Federal Writers' Project of the Works Progress Administration (North Carolina, Tennessee, Georgia). *These Are Our Lives*. Chapel Hill: University of North Carolina Press, 1939.

Fletcher, William. *Recording Your Family History: A Guide to Preserving Oral History Using Audio and Video Tape*. Berkeley, Calif.: Ten Speed Press, 1983, 1989.

Gluck, Sherna Berger. *Rosie the Riveter Revisited: Women, the War, and Social Change*. Boston: Twayne Publishers, 1987.

Krause, Corinne Azen. *Grandmothers, Mothers, and Daughters: Oral Histories of Three Generations of Ethnic American Women*. Boston: Twayne Publishers, 1991.

Miller, Merle. *Plain Speaking: An Oral Biography of Harry S. Truman*. New York: G.P. Putnam, 1974.

Ritchie, Donald A. *Doing Oral History*. New York: Twayne Publishers, 1995.

Ryant, Carl. "Oral History and the Family: A Tool for the Documentation and Interpretation of Family History." *Annual of the New England Oral History Association* 2 (1989–1990), 30–37.

Scobie, Ingrid W. "Family and Community History Through Oral History." *The Public Historian* 1 (1979), 29–39.

Terkel, Studs. *"The Good War": An Oral History of World War II*. New York: Pantheon, 1984.

———. *Hard Times: An Oral History of the Great Depression*. New York: Pantheon, 1970.

Terrill, Tom E. and Jerrold Hirsch, eds. *Such as Us: Southern Voices of the Thirties*. New York: W.W. Norton, 1979.

Tucker, Susan. *Telling Memories Among Southern Women: Domestic Workers and Their Employers in the Segregated South*. New York: Schocken Books, 1988.

ANALYZING HEIRLOOM DOCUMENTS

Benstock, Shari. *The Private Self: Theory and Practice of Women's Autobiographical Writings*. Chapel Hill: University of North Carolina Press, 1988.

Bias, Danielle, et al. "Scrapbooks and Albums, Theories and Practice: An Annotated Bibliography," <www.tulane.edu/~wclib/susan.html>.

Blais, Madeleine. "Division of Things Past: An Account of the Making and

Unmaking of a Family Album." *Lear's* 5, no. 11 (January 1993): 64–65, 84–85.

Budra, Paul and Betty Schellenberg, eds. *Part Two: Reflections on the Sequel*. Toronto: University of Toronto Press, 1998.

Bunkers, Suzanne L., ed. *Diaries of Girls and Women: A Midwestern American Sampler*. Madison: University of Wisconsin, 2001.

Bunkers, Suzanne L. and Cynthia A. Huff, eds. *Inscribing the Daily: Critical Essays on Women's Diaries*. Amherst: University of Massachusetts Press, 1996.

Carmack, Sharon DeBartolo. "Dear Diary." *Family Tree Magazine* 1 (June 2000): 24–28.

Culley, Margo, ed. *American Women's Autobiography: Fea(s)ts of Memory*. Madison: University of Wisconsin Press, 1992.

———. *A Day at a Time: The Diary Literature of American Women From 1764 to the Present*. New York: Feminist Press, 1985.

Film Study Center at Harvard University. "Martha Ballard's Diary Online." <www.dohistory.org/>, posted 2000.

Forbes, Harriette, comp. *New England Diaries, 1602–1800: A Descriptive Catalogue of Diaries, Orderly Books, and Sea Journals*. New York: Russell and Russell, 1967.

Garber, Marjorie. "I'll Be Back" (review of Paul Budra and Betty Schellenberg, *Part Two: Reflections on the Sequel*). *London Review of Books* 21, no. 16 (19 August 1999). Reproduced at <www.lrb.co.uk/v21/n16/garb2116 .htm>.

Goodfriend, Joyce D. *The Published Diaries and Letters of American Women: An Annotated Bibliography*. Boston: G.K. Hall, 1987.

Henry, Mark. "Diary Helps Man Follow in His Father's Footsteps." *The Press-Enterprise* (Redlands, Calif.), <www.pe.com/news/stories/061101/early11.s html>, posted 14 June 2001.

Johnson, Anne. "Our Quilting History: Signature Quilts," <http://womenfolk .com/grandmothers/friendqu.htm>, posted 1998 (no longer available).

Kagle, Steven E. *American Diary Literature, 1620–1799*. Boston: Twayne Publishing, 1979.

———. *Early Nineteenth-Century American Diary Literature*. Boston: Twayne Publishing, 1986.

———. *Late Nineteenth-Century American Diary Literature*. Boston: Twayne Publishing, 1988.

Matthews, William, comp. *American Diaries: An Annotated Bibliography of American Diaries Written Prior to the Year 1861*. Berkeley: University of California Press, 1945.

———. *American Diaries in Manuscript, 1580–1954: A Descriptive Bibliography*. Athens: University of Georgia Press, 1974.

Miller, Randall M. and Linda Patterson Miller. *The Book of American Diaries: From Heart and Mind to Pen and Paper—Day-by-Day Personal Accounts Through the Centuries*. New York: Avon Books, 1995.

Morine, Suzanne. "Anne Frank Diary Reference," <www.angelfire.com/journ al2/afdiary/>, posted 2000.

Princeton University Library. "Autograph Book Collection, 1825–1884," <http://libweb.princeton.edu:2003/libraries/firestone/rbsc/finding_aids/autograph/html>, posted 1997.

Rosenblatt, Paul C. *Bitter, Bitter Tears: Nineteenth-Century Diarists and Twentieth-Century Grief Theories*. Minneapolis: University of Minnesota Press, 1983.

Theophano, Janet. *Eat My Words: Reading Women's Lives Through the Cookbooks They Wrote*. New York: Palgrove, 2002.

Thomas, Laura. "Scrapbooks: 21st Century Lives Bound Together by 19th Century Art." *San Francisco Chronicle*, 21 July 2001.

Tucker, Susan. "Within a Scrapbook's Pages." *The Historic New Orleans Collection Quarterly* 15, no. 1 (Winter 1997): 6–7.

Van der Reyden, D[iane]. "Identifying the Real Thing." Prepared for the School for Scanning, National Park Service and Northeast Document Conservation Center, 11–13 September 1996, <www.scmre.org/analysis.htm>.

MEMOIR AND LIFE STORY WRITING GUIDES

Barrington, Judith. *Writing the Memoir: From Truth to Art*. Portland, Ore.: The Eighth Mountain Press, 1997.

Bender, Sheila. *Writing Personal Essays: How to Shape Your Life Experiences for the Page*. Cincinnati: Writer's Digest Books, 1995.

Carmack, Sharon DeBartolo. "Writing Your Life Story." *Family Tree Magazine* (January 2000): 40–47.

Chapin, Alice. *Reaching Back: A Workbook for Recording Your Life's Most Meaningful Moments to Share With Future Generations*. Cincinnati: Betterway Books, 1997.

Ledoux, Denis. *The Photo Scribe: A Writing Guide: How to Write the Stories Behind Your Photographs*. Lisbon Falls, Maine: Soleil Press, 1999.

———. *Turning Memories Into Memoirs: A Handbook for Writing Lifestories*. Lisbon Falls, Maine: Soleil Press, 1993. See also <www.turningmemories.com/>.

Neubauer, Joan. *From Memories to Manuscript: The Five-Step Method of Writing Your Life Story*. Salt Lake City: Ancestry Publishing, 1997.

Polking, Kirk. *Writing Family Histories and Memoirs*. Cincinnati: Betterway Books, 1995.

Rainer, Tristine. *Your Life as Story: Discovering the "New Autobiography" and Writing Memoir as Literature*. New York: Penguin Putnam, 1997.

Roorbach, Bill. *Writing Life Stories*. Cincinnati: Story Press, 2000.

Selling, Bernard. *Writing From Within: A Guide to Creativity and Life Story Writing*. Alameda, Calif.: Hunting House Publishers, 1988, 1998.

Zinsser, William, ed. *Inventing the Truth: The Art and Craft of Memoir*. New York: Houghton Mifflin, 1987.

FAMILY HISTORY WRITING GUIDES

Barnes, Donald R. and Richard S. Lackey. *Write it Right: A Manual for Writing Family Histories and Genealogies*. Ocala, Fla.: Lyon Press, 1983.

Gouldrup, Lawrence P. *Writing the Family Narrative*. Salt Lake City: Ancestry Publishing, 1987.

Hatcher, Patricia Law. *Producing a Quality Family History*. Salt Lake City: Ancestry Publishing, 1996.

Kempthorne, Charley. *For All Time: A Complete Guide to Writing Your Family History*. Portsmouth, N.H.: Boynton/Cook Publishers, 1996.

Mills, Elizabeth Shown. *Evidence! Citation and Analysis for the Family Historian*. Baltimore: Genealogical Publishing Company, 1997.

GENERAL WRITING, STYLE, EDITING, AND INDEXING GUIDES

American Society of Indexers. "Index Evaluation Checklist." Wheatridge, Colo.: ASI, <www.asindexing.org/site/checklist.shtml>, posted 2000.

Cheney, Theodore A. Rees. *Writing Creative Nonfiction*. Berkeley, Calif.: Ten Speed Press, 1987, 1991.

Fetters, Linda K. *Handbook of Indexing Techniques: A Guide for Beginning Indexers*. 2d ed. Fetters Infomanagement, 1999.

Gerard, Philip. *Creative Nonfiction: Researching and Crafting Stories of Real Life*. Cincinnati: Story Press, 1996.

Gibaldi, Joseph, ed. *MLA Style Manual and Guide to Scholarly Publishing*. New York: Modern Language Association, 1985, 1998.

Gutkind, Lee. *The Art of Creative Nonfiction: Writing and Selling the Literature of Reality*. New York: John Wiley and Sons, Inc., 1997.

Hatcher, Patricia Law and John V. Wylie. *Indexing Family Histories: Simple Steps For a Quality Project*. Arlington: National Genealogical Society Special Publication, 1994.

Higham, Robin, et al. *A Brief Guide to Scholarly Editing*. Manhattan, Kans.: Sunflower University Press, 1982.

Mulvany, Nancy C. *Indexing Books*. Chicago: University of Chicago Press, 1994.

Plotnik, Arthur. *The Elements of Editing: A Modern Guide for Editors and Journalists*. New York: Macmillan Publishing Co., 1982.

University of Chicago Press. *The Chicago Manual of Style*. 14th ed. Chicago: University of Chicago Press, 1993. See also <www.press.uchicago.edu/Misc/Chicago/cmosfaq.html>.

COPYRIGHT

Cogswell, Robert. *Copyright Law for Unpublished Manuscripts and Archival Collections*. Chicago: Society of American Archivists, 1992.

Fishman, Stephen. *The Copyright Handbook: How to Protect and Use Written Works*. Berkeley, Calif.: Nolo.com, 2000.

———. *The Public Domain: How to Find and Use Copyright-Free Writings, Music, Art, and More*. Berkeley: Nolo.com, 2000.

Library of Congress Copyright Office. *Copyright Law of the United States of America*. Washington, D.C.: United States Copyright Office, 2000.

Stim, Richard. *Getting Permission: How to License and Clear Copyrighted Materials Online and Off*. Berkeley, Calif.: Nolo.com, 2000.

NONFICTION BOOK PROPOSALS AND PUBLISHING OPPORTUNITIES

Association of American University Presses (AAUP). *AAUP Directory, 2000–2001*. Chicago: University of Chicago Press, 2000.

Derricourt, Robin. *An Author's Guide to Scholarly Publishing*. Princeton, N.J.: Princeton University Press, 1996.

Herman, Jeff and Deborah M. Adams. *Write the Perfect Book Proposal: Ten Proposals That Sold and Why*. New York: John Wiley and Sons, 1993.

Larsen, Michael. *How to Write a Book Proposal*. Cincinnati: Writer's Digest Books, 1985.

Lyon, Elizabeth. *Nonfiction Book Proposals Anybody Can Write: How to Get a Contract and an Advance Before Writing Your Book*. Hillsboro, Ore.: Blue Heron Publishing, 1995.

Moore, Marilyn M. "So You Want to Write a Cookbook: Some Tips to Get You Started," <www.foodnet.com/epr/sections/writers/cookbook/cookbook.html>, posted 1995.

Ohi, Debbie Ridpath. *Writer's Online Marketplace: How and Where to Get Published Online*. Cincinnati: Writer's Digest Books, 2001.

Parsons, Paul. *Getting Published: The Acquisition Process at University Presses*. Knoxville: University of Tennessee Press, 1989.

Smith, Mack E. and Sara Freeman Smith. *How to Self-Publish and Market Your Own Book: A Simple Guide for Aspiring Writers*. Houston: UR Gems Group, 1998, 2001.

William and Mary Quarterly. "Some Guidelines for Preparing Documents for Publication in the *William and Mary Quarterly*," <www.wm.edu/oieahc/WMQ/prep.html>.

Wilson, Richard S. *Publishing Your Family History on the Internet*. La Habra, Calif.: Compuology, 1999.

Wolfe, J. Kevin. *You Can Write a Cookbook*. Cincinnati: Writer's Digest Books, 2000.

SELECTED GENEALOGICAL RESEARCH GUIDES

Bentley, Elizabeth Petty. *The Genealogist's Address Book*. 4th ed. Baltimore: Genealogical Publishing Company, 1998.

Carmack, Sharon DeBartolo. *Organizing Your Family History Search*. Cincinnati: Betterway Books, 1999.

Eichholz, Alice, ed. *Ancestry's Red Book: American State, County, and Town Sources*. Rev. ed. Salt Lake City: Ancestry Publishing, 1989, 1992.

Everton, George B., comp. *The Handy Book for Genealogists*. 10th ed. Logan, Utah: Everton Publishers, 1991.

Greenwood, Val D. *The Researcher's Guide to American Genealogy*. 3d ed. Baltimore: Genealogical Publishing Company, 2000.

Jones, Henry Z. *More Psychic Roots: Further Adventures in Serendipity and Intuition in Genealogy*. Baltimore: Genealogical Publishing Company, 1997.

———. *Psychic Roots: Serendipity and Intuition in Genealogy*. Baltimore: Genealogical Publishing Company, 1993.

National Endowment for the Humanities. *My History is America's History: Fifteen Things You Can Do to Save America's Stories*. Washington, D.C.: National Endowment for the Humanities, 1999. See also <www.myhistory.org>.

Smith, Juliana Szucs. *The Ancestry Family Historian's Address Book*. Salt Lake City: Ancestry Publishing, 1997.

Sturdevant, Katherine Scott. *Bringing Your Family History to Life Through Social History*. Cincinnati: Betterway Books, 2000.

Szucs, Loretto Dennis and Sandra Hargreaves Luebking, eds. *The Source: A Guidebook of American Genealogy*. Salt Lake City: Ancestry Publishing, 1997.

SELECTED HISTORICAL RESEARCH GUIDES

American Association for State and Local History (AASLH). *Directory of Historical Organizations in the United States and Canada*. 15th ed. Walnut Creek, Calif.: AltaMira Press, 2001.

Baird's Manual of American College Fraternities. Menasha, Wisc.: 1949.

Freidel, Frank, ed. *The Harvard Guide to American History*. Rev. ed. Cambridge: Harvard University Press, 1974.

Gibaldi, Joseph, ed. *MLA Handbook for Writers of Research Papers*. 5th ed. New York: Modern Language Association, 1977, 1999.

Hamer, Philip M., ed. *A Guide to Archives and Manuscripts in the United States*. New Haven: Yale University Press, 1961.

Hirsch, E.D. Jr. *Cultural Literacy: What Every American Needs to Know*. Boston: Houghton Mifflin, 1987.

Kyvig, David E. and Myron A. Marty. *Nearby History: Exploring the Past Around You*. Nashville: American Association for State and Local History, 1982.

Library of Congress. *National Union Catalog of Manuscript Collections* (NUCMC). Washington, D.C.: Library of Congress, 1959–present. See also <http://lcweb.loc.gov/coll/nucmc/nucmc.html>.

Macmillan Information. *The College Blue Book*. New York: Macmillan, annual.

Mann, Thomas. *The Oxford Guide to Library Research*. New York: Oxford University Press, 1998.

Marius, Richard and Melvin E. Page. *A Short Guide to Writing About History*. 4th ed. New York: Longman, 2001.

Metter, Ellen. *Facts in a Flash: A Research Guide for Writers*. Cincinnati: Writer's Digest Books, 1999.

———. *The Writer's Ultimate Research Guide*. Cincinnati: Writer's Digest Books, 1995.

Modern Language Association. *American Literary Manuscripts*. Austin: University of Texas Press, 1960–1961.

Morris, Jeffrey B. and Richard B. Morris, eds. *Encyclopedia of American History*. 7th ed. New York: HarperCollins, 1953–1996.

National Historical Publications and Records Commission (NHPRC). *Directory of Archives and Manuscript Repositories in the United States*. 2d ed. Phoenix: Oryx Press, 1988.

Robbins, J. Albert, et al. *American Literary Manuscripts: A Checklist of Holdings in Academic, Historical, and Public Libraries, Museums, and Authors' Homes in the United States*. Athens: University of Georgia Press, 1977.

Rodenhouse, Mary Pat, ed. *HEP Higher Education Directory*. Falls Church, Va.: Higher Education Publications. Annual.

Trinkle, Dennis, et al. *The History Highway: A Guide to Internet Sources*. Armonk, N.Y.: M.E. Sharpe, 1997, 2000.

CATEGORIZING GENERATIONS

Howe, Neil and William Strauss. *Millennials Rising: The Next Great Generation*. New York: Random House, 2000.

———. *13th Gen: Abort, Retry, Ignore, Fail?* New York: Random House, 1993.

———. *The Fourth Turning: An American Prophecy*. New York: Broadway Books, 1997.

———. *Generations: The History of America's Future, 1584 to 2069*. New York: William Morrow, 1991.

CITED ARTIFACTS/SOCIAL HISTORY

Allen, Alistair and Joan Hoverstadt. *The History of Printed Scraps*. London: New Cavendish Books, 1983, 1990.

Jackson, H. J. *Marginalia: Readers Writing in Books*. New Haven: Yale University Press, 2001.

Judd, Peter Haring. *The Hatch and Brood of Time: Five Phelps Families in the Atlantic World, 1720–1880*. Boston: Newbury Street Press, 1999.

Nickell, Joe. *Pen, Ink, and Evidence: A Study of Writing and Writing Materials for the Penman, Collector, and Document Detective*. Lexington: University Press of Kentucky, 1990.

Rickards, Maurice. *Encyclopedia of Ephemera: A Guide to the Fragmentary Documents of Everyday Life for the Collector, Curator, and Historian*. New York: Routledge, 2000.

Simons, D. Brenton and Peter Benes, eds. *The Art of Family: Genealogical Artifacts in New England*. Boston: New England Historic Genealogical Society, 2002.

Ulrich, Laurel Thatcher. *The Age of Homespun: Objects and Stories in the Creation of an American Myth*. New York: Alfred A. Knopf, 2001.

Index

Note: This index contains integrated references to document types, equipment and resources, historical events, methodologies, proper names, and social history topics.

Explore your family history with Betterway Books!

Crafting Your Own Heritage Album—Keep your family's memory alive! Learn how to capture and preserve the precious photos and keepsakes of your family history for years to come. Easy-to-follow instructions and page after page of elegant and imaginative ideas teach you how to make more than a scrapbook—you'll create a treasured heirloom and priceless family resource.
ISBN 1-55870-534-1, paperback, 128 pages, #70457-K

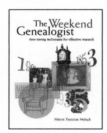

The Weekend Genealogist—Maximize your family research efficiency! With this guide, you can focus your efforts in searching for family documents while still gaining the best results. Organization and research techniques are presented in a clear, easy-to-follow format perfect for advanced researchers *and* beginners. You'll learn how to work more efficiently using family history facilities, the Internet—even the postal service!
ISBN 1-55870-546-5, paperback, 144 pages, #70496-K

The Genealogist's Computer Companion—Master the basics of online research and turn your computer into an efficient, versatile research tool. Respected genealogist Rhonda McClure shows you how, providing guidelines and advice that enable you to find new information, verify existing research, and save valuable time. She also provides an invaluable glossary of genealogical and technical terms.
ISBN 1-55870-591-0, paperback, 192 pages, #70529-K

Your Guide to the Family History Library—The Family History Library in Salt Lake City is the largest collection of genealogy and family history materials in the world. No other repository compares for both quantity and *quality* of research materials. Written for beginning and intermediate genealogists, *Your Guide to the Family History Library* will help you use the library's resources effectively, both on site and online.
ISBN 1-55870-578-3, paperback, 272 pages, #70513-K

Your Guide to Cemetery Research—Cemeteries can help fill the holes in your precious family history! With this book, you'll learn how to determine when and where a person died, locate the exact cemetery in which a family or individual is interred, analyze headstones and markers, interpret funerary art and tombstone iconography, and more!
ISBN 1-55870-589-9, paperback, 272 pages, #70527-K

Preserving Your Family Photographs—Learn how to care for your family photograph collection by applying the concepts used by conservators and photo curators every day. Maureen Taylor shows you how to organize your photographs for both family history research and display, create a scrapbook using archive quality guidelines, select a restoration expert to restore damaged photos, use photo identification techniques, and more.
ISBN 1-55870-579-1, paperback, 256 pages, #70514-K

Long-Distance Genealogy—Gathering information from sources that can't be visited is a challenge for all genealogists. This book will teach you the basics of long-distance research. You'll learn what types of records and publications can be accessed from a distance, problems associated with the process, how to network, how to use computer resources, and special "last resort" options.
ISBN 1-55870-535-X, paperback, 272 pages, #70495-K

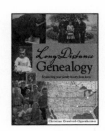

Your Guide to the Federal Census—This one-of-a-kind book examines the "nuts and bolts" of census records. You'll find out where to view the census and how to use it to find ancestors quickly and easily. Easy-to-follow instructions and case studies detail nearly every scenario for tracing family histories through census records. You'll also find invaluable appendixes, a glossary of census terms, and helpful reference charts.
ISBN 1-55870-588-0, paperback, 288 pages, #70525-K

These and other fine titles from Betterway Books are available from you local bookstore, online supplier or by calling (800) 221-5831.